Return to Vienna

**THE SPECIAL OPERATIONS EXECUTIVE
AND THE REBIRTH OF AUSTRIA**

Peter Dixon

Cloudshill Press
Cheltenham and London

Copyright © 2023 by Peter Dixon.

All rights reserved. No part of this publication may be reproduced, distributed or transmitted in any form or by any means, including photocopying, recording, or other electronic or mechanical methods, without the prior written permission of the publisher, except in the case of brief quotations embodied in critical reviews and certain other noncommercial uses permitted by copyright law. For permission requests, write to the publisher, addressed "Attention: Permissions Coordinator," at info@cloudshillpress.com.

Every reasonable effort has been taken to trace copyright holders of material reproduced in this book, but if any have been inadvertently overlooked the Publisher would be glad to hear from them.

Cover design by James Morgan. Cover Image adapted from 'Parachutist', by Guenther Dillingen, published at pixabay.com, in the Public Domain under Creative Commons CCO 1.0.

Copyright details are provided in the List of Images, whose content is deemed to be part of this copyright page.

Peter Dixon asserts his moral right to be identified as the author of this book.

Published by Cloudshill Press LLP Registered Office: 27 Old Gloucester Street, London WC1N 3AX United Kingdom

www.cloudshillpress.com. Please contact by email via info@cloudshillpress.com.

Book Layout ©2017 BookDesignTemplates.com

Ordering Information: for quantity sales. Special discounts are available on quantity purchases by corporations, associations, and others. For details, contact the "Special Sales Department" via info@cloudshillpress.com.

Return to Vienna / Peter Dixon. —1st ed.

ISBN (paperback) 978-1-9160273-9-8

ISBN (hardback) 978-1-915842-00-8

ISBN (ebook) 978-1-9160273-7-4

Contents

Foreword 1

Introduction 3

A Jewish Soldier 5

The Long Road Home 23

Approaching Storm 43

Espionage and Sabotage 59

Early Days 77

Working from Outside 101

The Slovenian Route 129

Out of Italy 145

Final Push 167

Endgame 189

Conclusion 213

Acknowledgements 221

Dramatis Personae 223

Chronology 229

Glossary 233

Sources and Further Reading 237

Index 243

Bibliography 252

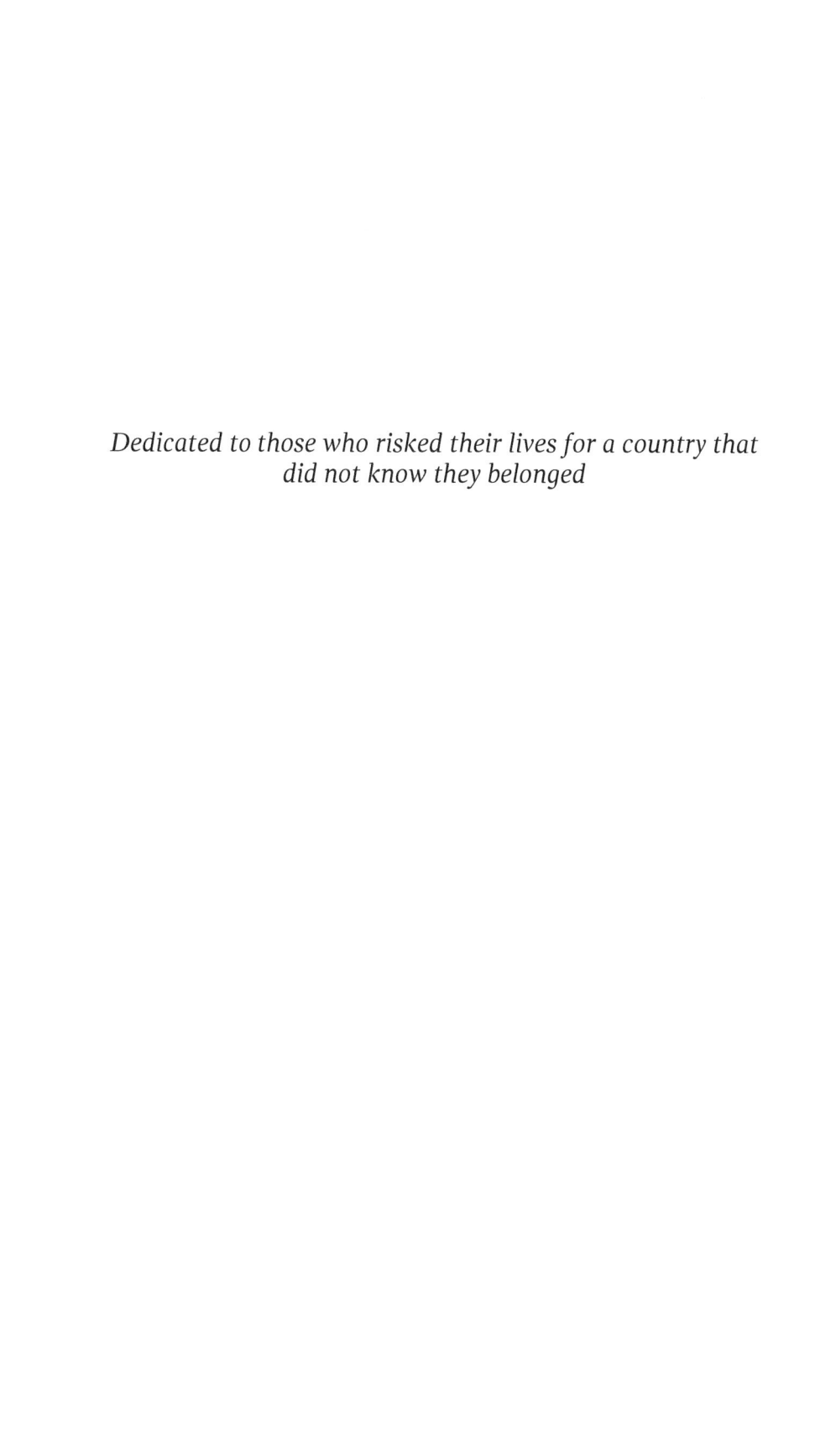

Dedicated to those who risked their lives for a country that did not know they belonged

Es ist an uns heute, den Glauben an die Unbesiegbarkeit des Geistes trotz allem ... unerschütterlich aufrechtzuerhalten.

Today, it is for us steadfastly to maintain faith in the invincibility of the spirit

– Stefan Zweig, 1941

Foreword

By Michael Zimmermann
Austrian Ambassador to the United Kingdom

The period from 1938 to 1945 saw the darkest moments in Austrian history. With initially widespread support among the population, the Nazi Regime brutally persecuted minorities and political opponents during its seven years of rule in Austria and sent 65,000 Austrian Jews to their death in the Holocaust. Following the defeat of Nazi Germany by the Allies, the Republic of Austria re-emerged as an independent State, yet under occupation for another decade. The Austrian State Treaty, signed at the Schloss Belvedere on 15th May 1955, prepared the way for the development of Austria as a consolidated and prosperous democracy in the heart of Europe.

The United Kingdom, as Allied power and signatory of the State Treaty, plays an important role in this history. Peter Dixon's book delivers a fascinating account of the Austrian Section of the Special Operations Executive (SOE): its many disappointments and its few successes, but above all its persistence. It is a story of a small group of women and men who would not have their faith in Austria destroyed, despite the overwhelming domination of the Nazi regime. Many of them had been forced to leave in the 1930s. They believed that Austrian independence was worth fighting for and that Nazi dominance could be undermined. Peter Dixon highlights the role played by the SOE in influencing British and Allied policy towards the future of Austria after the war, leading to the Moscow Declaration of

1943 and the eventual re-establishment of the Republic of Austria. This story illustrates the turbulent history of Austria, and of British-Austrian relations, in the first half of the past century. It forms part of a wider effort of historians and writers, many of them from the United Kingdom, to reappraise important historical episodes and draw the right lessons from them. As Austrians, we consider this outside view immensely valuable as we try to grapple with our own past and continue to work for reconciliation with the victims of the Nazi regime.

Today, the relations between the United Kingdom and Austria are better than ever. Through political cooperation, trade and investment, tourism and other people-to-people links, a genuine friendship between the two countries has developed in the post-war period. I sincerely hope that the sacrifices and contribution of courageous women and men, such as those described in the following pages, will not be forgotten.

February 2023

Introduction

EARLY IN THE SECOND WORLD WAR, Austrian exiles in Britain were seen as 'enemy aliens', indistinguishable from Germans. After all, Hitler had annexed Austria and turned it into an integral part of the greater *Reich*. When German troops marched into Austria on 12th March 1938, Austria ceased to exist. Refugees who arrived in Britain were interned on the Isle of Man or deported to Canada and Australia. Many thousands of Austrians eventually overcame these obstacles to fight on the Allied side, determined to defeat Nazi domination of their country. Often they enlisted in the Pioneer Corps and were given menial tasks: building bridges, roads, airfields and hutted camps.

Some, though, joined units that made better use of their language skills. A few found their way into the Special Operations Executive, the secret organisation formed by Winston Churchill to 'set Europe ablaze'. There, a small two-woman part of the German Section was dedicated to Austria. 'Dedicated' is the right word, for these two young women had lived for years in Vienna and loved Austria and its people. Rightly or wrongly, their experience had convinced them that a good number of Austrians would be willing to resist Hitler.

Just as for occupied countries like France and Belgium, SOE trained the Austrian men to operate undercover as secret agents in their homeland, carrying out sabotage and organising resistance. Only in this way could the Allies undermine Nazi rule in Europe and elsewhere. But in Austria, a country with powerful Nazi support where few individuals were willing to resist the regime, infiltrating agents was doubly difficult. The efforts of the tiny section of SOE that dealt with Austria did not significantly alter the course of the war. Few of the courageous agents made it home to Austria. And many who did return were killed.

Taking a British viewpoint, this book tells the stories of the small group of men and women in SOE, Austrians and foreigners, who kept the idea of Austria as an independent nation alive, not least to contribute to the collapse of Hitler's Germany. It is the story both of Austrian fighters who served with the Allies, inside and outside Austria, and of those who supported them. One man, a Viennese Jew, represents a microcosm of this history. He called himself Charles Kennedy.

CHAPTER 1

A Jewish Soldier

Blind Drop

JUST BEFORE MIDNIGHT ON 23ʳᴅ MARCH 1945, Second Lieutenant Charles Kennedy faced a serious problem. The Halifax bomber of No 148 Squadron from which he was about to jump was approaching the drop zone, but he had noticed something amiss. His leg strap was not properly connected.

The webbing strap attached a bag to his leg, only to be released once he was suspended below the parachute canopy. The bag—containing his equipment—would then fall away from his body, attached to his harness by a long rope. It would hit the ground a few seconds before Charles did, reducing the shock of his landing. But the link did not seem secure.[1]

Over the engine noise, Charles shouted to the dispatcher for help. The minutes ran out as they tried to make the strap secure. It was time to jump. The improvised repair would have to do.

The aircraft's captain, Pilot Officer Don Atkins, illuminated the red light,[2] then the green. Planners had carefully examined air reconnaissance photographs of the area and pronounced it suitable, but there was no reception party. Charles was jumping 'blind'. He dropped through the 'joe hole' in the aircraft's floor into the looming darkness below. Immediately, the slipstream snatched him away from the aircraft. The makeshift mend gave way, the bag tore from his leg. As it fell, the sudden tug snapped the rope attached to Charles' harness. The bag disappeared into the darkness and Charles was left with an empty rope trailing from his body. With the bag went much of his equipment, carefully prepared for his mission. Most importantly, he no longer had his W/T set: the radio, concealed within a portable gramophone, with which he was to contact the Special Operations Executive base in Italy.[3]

There was good news, though. The weather and visibility were perfect, and Charles landed right on target, undetected and without injury. His lonely drop zone was on the wooded mountain ridge known as the Manhartsberg, just seven miles from the nearest town, Krems an der Donau, where the Krems river joins the Danube. Theo Neumann, a Viennese socialist and now an SOE agent, had suggested the location. In better times, Theo had enjoyed vacations at his family's summer house there.[4]

Map of Austria, 1930s

Charles immediately drew together and hid his billowing parachute. He stripped off his parachutist's coverall, under which he wore a civilian suit with Austrian tailor's labels, and added it to the hide. Then he started searching for the missing leg bag. Apart from the radio, the bag contained the signal code plan known as *Mario*, through which he would ensure that contact with Italy was secure, and essentials like ammunition, spare clothing and forged food coupons. Without the last, he might starve. After over four hours of searching, dawn approached and the risk of discovery increased. Charles abandoned the search and set off for the forty-mile journey to his destination: Vienna. He was going home.

Charles Kennedy's name could not have sounded more English, but it was a recent invention. Like many Austrians who had joined the Allied fight against the Nazi regime, Charles had assumed a new identity, a *nom de guerre*. His real name was Leo Hillman, and he was a Viennese native of Jewish extraction.[5] He had joined the British Army's Pioneer Corps in Palestine in January 1940 and his return to Austria was far more than a homecoming. His task was to implement Operation *Electra*.

Originally planned for a parachute drop during the January or February 1945 moonlit periods, the operation's primary aim was to contact the Austrian Social Democrat underground movement in Vienna, establish a relationship between them and their Austrian colleagues in exile, and offer any support they might need.[6] A trained radio operator and a native of the city, Hillman was the ideal man for the mission.

With hindsight, we know today that in March 1945 the war in Europe had only weeks to run. Allied commanders then were confident of victory but did not know how long it might take. So the Special Operations Executive, the organisation created by Winston Churchill to undermine Nazi domination, kept the pressure on. And Leo Hillman took the train to Vienna.

Freeing the Homeland

Leo Hillman parachuted into his homeland under an assumed name and travelled by train to Vienna under another.

A decade later, after seven years of Nazi domination and ten of Allied occupation on the front line of the Cold War, the occupiers and the Austrian government signed the Austrian State Treaty. On 27th July 1955, it came into effect and Austria again became a sovereign state. British undercover agency the Special Operations Executive had played a modest part in the process that led Austria back to independence.

The Hillman-Kennedy narrative is one of countless stories that together represent the part played by Austrians in the fight against Hitler, in part through their involvement with SOE. Leo was among the Austrian refugees and exiles, many of them Jewish, who gravitated to SOE. His story is a microcosm of the whole: the persecution under Adolf Hitler of Jews and opponents of the Nazi regime; flight into exile for those who escaped imprisonment and death; determination to join the battle against the Nazis; service in the Pioneer Corps and other parts of the British Army; discovery by SOE 'talent scouts'; tough training and detailed preparation; dangerous missions into the homeland; intimate involvement at the front line of the nascent Cold War; and witnessing the rebirth of an independent Austrian nation.

Goodbye Austria

Leo Hillman was coming back to Vienna after an absence of five years. Born in August 1923 to Dora Hillmann, who, like her husband Adolf originated in Poland, Leo had grown up in the city. A furrier, Adolf ran a shop in the Währing district of northwest Vienna.[7] When he was born, that first name did not have today's connotations. The family lived near the shop and, like other Jewish shop owners, suffered from the hostility that increased through the 1930s. Leo would later claim that he had been imprisoned in Vienna for 'Nazi-baiting'.

The Fascist and anti-Semitic undercurrent progressively grew as Chancellor Adolf Hitler strengthened his grip on power in neighbouring Germany. On 12th March 1938, the trend came to a head. German tanks rolled across the border, the first military move in implementing the *'Anschluss'*, the annexation of Austria. Hitler declared that the sovereign state of Austria no longer existed. It was now simply a province of *Grossdeutschland*, Greater Germany. The Nazis called it the *Ostmark*.

The *Anschluss* already enjoyed substantial popular support among Austrians. But the Nazis made sure the takeover would succeed. Undercover agents and Austrian Nazis had prepared the ground well, rioting and disrupting life on Vienna's streets. Hitler demanded that Austrian Chancellor Kurt von Schuschnigg resign and hand power to the Austrian National Socialists. Meanwhile, German troops were on the way. Within days, the Gestapo rounded up thousands of Jews and opponents of Nazi rule and shipped them off to overcrowded concentration camps. The Nazis excluded Jews from the Austrian economy and culture, making them do menial and humiliating tasks. Jewish businesses were seized or bought up for a pittance. Many Jews were killed. Others fled abroad.

Hitler had already taken back the *Rheinland* in western Germany, 'stolen' from the Germans as part of the Treaty of Versailles at the end of the 1914-18 War. But for him, incorporating Austria was a priority. He had risen from his origins in the Austrian village of Braunau am Inn to become the most powerful man in Germany and eventually in Europe. In *Mein Kampf*, he wrote that it was essential for Austria 'to return to the great mother-country'. In March 1938, it did.

Jews in Austria were as Austrian as those who now attacked them. But for them the following months were even more of a nightmare than before. Violent persecution became increasingly brazen. As 1939 developed, Jews feared for their lives. Those who could do so left.

Among them were the Hillmanns. They may have been forced by Nazi intimidation to close the fur shop, or simply have felt it was too dangerous to stay. Soon after the world said goodbye to an independent Austria, the family bade farewell to their homeland and fled. Leo's parents ended up interned in Mauritius.[8] Some time after leaving Vienna, Leo left them and followed a different route. For a while, he hid in a Catholic monastery in France. But his next move showed his taste for adventure. In late 1939, a few weeks after his sixteenth birthday, he joined the French Foreign Legion.[9]

Pioneers and Raiders

Leo Hillman did not stay long with the French. Where he travelled and whom he fought against during the turbulent autumn of 1939 is uncertain. Anonymity is a principle of the Legion.[10] During that winter, Leo made his way to Palestine. Private Hillman, as he became, joined the Auxiliary Military Pioneer Corps (AMPC) in Palestine on 11th January 1940. Early in the war, this labour force was the only element of the British forces where 'enemy aliens' could serve. No. 1 (Palestine) Company AMPC formed up at the Palestinian village of Al-Sarafand, near Haifa, and comprised 650 Arabs and Jews, the latter from all over Europe. They worked well together.[11] It was just as well, for within weeks they were on their way to France. Leo and his comrades worked on railway and road construction near the town of Rennes in Brittany. Retreating from the advancing German juggernaut, No 401 (Palestine) Company AMPC took ship for England in two trawlers on 17th June and arrived at Weymouth.

Their commander, Major Henry Cator, had earned a Military Cross in the 1914-18 War. He sympathised with the ambitions of most of his men for a more active role in fighting the Germans. He understood that the Pioneer Corps' primary role—building bridges and airfields, laying roadways and digging out fortifications—did not satisfy them. After a few weeks, Cator had persuaded the War Office to give the unit a combat role. They sailed on 6th August 1940 back to Palestine.

Europe between the wars

In Cairo, General Sir Archibald Wavell had already decided to form Commandos—military units trained for hit-and-run raids into enemy territory—in the Middle East. Henry Cator was authorised to raise No 51 (Middle East) Commando from his Palestinian AMPC Company. From the Jews and Arabs who volunteered, he selected the best 300 men; Leo Hillman was among them. Just as the basic ranks of artillerymen are called 'gunners' and engineers 'sappers', the men became known as 'raiders'.

As the men started training at Geneifa, east of Cairo, their toughness and enthusiasm impressed their British Army instructors. They learned to build and sail rafts on the Sweetwater Canal, to board and deploy from boats and submarines on the Great Bitter Lake, to survive long desert marches and to work with demolition charges. Expecting to operate in the Mediterranean, they were surprised to be ordered to Eritrea.

The fully trained 51 Commando sailed from Suez to Port Sudan and spent three weeks at Gedaref adjusting to the climate. In Khartoum, Cator received orders to begin patrols and ambushes in support of British and Indian troops that were pushing back the occupying Italian army. As the divisional history put it, '51 Palestine Commando, a tough and aggressive agglomeration of Jews and Arabs under British officers, were taken under command'.

Using Sudanese camels and Cypriot mules for transport, for the next two months Raider Leo Hillman and his comrades seized and occupied water holes, a vital resource. They stormed vertiginous hills, to attack and hold enemy observation posts that were endangering the main forces. The final decisive battle in Eritrea took place on 25th March 1941, as 51 Commando supported the 5th Indian Division in their successful seizure of the Keren battlefield.

After a month's recuperation, 51 Commando was on the move again, this time into Abyssinia, today's Ethiopia. Supported by Colonel Orde Wingate's *Gideon Force*, Emperor Haile Selassie had entered Ethiopia in January with Ethiopian irregulars, who conducted a guerrilla campaign against the Italian occupation. 51 Commando supported the Allied advance against strong Italian resistance, with patrols, ambushes and diversions. In heavy rain and inhospitable terrain, the Commando kept up the pressure. They patrolled aggressively in the areas still held by the Italians, until all but a few remaining small groups surrendered, after the Allied victory at Gondar in November 1941.

51 Commando achieved remarkable success as it played its part in the first Allied strategic victory of the war, defeating the Italian occupiers of Ethiopia and restoring the Emperor to his throne in Addis Ababa. The tough, disciplined and highly motivated troops courageously infiltrated behind enemy lines in the mountainous terrain. Medal awards recognised many acts of bravery.[12]

Raider Hillman played his part in the unit's efforts but was not singled out as an individual. That would change. As 51 (Middle East) Commando returned to Egypt for leave and eventual disbandment, Leo moved on to a new and much more hazardous role.[13]

Austrian Desert Hero

Private Leo Hillman was rather short and stout. His gold-rimmed spectacles made him look more like a young professor than a combat-hardened soldier. When he opened his mouth to speak in his newly acquired English and introduced himself in a sardonic tone as 'Baron von Schnitzelberger', the splendid cockney accent was incongruous.

Like many other Austrian and German volunteers in the British armed forces, Leo himself chose his new name. The discovery of real names could be hazardous to families back home. Add to that nicknames and the field aliases used during operations, and the results can be confusing. But to his comrades in the desert, he was Charlie Hillman. His love of eating earned him a corpulent figure and the nickname 'Chunky'.

'Chunky' Hillman was a determined, capable and popular soldier. His popularity waned somewhat when he chewed garlic, a habit he had picked up in the French Foreign Legion. His friend Fred Warner claimed that the smell was so bad that others would not sit with Leo at meals. It was not Leo's odour, though, that interested Captain

Herbert Buck as he searched Palestine for recruits for a new secret unit. It was the language.[14]

A gifted linguist and a German-speaker, Buck had escaped from *Afrikakorps* captivity in late 1941 dressed in a purloined German uniform, crossing the desert to reach Allied lines by hijacking German vehicles and leaving the drivers trussed up by the roadside. The exploit sparked a novel idea in his Oxford-educated mind. Soldiers who spoke German fluently could don *Afrikakorps* uniform and penetrate behind enemy lines. Thus was born an unorthodox but potentially highly effective unit, operating under the cover name of Special Interrogation Group (SIG). According to the Middle East Commando Depot's War Diary for 17th March 1942, a Captain Buck arrived, 'to select German-speaking personnel with a view to certain work'.[15] Private Leo Hillman was one of the Jewish volunteers selected for that work.

Barely three dozen strong, the tiny unit trained intensively in Egypt for its highly dangerous mission. Captain Buck pulled no punches as he briefed them on their prospects. If captured, the men would be doubly condemned. Soldiers operating behind enemy lines out of uniform—or in German uniform—would be treated as spies and executed. If the SIG men were discovered to be Jewish, an even worse fate awaited them.

During the unit's three months of training, camp routine was all in German. Leo and his friends concocted and memorised assumed identities. They carried photographs and letters from fictitious lovers 'back home' and familiarised themselves with procedures, personalities and slang in Erwin Rommel's *Afrikakorps*. The men used captured German vehicles, weapons and equipment. On their first missions, they primarily sought intelligence. Dressed as German military police, Captain Buck, Leo Hillman and 'Tiffen' Tiefenbrunner set up temporary roadblocks and interrogated vehicle occupants to glean operational details. They entered German and Italian camps and mingled with soldiers as they stood in line for meals and even wages.

'Bertie' Buck had not only relied on Jewish refugees in seeking recruits for SIG. He had also toured prisoner-of-war camps to look for likely candidates. He found two PoWs: *Feldwebel* Walter Essner and *Unteroffizier* Heinrich Bruckner. Both expressed vehement opposition to the Nazis.[16] They had both served in the French Foreign Legion before being picked up for the *Afrikakorps* and later captured by the 8th Army. Bruckner was blond, aggressive and brash. Essler was quiet and easy-going. Some of Buck's men were doubtful, but the captain insisted the insider knowledge of Rommel's force in North Africa would be priceless. And he wanted to take the pair on operations. The SIG's first major mission would show how wrong he was.

In mid-1942, while the Desert War in North Africa was in full flood, the strategically crucial island of Malta was under constant attack as Allied convoys battled to break through and relieve the beleaguered defenders. 'There is no need for me to stress the vital importance of the safe arrival of our convoys at Malta,' wrote Winston Churchill on 2nd June.[17]

Meanwhile, Captain David Stirling was gaining fame, or infamy, within the Cairo Headquarters as an annoyingly unconventional but imaginative officer. His concept of small raiding parties, which eventually gained worldwide renown as the Special Air Service, had gained acceptance by Lieutenant-General Neil Ritchie, commanding 8th Army. 'Top cover' from Ritchie allowed Stirling to build up a small force. As attacks on Malta intensified and convoys failed to get through, the Director of Military Operations ordered Stirling to make a plan to relieve the pressure. Stirling delivered the plan twenty-four hours later: the SAS would destroy aircraft on the ground, so that they could not pose a threat to Malta. In total, they would attack eight airfields, on the night of 13th/14th June. Three were at Derna and Martuba, deep in enemy territory 100 miles west of Tobruk. Stirling had one major concern: how would the SAS patrols get there? Then a Cairo staff officer told him about the SIG. David Stirling called Bertie Buck to Cairo to discuss a novel proposal for a raid on the two airfields. SAS troops would infiltrate across Axis lines disguised as POWs, with German-speaking SIG men 'guarding' them. Buck jumped at the chance to show the SIG's mettle.

The various groups made their rendezvous at the isolated oasis of Siwa, in the Western Desert some 350 miles from Cairo. On 6th June, they moved out, with a patrol of New Zealanders from the Long Range Desert Group, expert navigators in the sandy wastes, as their guides. Four days further into the desert, the SIG men donned their *Afrikakorps* uniforms and assumed their characters. The Free French SAS 'prisoners', commanded by Lieutenant Augustin Jourdain, kept their weapons hidden. At one guard post, a German NCO warned them that British Commandos might be in the area, so they took his advice and sought the 'safety' of an *Afrikakorps* transit camp, taking on fuel and stores overnight. Not knowing the new password for the month of June, they bluffed it out of an Italian guard.

On the afternoon of 13th June, Jourdain and Bruckner reconnoitred airfields at Derna, finding Messerschmitt Bf 110 and Junkers Ju 87 Stuka aircraft parked in the open. Jourdain and Buck made their plans, dividing the SIG men and the French SAS between them. Buck and his group would attack Martuba, Jourdain's party would strike at Derna. Leo Hillman was with Buck.

But there were two major snags. Back in Cairo, Colonel Bonner Fellers, Military Attaché in the American Embassy, was sending detailed reports on British military operations and plans to Washington. He doubted the security of the State Department 'Black Code' he was using, but was told to continue using it. He was right to be suspicious. The *Servizio Informazioni Militare* (SIM), the highly efficient Italian military intelligence service, had burgled the US Embassy in Rome in 1941, before the USA entered the war, and stolen the codes. As a result, Rommel knew the dates of the planned raids.[18] That was bad enough, but worse was to come.

As Augustin Jourdain's party was on its way to attack Derna, Bruckner was driving their truck. Suddenly, he announced that there was a problem, jumped down and disappeared into the darkness. He returned with a patrol of German soldiers, who surrounded the truck and demanded that the 'prisoners' come out. Realising that they had been betrayed, the SIG men and the French SAS opened up with machine pistols and threw grenades, but they were overcome. Most were killed or captured. Jordain was wounded but escaped in the confusion and made it back to the rendezvous with Buck's party.[19]

The word that the mission had failed, the SAS troopers 'betrayed by the SIG', spread rapidly through the Middle Eastern special forces grapevine and led to a steep decline in trust. It was not entirely fair. While Jourdain's patrol was being betrayed and wiped out, Buck's party—including Leo Hillman—successfully attacked the airfield at Martuba, destroying twenty-seven German aircraft.

That was one small contribution to Malta's survival, but the desert war was not going well. As Leo and his remaining comrades struggled back across the desert to Cairo, Rommel's advance seemed unstoppable. The strategically significant port of Tobruk fell to the *Afrikakorps* on 21st June 1942.

Tobruk

The port of Tobruk was a key asset for Rommel as his forces pressed eastwards. Anything that might interrupt his flow of supplies would contribute to stopping him. The atmosphere in Cairo was close to panic. As the British in Cairo prepared for evacuation and burned secret documents, 1st July 1942 became known as 'Ash Wednesday'. Rommel did not reach Cairo, though, and the tide of the Desert War turned. Options opened up. One of them was Operation *Agreement*, planned for mid-September as a means of weakening Axis forces, by destroying harbour facilities, airfields, ships, fuel and other supplies.

Perhaps the best-known account of the June 1942 raid on Tobruk is the 1967 film starring Rock Hudson and George Peppard, which is a fine adventure movie but bears little relation to actual events. Several more accurate accounts are in print,[20] but the focus here is on the role of Leo Hillman and his SIG comrades.

Tobruk was a hard nut to crack, its harbour approaches mined and its garrison 17,000 strong. David Stirling and Lieutenant-Colonel John Haselden, a former cotton trader who was now an SAS commander, had proposed a surprise hit-and-run raid by a relatively small party. But the plan grew and grew. By the time the joint planners had finished with it, it had become a large and excessively complex land-sea operation with optimistic expectations. That Winston Churchill was in Cairo at the time probably did not encourage prudent planning.

The desert group, under Haselden's command, would be known as 'Force B'. After the Bruckner betrayal, the SIG's reputation was tarnished. Even so, the 'prisoners under escort' concept was sound and was a key part of Haselden's plan. But through Bruckner's information the Germans were aware of the ploy. Haselden's Force B assembled at Kufra Oasis, a hub on the ancient trade routes between Libya, Chad and Sudan.

Arriving there in a Bristol Bombay aircraft, Buck and his men looked and acted like German soldiers. The 'SIG betrayal' had not been forgotten, and the underlying mistrust of Palestinian Jews did not improve their reception by the other soldiers. Leo Hillman worked with the others to change the appearance of the trucks: painting the *Afrikakorps* symbol of a swastika and a palm tree on the doors; adding 'booty' markings to give the impression that these were captured British vehicles.

After a 600-mile desert crossing in eight three-ton trucks, guided by the Long Range Desert Group, the time came for Bertie Buck and his men to play their part. The SIG party was small. With Buck were German-speaker Lieutenant David Russell and five 'guards': Opprower, Goldstein, Berg, Rohr, Rosenzweig and Leo Hillman. Leo was using the name 'Steiner'.[21]

Buck drove the lead vehicle, one SIG member each of the following trucks. Approaching Tobruk and emerging from the sand on to a hard surface, they joined the stream of Axis traffic on the highway. At an Italian checkpoint, Buck casually waved the convoy's forged papers and was just as casually waved through. The 'German' SIG drivers exchanged insults with the Italian soldiers and successfully brought their eighty 'prisoners' through several sentry posts. As the commandos climbed down from the trucks and set about their individual missions, Buck and the SIG men stayed with John Haselden, taking over a remote villa on the coast and interrogating the surprised Italian occupants about local defences. The 'Italian Villa' became Haselden's command post.

Having successfully implemented their bluff, the SIG were free for other tasks. They attacked and neutralised several machine gun and anti-aircraft positions. Part of Haselden's plan was to release Allied PoWs thought to be in Tobruk, and Buck went off in search of them. But the Allied incursion was not going unnoticed. Leo and his friends held the positions they had seized against the increasing pressure of counter-attacks. Meanwhile, the other parts of Operation *Agreement* were falling apart. Inadequate landing craft, signals on landing beaches sent too late, underestimated resistance to a major attack: all contributed to the failure of the planned reinforcements to come ashore.

Haselden reluctantly ordered a withdrawal. Bertie Buck passed an order to the SIG men to get rid of their German uniforms and documents, and destroy most of the trucks. Some of them stripped uniforms from fallen British men and became Allied soldiers again. Leo Hillman did not have time to do so; he was still ostensibly German.

As dawn approached, they fell back to the Italian Villa, loaded casualties on to a truck and attempted to break out through the closing net. Seeing that Italian soldiers manning a machine gun blocked the way out, Haselden set out to tackle them. Buck, Hillman and two others rushed to help him. Haselden's courageous attack allowed the truck to get through, but he was shot and fell. Second Lieutenant 'Mac' MacDonald, a New Zealander, tried to drag him clear. At that moment, a grenade hit Haselden and killed him instantly. MacDonald barely escaped the same fate. Private Rohr lay wounded and Leo Hillman, his weapon empty, dragged him back under fire.

Buck, Hillman and MacDonald, with the wounded Rohr in tow, found the truck gone and their way ahead blocked. They took their only escape route and headed for the beach. They split up. Buck took Rohr further into enemy territory, in the hope of bluffing their way through and stealing a vehicle. They were captured, and Buck spent three years in German PoW camps.

At the beach, Leo Hillman joined up with Lieutenant Tommy Langton of the Special Boat Squadron, who was looking for a way out of the debacle for the small group of men he had gathered around him.[22] Finding that Langton's Motor Torpedo Boat's engines would not start, the small party took the only other way out: into the desert. Leo hobbled to keep up, his foot injured. Thirsty and starving, they travelled at night and hid by day. Friendly Arabs sheltered them and passed them from settlement to settlement. Leo Hillman's language skills were an asset, as was his irrepressibly cheerful attitude. It took two gruelling months and nearly 400 miles of walking for Langton's depleted group—now numbering four—to reach Allied lines.[23] Leo's role was described in the citation Langton wrote for the award of the Military Medal:

> On Sept. 13th, 1942 Pte. Hillman, then a member of the Special Investigation Group (*sic*), formed part of the force which entered Tobruk from KUFRA under Lt. Col. Haseldon (*sic*). Hillman was dressed in German uniform and it was his job to speak to any enemy guarding check posts on the road, and get the party through in their trucks. When action started Hillman was in Capt. Buck's party which, still in German uniform, took the first objective. The next morning after reinforcements had failed to land, I saw Hillman with one or two others and Lt. Col. Haseldon holding off and actually advancing on enemy who were greatly superior in numbers. The others made for the trucks, but Hillman refused to leave the Col. and attacked with him, killing several Italians and forcing others to run. When within a few yards of the enemy Lt. Col. Haseldon was hit and rolled over. Hillman went up to him and called his name several times. Not until he was certain that Lt. Col. Haseldon was killed did he come back to join us on board the stranded M.T.B. Here he kept the guns supplied with ammunition until no more could be found on board and then took to the hills with my party when it was apparent that no more could be done. For the next nine weeks during which we were endeavouring to get back to our own lines, Hillman showed courage, endurance and cheerfulness which was a great example to the rest of us. This in spite of the fact that the soles of his boots were torn off during the action and he tore his feet badly on the barbed wire perimeter defences at Tobruk on the first night of our journey, causing sores which were still open when he reached hospital nine weeks later. Whenever enemy positions were encountered Hillman showed the greatest calmness and courage. He was entirely responsible for persuading the Arabs to give us food

etc. I have no hesitation in saying that without his example and help we would have had very little chance of escaping successfully. Hillman has been in action with Capt. Buck's party in German uniform on a previous occasion, and was in the East African campaign with No. 52 Commando (*sic*).[24]

The over-ambitious Operation *Agreement* had failed. Three Royal Navy ships had been sunk, almost 800 men killed or captured. But the apparently unremarkable Leo Hillman had proved himself a resourceful and courageous soldier, at the age of just nineteen. Much had changed in his life. It was also here that he took on a new name. Concerned that the Germans already knew too much about him through Heinrich Bruckner, he asked his fellow-escapers to call him Kennedy. It was the name he would use on his return to Austria.

---

[1] The narrative of Kennedy/Hillman's operation is based on the Operation *Electra* reports in his personal file at the British National Archives (TNA), reference HS 9/711/2, the 148 Squadron Operations Record Book entry in TNA AIR 996/30 and reports in TNA HS 6/17-22. Additional information has been clarified or confirmed from Peter Pirker, 'a credit to the British army and to his own country, which is Austria': *Dokumente zu Leo Hillmans Kampf gegen den Nationalsozialismus, Täter: Österreichische Akteure im Nationalsozialismus* (2014). www.doew.at and Peter Pirker, *Subversion deutscher Herrschaft: der britische Kriegsgeheindienst SOE und Österreich*, Zeitgeschichte im Kontext (Goettingen: Vienna University Press, 2012).
[2] More on the Atkins crew is at http://www.operationdarkofthemoon.org.uk.
[3] The special operations element of SOE was initially known as SO2, but for simplicity the term SOE is used throughout. The propaganda element, SO1, became the Political Warfare Establishment and the planning element, SO3, withered on the vine.
[4] Peter Pirker, 'a credit to ...', 2014.
[5] Nick Van Der Bijl suggests he was 'born Leo Loebel in Vienna to prominent Jewish Socialists' (Nicholas Van der Bijl, *Sharing the Secret: the history of the Intelligence Corps 1940-2010* (Pen & Sword Military, 2013), but Dr Peter Pirker has verified that he was born Leo Hillmann (Peter Pirker, 'a credit to ...', 2014, Note 3). To avoid confusion the anglicised spelling 'Hillman' will be used here. In what follows, the choice of which of the multiple possible names to use will depend on which seems most natural for the individual's personal story. After an initial explanation, a single name will be used for consistency.
[6] TNA HS 6/17, various dates; HS 6/19, 2nd January 1945.
[7] Peter Pirker, 'a credit to ...', 2014.

[8] They were probably among the 1,580 persons who were interned on Mauritius, most of whom eventually settled in Palestine in August 1945 (Aharon Zwergbaum et al, 'Mauritius,' in *Encyclopaedia Judaica*, ed. Michael Berenbaum and Fred Skolnik 2nd (Detroit, MI: Macmillan Reference USA, 2007)).

[9] Fred Warner, *Don't You Know There's a War On?*, unpublished, TNA HS 6/23, HS 9/711/2.

[10] He probably served in the so-called *régiments de marche de volontaires étrangers* (RMVE, Marching Regiments of Foreign Volunteers), formed in September 1939 in the face of the German threat; 40% of the men in the sparsely equipped units were Jewish (Douglas Porch, *The French Foreign Legion: a complete history of the legendary fighting force* (London: Macmillan, 1991), p.445). When the 'phoney war' came to a sudden end in May 1940, the RMVE fought bravely to defend continental France. Other Legion units had fought in Norway where, according to his friend Fred Warner, Leo served with them (Fred Warner, 1985). However, by then Hillman was already in Palestine.

[11] This and the following six paragraphs are based partly on http://www.commandoveterans.org/51MECommando1941, by Harry Fecitt MBE TD, accessed 25th May 2021.

[12] Captain John Lapraik was awarded an Immediate Military Cross and Raider Sandor Landler the Military Medal.

[13] Brigadier H W Wynter, *Special forces in the Desert War, 1940-1943* (Richmond: Public Record Office, 2001), pp.305-306.

[14] Fred Warner, 1985.

[15] TNA WO 218/159. Authors differ about the precise details of the events surrounding the SIG. Although Virginia Cowles (Virginia Cowles, *The Phantom Major: the story of David Stirling and the SAS Regiment* (London: Grafton, 1988, 1958)) did not have access to more recently opened files in 1958, nor to information from German and Italian archives, she was able to interview and/or consult the private papers of some of the individuals involved. These included Leo Hillman, Augustin Jourdain and David Stirling. On the other hand, files opened later may have allowed authors like John Sadler (John Sadler, *Operation Agreement: Jewish commandos and the raid on Tobruk* (Oxford: Osprey Publishing, 2016)) and Damien Lewis, who describes the exploits of the SIG in dramatic fashion in Damien Lewis, *SAS Ghost Patrol: the ultra-secret unit that posed as Nazi Stormtroopers* (London: Quercus, 2017), to correct details. In what follows, where versions differ and I have been unable to verify details from contemporary primary documents, I have used the one that best fits the context.

[16] Damien Lewis suggests that Essner and Bruckner had been flown to Britain after capture and 'turned' at the Combined Services Detailed Interrogation Centre, 'Camp 020', Damien Lewis, 2017, p.96. No primary source has been found to confirm this.

[17] Virginia Cowles, 1958.

[18] 'Colonel Bonner Fellers, the U.S. military attaché in Cairo, 'was given full access to everything in the 8th Army and he sent back detailed reports on it all to Washington.' Unbeknown to Fellers, Axis intelligence read the reports: within eight hours the most secret data on British 'strengths, positions, losses, reinforcements, supply, situation, plans, morale etc' were under the gimlet eyes of Adolf Hitler, Benito Mussolini, and Field Marshal Erwin Rommel.' C. J. Jenner, 'Turning the Hinge of Fate: Good Source and the UK-U.S. Intelligence Alliance, 1940–1942', *Diplomatic History* 32, no. 2 (2009): p.165. Ironically, it was through 'Ultra' intercepts that the British were able to warn the Americans about Fellers' communications being compromised, but not until 12th June. Too late, the leak was plugged on 29th June.

[19] According to a message intercepted by the Allies, Adolf Hitler issued a order, apparently as a result of these events and 'not to be forwarded in writing'. Officers were to be briefed verbally that 'the severest measures' were to be taken against 'German political refugees' operating with the Allies in Africa. They were to be 'immediately wiped out in battle', but if they escaped this fate, 'a military sentence is to be pronounced by the nearest German officer and they are to be shot out of hand, unless they have to be temporarily retained for intelligence'. Cited in John Sadler, 2016, p.20. In November 1942, Adolf Hitler's *Kommandobefehl* would direct that all Allied soldiers operating behind Axis lines, whether in uniform or not, were to be executed.

[20] For example, Colin Bierman and Colin Smith, *Alamein: war without hate* (London: Viking, 2002), Gordon Landsborough, *Tobruk Commando: the raid to destroy Rommel's base* (London: Greenhill, 1989, 1956), Peter C. Smith, *Massacre at Tobruk: the story of Operation Agreement* (London: Kimber, 1987) David Jefferson, *Tobruk: a raid too far* (London: Robert Hale, 2013) and John Sadler, 2016.

[21] I am grateful to Alan Ogden for information on Russell, who later joined SOE and operated in Romania, where he was robbed and murdered.

[22] G B Courtney, *SBS in World War Two: the story of the original Special Boat Section of the Army Commandos* (London: Hale, 1983), pp.71-77. A briefer account is also in Barrie Pitt, *Special Boat Squadron: the story of the SBS in the Mediterranean* (London: Corgi, 1985, 1983).

[23] Brigadier H W Wynter, 2001, pp.347-348.

[24] TNA WO 373/46/64. Award announced in London Gazette on 11th March 1943.

CHAPTER 2

The Long Road Home

Hillman in SOE

WITHOUT BERTIE BUCK TO PLEAD ITS CAUSE to sceptical staff officers, the future of the Special Interrogation Group was bleak. Injured and on the run for several days, Buck had been captured near Tobruk, shipped to Italy and then to Germany. After escaping and being recaptured twice, he was put under special watch and spent the rest of the war as a prisoner. As Leo Hillman recuperated in a Cairo hospital, he learned the Army had disbanded the SIG after the abortive Tobruk raid. Most of his comrades had returned to the Pioneer Corps, but Leo wanted something more active. He somehow persuaded David Stirling to accept him into No 1 SAS Regiment. Stirling was captured in January 1943, but SAS jeep patrols continued to crisscross the Western Desert, raiding airfields, destroying supply trucks and cutting telephone lines.[1]

Why and how Leo Hillman transferred from the SAS to the Special Operations Executive is unclear. It may be that his language skills and his determination to return to Austria filtered through to the SOE representatives in Cairo, looking out for likely candidates. And the situation in North Africa had changed. In mid-1943, the Allies had already turned the tables in the Desert War and the *Afrikakorps* was retreating from Montgomery's 8th Army in the east. Blocked by Anglo-

American forces to the west in French North Africa following the Operation *Torch* amphibious landings, the last Axis forces in North Africa surrendered in May 1943. Attention turned to the Mediterranean. The Allies invaded Sicily on 9th July, Mussolini was arrested and, in September, Italy signed an armistice with the Allies. Allied troops made their tortuous and bloody advance through mainland Italy against tough Italian Fascist and German opposition. For Leo, the right place for an Austrian anti-Nazi would be Austria.[2]

Leo joined SOE for training as a wireless operator. He learned to encode and decode ciphers, to transmit coded messages in rapid Morse code, to include secret 'hints' to show if he was transmitting under duress, and to keep messages short. The *Gestapo*'s radio detectors would need time to triangulate the transmissions and locate his hiding place.[3]

The young women who would be at the receiving end—in Britain, in North Africa or eventually in Italy—would listen in to students' Morse transmissions and learn to recognise their transmission 'fingerprint': their 'fist'. These skilled operators, most of them members of the deceptively named First Aid Nursing Yeomanry, the FANY, could often discern whether an impostor had taken over an agent's radio.[4]

To Italy

By the summer of 1944, Leo had completed his training as a 'W/Op' and arrived in Italy. The Allies were still making their painful progress against an effective Fascist defence in the north. Further south, SOE had established its base at Monopoli, twenty miles southeast of Bari on the east coast, mounting operations into distant Poland, Yugoslavia, the Balkans and Austria. The SOE organisation in Italy became known as No 1 Special Force, code name *Maryland*.

Just as in Palestine and at *Massingham*, the secret SOE base near Algiers,[5] No 1 Special Force set up a localised and shortened version of the training process developed at SOE's vast network of stations in Britain. SOE requisitioned dozens of apartments and villas in southern Italy to replicate the entire UK system: paramilitary tactics, wireless operator training, parachuting, undercover operations, 'finishing' schools and holding schools.[6]

In late summer 1944, Leo Hillman joined others destined for operations in Austria at 'Villa Rossa', a 'fine Italian villa' surrounded by vineyards, well away from other buildings and 'on top of a hill overlooking the town of Fasano and the Adriatic Sea'. When the grapes had ripened, the men could lean out of their bedroom windows and pick them. The villa's population was in constant flux, as agents came and went, some being inserted by sea or air behind German lines in northern Italy. When Leo arrived at the 'Hotel Seaview', as his new comrades called it, he gained the nickname 'Poldi'. He looked nothing like a hardened agent; 'everything about him was round—his face, his nose, his body—and to complete the look, his legs were short.' When Major 'Jimmy' Darton, the German Section representative in Italy, arrived at the villa to present him with the Military Medal, the others changed their view of him'.[7]

One of SOE's 'very capable' field security sergeants was in charge of the villa. This was probably Sergeant Beaumont, who had joined SOE in February 1941 as a member of No 65 Field Security Section.[8] His job was to keep an eye on the men, but he 'had the most wonderful sense of humour and the kindest disposition', according to Leo's Hamburg-born friend Fred Warner. 'Nothing could ruffle him' and 'he surely did not have an easy time, as we were a difficult crowd, hard to please and full of our own importance'.[9]

The trainees ate well. A local woman provided excellent Italian food, while her two sons did housework, washing and other jobs. The younger son was a tailor. The plan for Leo and others bound for Austria had been to parachute into Yugoslavia, where SOE officers were working with the partisans led by General Josip Broz, known as Tito. But the political situation in Yugoslavia was becoming more complicated. Tito was happy to accept supplies from the western Allies, but less willing to help get agents through to Austria. So the trainees continued to train and keep fit as they waited for other options to present themselves. Although they were NCOs—Leo was a corporal—they had the acting rank of Second Lieutenant, an advantage when they socialised in the Italian towns. They often spent off-duty time at the Hotel Imperiale in Bari, which had become the British Officers' Club and Transit Hotel. Its temporary manager, an Austrian refugee freed from an Italian internment camp, treated them well. In the evenings at the villa, they found time to play bridge. One defector from the *Wehrmacht*, the son of a German ambassador, was the finest bridge player Warner had ever met. A short leave trip to the newly liberated Rome included contacting the Austrian community there, a visit to the Sistine Chapel and an evening at the opera to hear Puccini's 'Tosca'.

Despite the leisure, the waiting time in Italy was deeply frustrating for the Austrians. Some, recruited from PoW camps in Italy or Egypt, had to go through training. But men like Leo Hillman were already fully trained in undercover operations. They had to be kept up to scratch while they waited for deployment. For many of them, the waiting lasted months. Under Operation *Clowder*, SOE worked hard to get agents into Austria through Carinthia. The uncooperative attitude of Tito's Yugoslavian partisans made this more and more difficult. Setting up a reception party in Austria itself for parachuting was impossible. The only option was a 'blind' drop, and the combination of Austrian terrain and winter weather offered few windows of opportunity for that.

Meanwhile, Leo and his friends planned and trained. Several motorcycles were kept at the villa for the men to use, but the inexperienced riders wrecked most of them. Apart from long route marches, they practised firing, stripping and reassembling a range of Allied and enemy weapons. The Royal Air Force airfield at Brindisi was the site for parachute practice, including working with the secret 'Eureka' navigation aid, with which a ground party could guide an aircraft accurately to a drop zone. In the southern Italian mountains, they learned mountaineering skills and skiing. The Allies had rapidly formed a Mountain Warfare School near the town of Sepino, where experienced American and British soldiers shared their expertise.

Building on his previous SOE training, Leo Hillman took part in extra courses to bring his knowledge up to date. In September 1944, he was on a 'finishing school' course with three other Austrians and Germans. They learned the skills they would need to survive undercover in Austria, even though they hoped to be operating in British uniform. They learned how to organise an undercover group, to avoid detection, to stick to a cover identity and to become skilled burglars. Instructors taught them the current uniforms and insignia of Nazi security forces and drilled them in resisting interrogation. In local Italian towns, the students set up dead letter boxes and safe houses, while SOE field security NCOs acted as contacts or tried to follow them through crowded streets. Lessons were learned, and it paid to take them seriously.[10]

By October 1944, Leo was on a specialist wireless (radio) operator, or W/Op, course at *Maryland*'s wireless school close to the villa in Selva di Fasano, known to SOE as 'Hillside'.[11] He refreshed his Morse code skills and learned to use the codes that would keep his transmissions secure. Apart from encrypting the messages, the operators used codewords for locations, people and formations. Leo would transmit from '*Ilford*' (Austria) to '*Tooting*' (Italy). In November, he was at the Austrian 'holding school' in Italy, where the final preparations for his mission were made.[12] Leo's conducting officer briefed him on his precise mission, on the current military and political situation, and on the people he was to contact in Vienna. He memorised his cover story and was tested on the details. He was given the opportunity to write a will and offered a cyanide capsule as an alternative to undergoing torture. Leo was ready.

But Leo continued to wait, his hope building during the few nights in each month when the moon was bright enough for parachute drops. Christmas came and went, the weather atrocious. On 11th January 1945, SOE made a firm plan to drop Leo during the next moon period. No aircraft was available during January, so they attempted the mission on the night of 20th/21st February. Cloud covered the drop zone, and the aircraft turned back. More frustration.[13]

It was not until the night of 23rd March, months after Leo's arrival in Italy, that the constellation of moonlight, weather and aircraft availability came together and allowed his mission to go ahead.[14] As he searched in the Manhartsberg forest for his missing radio and personal equipment, and then realised that the search was hopeless, Leo Hillman—alias 2nd Lieutenant Charles Kennedy, alias *Obergefreiter* Gerber—was determined that he would make every remaining day count.

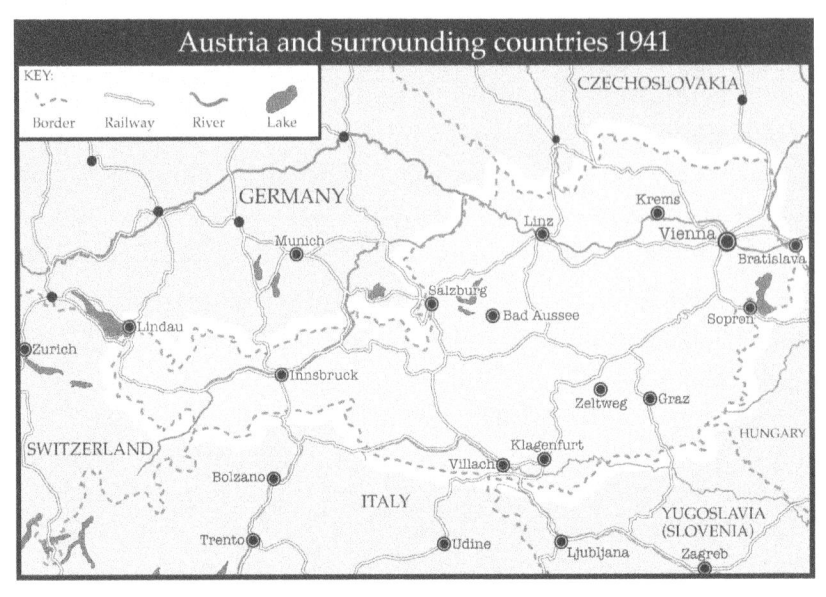

Map of Austria and neighbouring countries

Obergefreiter Gerber

When Leo Hillman boarded the Vienna train at Krems on the morning of 24th March 1945, he was masquerading as a former *Wehrmacht* soldier, discharged after suffering a duodenal ulcer in North Africa. If the *Gestapo* stopped him on the station platform, he would be to them a former junior soldier called Gerber.[15]

His carefully memorised 'legend' gave him a new persona. According to his *Wehrpass*, his forged military identity card, 'Gerber' had been conscripted into the *Wehrmacht* reserve in Vienna on 2nd June 1939. Along with the rest of his age group, he was called up in November and joined the 1st Company of the 304th Infantry Battalion, at Plauen, in Saxony. The pattern of *Wehrpass* available to the SOE forgers was first issued in 1942, so they had copied details of a 'lost'

1939 original on to the newer form, using two different styles of handwriting. Using intelligence about German formations, they had recorded on the document that the unit in which 'Gerber' was serving had changed its name on joining Erwin Rommel's *Afrikakorps* to become the 104th Panzer Grenadier Battalion. Where possible, SOE in London passed on the names of the regimental commanding officers and details of where the battalion had served. 'Gerber' had been taken ill on 12th December 1942. After some time in a field hospital, *Feldlazarett* 667, he was evacuated via Naples to a military hospital in Kaiserslautern in Germany. Discharged there from military service but fit for civilian employment, he had returned to Vienna and reported to the *Gestapo*. Alongside the *Wehrpass*, the forgers had provided a driving licence, a *Bundeswehr* discharge certificate—the *Entlassungschein*—and papers to show that he was a *Gestapo* employee. These would help him gain entry to *Gestapo* headquarters.

Leo had had to memorise these fictional details, and more, during his time at the SOE outpost in Italy, but they were tailored to his extensive knowledge of living as a German soldier in the desert war. His former service in the SIG served him well.

Districts of Vienna, 1938

Operation *Electra*

Leo Hillman arrived at the *Westbahnhof* in Vienna without running into any further trouble, blending into the crowd at the station. He walked through city streets, familiar from his boyhood, to an address on the Domikanerbastei in Vienna's central district.[16] His task was to contact any social democrats who were resisting the Nazis and assist them with weapons and any other aid they might need. Austrian socialists in exile had passed him the name of Karl Tambornino, a prominent and influential socialist, as a first point of contact.[17]

At the address, he met Tambornino, who greeted him with suspicion. The socialist movement, said Karl, was 'practically non-existent, since most of its active members had been arrested' a few weeks earlier.[18]

Other potentially dangerous individuals had been swept up in the general conscription to the *Volkssturm*, Hitler's last-ditch 'force' of boys and old men. In an atmosphere of deception where *agents provocateurs* and *Gestapo* informers were common, Tambornino's suspicion was justified. Slowly, though, Leo got him to open up and admit to his illicit socialist connections. In fact, he had been leader in Vienna's District IV of the *Republikanischer Schutzbund,* a banned paramilitary arm of the Social Democratic Workers' Party (SDAPÖ). Arrested in 1934, he had spent eighteen months in prison. He believed he was under constant surveillance by the *Gestapo*.[19]

The resistance movement still had a few active members, allowed Karl, and he was in touch with them. He passed Leo on to another address, on the Schubertring, where he could stay in reasonable safety.[20] Tambornino's wife gave Leo some food coupons, so that he could feed himself for the next few days.

No doubt carefully watched by his new friends, Leo stayed at this safe house while the *Widerstandsbewegung*, the resistance movement, decided how to use his expertise. Without his radio, the original plan of establishing contact with the British and the Austrian exiles was unworkable. Things were moving too quickly. The Red Army was almost at the gates of Vienna. How could the Nazi defence best be undermined?

Leo met with a resistance leader at a secret location and explained how they could harass and terrorise the SS and *Wehrmacht* defenders. Also, Leo explained, he planned to mount a raid on the *Gestapo*'s Vienna headquarters, the Hotel Metropole, in order to take hostages and capture files before they could be destroyed. These were his orders from Major 'Jimmy' Darton, as 'a matter of paramount importance'.[21]

Impressed, the resistance leader put 130 of his men under Leo's command. Most were young Austrian deserters from the *Wehrmacht*, who were highly disciplined and ready to obey Leo's orders. The men had limitless enthusiasm but lacked organisation and the ability to plan attacks in detail. Over the brief period he had available, Leo successfully corrected that. He had to hide them in cellars and bombed ruins, as none of them had any papers. Even Leo, as his *alter ego* the medically unfit *Obergefreiter* Gerber, was in danger of being stopped on the street and 'recruited' for the *Volkssturm*. The *Gestapo* patrolled constantly and challenges were frequent.

Memorial on the site of the former Hotel Metropole, Morzinplatz, Vienna

The raid on the Hotel Metropole became more urgent after Leo infiltrated the building with one of his new comrades to gain intelligence. During the clandestine reconnaissance visit, he heard the *Gestapo* planned to evacuate the hotel on Easter Day, Sunday 1st April. But this was the day planned for his raid. Leo quickly firmed up the plan, which owed a great deal to his SIG experience in North Africa. A two-ton truck and a car would deliver twenty-five men disguised as SS soldiers to carry out the raid, then wait with engines running until the raiders emerged. But hours before the planned operation Leo learned the SS had requisitioned both vehicles during Saturday night. He had to call off the operation.

On the same day, disappointed but undeterred, Leo attended a secret meeting of the resistance leaders, as close as he got to any coordinated Viennese movement. Essentially, there was no overarching control, and the different groups followed their own instincts. But the pace was quickening. *SS-Oberst-Gruppenführer* Sepp Dietrich had retreated from Hungary and took over the defence of Vienna. The underground leaders agreed to intensify sabotage and propaganda, and Leo's group set to work. During Monday night, they distributed leaflets across the city. Printed on portable presses in private houses or secretly by employees of printing works, some of the leaflets incited more sabotage from Viennese civilians, who were being forced to dig trenches and build barricades. Others called on the SS and *Gestapo* to leave Vienna and save it from devastation, warning that those who committed atrocities would be held responsible. Leo wrote some texts himself and believed that they played a considerable role in eroding Nazi morale and bringing about the collapse of the German defence of Vienna.

SOE had provided Leo with operational funds amounting to 10,000 *Reichsmark* and 300 US dollars, which he used to buy arms for his group. He had been able to contact soldiers at the nearby Rennweg barracks and persuade them to sell weapons and ammunition to the resistance. The prices were high.

On Tuesday, 3rd April, armoured cars patrolled the streets of Vienna during the day, but Leo Hillman and his 130 men were out that night, attacking military command posts and Nazi party offices. At 10.00 pm, Soviet shells fell on the city, the start of the battle of Vienna. Austrian *Wehrmacht* and *Volkssturm* soldiers deserted *en masse*, provided with shelter and civilian clothing by city-dwellers. Refugees were fleeing the city, using any means of transport they could lay their hands on, or walking with handcarts. Lines of traffic blocked the roads and resistance snipers fired on any Nazis recognisable in the chaos.

By the next weekend, the Red Army had reached the south-eastern suburbs of the city. At midnight on Saturday, 7th April, Leo joined a final meeting of the resistance group leaders and was able to report that he had received even more weapons from the barracks than he had hoped. They decided to wage open and merciless war against the SS.

Next morning, Leo divided his troops into well-equipped groups of seven or eight men. Before a group left its hiding place, he briefed them on the task and got them to think through what they would do if things went wrong, something they had not considered before his arrival. The groups attacked supply lorries with anti-tank weapons, preventing ammunition from reaching the SS troops as they retreated through the city streets. Sometimes Leo went with a group on its mission, including an attack on a prominent Nazi named Schweiger at his home in the Paulusgasse-Landstrasse. He set light to the vehicle of a Nazi Party member, both to thwart the man's escape from Vienna and to show the resistance fighters how easily a vehicle could be burnt out with limited resources, albeit with a certain amount of personal risk. Leo had learnt these and many other skills during his SOE training.

Eventually the SS were squeezed between the advancing Red Army and the resistance fighters to their rear. SS pressure on the resistance fighters increased, and they fell back to defend a few city blocks close to the Schlachthausgasse and the Rennweg barracks, hoping to be relieved by the Russians. A small group of *Wehrmacht* deserters successfully repelled 'at least three furious attacks'. The SS 'only succeeded in forcing the door of the house at 15, Schimmelgasse and murdering a youth of fifteen in front of his terrified mother'.

Some of Leo Hillman's men subsequently caught the murderer and shot him.

As Leo and a group of his men were defending the building at 3, Paulusplatz, under siege by two SS companies, he could see that the situation was becoming critical. He decided to make his way to the Russian lines and ask the Red Army for assistance. Leo later reported the events of the subsequent 'exciting half-hour':

> I left the building, which was besieged by SS troops, accompanied by one of my men who spoke Russian. We slipped through a back door into the open and by crossing two courtyards and jumping over a couple of walls we reached Schlachthausgasse, where I shot an SS-man who tried to stop us.
>
> Heavy fire was still being exchanged, and as we approached the abattoir at St. Marx we were met with a shower of bullets. I had taken a piece of white cloth with me and the fire stopped as soon as I waved it several times. Several heavily armed Russians appeared and my interpreter explained to them who we were and that we needed help at once. Taken to their HQ, I repeated my request to an officer who spoke some English. This request was immediately granted and a company ... supported by a self-propelled gun was detailed to deal with the SS. We reached our destination at the double only to find out that the enemy had fled at the approach of the Russians.[22]

Fighting was still going on in Vienna when Leo received a formal invitation to visit the Red Army's Corps HQ. From there he was taken to a divisional security section, accompanied by three resistance leaders. The Russians treated him with respect and courtesy, as he told them his story and passed a message from the Social Democratic Party, which 'welcomed the Red Army and called for the total destruction of Hitlerism'.

Prisoner of our friends

The Russian courtesy had limits. While the USSR, the USA and Britain were allies, the friendly alliance was tempered with mutual suspicion. The Allies had agreed the division of Austria into occupation zones and the joint administration of Vienna. They would eventually implement this arrangement as agreed, but for now the Russians were keeping the Americans and British well away from the capital.

As a 'guest' of the Red Army, Leo Hillman was kept in 'protective custody' and watched closely. The resistance leaders who had accompanied him gave names and addresses of prominent Nazis, who were arrested within hours. Leo went with Russian field security men to the apartments of those arrested and helped them seize documents linking the residents to the Nazi party and the *Gestapo*.

After three weeks Leo was brought before General Aleksei Blagodatov, the Red Army Commandant of Vienna, who packed him off to a transit centre in Vienna Neustadt. Here he was effectively a non-person without papers, a minnow tossed into the sea of displaced persons. It was an unpleasant experience.

With no means of proving his identity, Leo had no choice but to remain in Soviet-controlled Vienna until he could contact the British. Members of the resistance gave Leo a place to stay in safety, but it did not last long. The Soviet secret police, the NKVD, raided the apartment on 21st May on the strength of a confidential tip-off. They arrested Leo, along with one of the resistance fighters who were sheltering him. At NKVD headquarters, reported Leo later, 'we underwent a close interrogation, in the course of which I was threatened with shooting if I did not confess to be a Fascist spy'. After a phone call to the Russian military authorities who knew about Leo, his captors released him. In his absence, though, the flat had been searched. The searchers, led by Viennese functionaries of the Communist Party, had stolen the remaining 2,500 Reichsmark and 280 dollars of his operational funds. Leo's protests about the theft were in vain.

A few days later, he was again arrested. He had moved to an apartment on the Opernring, having seized the opportunity of transport out of Vienna. In the chaotic and repressive Viennese environment of May 1945, Leo was desperate to get back to SOE. He had met Lieutenant Madeleine Boncompagnie, a Belgian woman in British uniform who turned out to be a member of the Special Allied Airborne Reconnaissance Force, the SAARF. Her task was to organise transport to Vienna for former political prisoners released from Dachau concentration camp. She had offered him a ride to Linz, on the demarcation line between the Soviet- and US-occupied zones, and the Opernring apartment was a step closer to his goal.

Unfortunately, the building's janitor had reported 'foreigners staying here unregistered'. On the morning of Monday, 28th May, three plain-clothes agents of the *Staatspolizei*, now under the Soviet thumb, took Leo to police headquarters. Thirty-six hours later, he was interrogated and, despite naming prominent Viennese who would vouch for him, he was bundled off to the notorious '*Liesl*' prison. Food in Vienna was scarce, food for prisoners almost non-existent. Leo spent six weeks of starvation in a cell shared with nine Nazis. On 9th July, the police released him with apologies. His wristwatch was long gone from the file in which it had been left. For the next two weeks, Leo kept his head down in another Vienna apartment and hoped that the message he had given to the Belgian SAARF officer had got through to SOE.

'I, Lieut. C V Kennedy (General List), am in Vienna and have no chance to return', the handwritten message read, and continued:

> Since I haven't any documents to prove my British identity, I am under the constant threat of being shot by the Russians. I've been arrested twice by them. The Russians refuse to let me through their lines to reach my own people. ... Will you please pass following message on to ME 43:
>
> Am awaiting my rescue from Vienna. Am OK. But short of food and cannot obtain any. Send news or documents to the 'British-American Relief Comittee (sic)', Wien, Metternichgasse Nr 10. I am registered there but cannot get any help without documents.[23]

This message, arriving on 28th June, was the first sign that Leo Hillman was still alive. Unconfirmed or not, it was good news, for SOE had feared Hillman/Kennedy dead. Soon afterwards, the news was confirmed by a different route. The War Office in London received a message on 8th July from the British Military Mission in Hungary and passed it to SOE:

Greek military personnel recently arrived here from Vienna reports following. Lieut Charles Victor Kennedy, British parachutist age 28, has been detained by Austrian military authorities for last two months following denunciation. Still held 27th June at HQ on Elisabeth Promenade West 153 Vienna.

The lack of urgency in getting Leo's handwritten message to SOE—a four-week delay—may have been caused by Lieutenant Boncompagnie's comments. According to her boss at SAARF, she had 'a very bad impression of this person, whose story did not appear to hang together'. Truth can be strange.

For the remainder of his time in Vienna, Leo Hillman was relieved to remain unarrested. He somehow got to the inter-Allied demarcation line and reported to the US military. The SOE unit in Austria heard on 10th August that he was 'safe at Linz with the Americans' and two days later reported 'Kennedy safe with us at Klagenfurt'.

Leo Hillman was awarded the Military Cross for his action in Vienna. According to the citation,

> This officer was parachuted alone into Austria in March 1945 and immediately made his way by train to VIENNA. This journey was carried out in the face of great *Gestapo* activity and could never have been accomplished without immense determination and courage on the officer's part. On arrival in VIENNA, by the exercise of outstanding skill and personality, he established personal command over some 400 (sic) Austrian deserters and evaders whom he armed, equipped and organised into a guerrilla force. This force operated against the SS and Nazi officials during the last 10 days before the Russian entry into Vienna, and was effective in preventing demolitions and fires started by the fleeing SS. Lt Hillman and his personal squad rounded up some 100 SS men and handed them over to the Russian troops.
>
> Throughout the whole of this period it was this officer's personal skill, bravery and determination which held together the otherwise unorganised effort of these 400 Viennese resisters. His life was permanently in danger but his personal example induced many Viennese to take offensive action which they would otherwise not have done. Lt Hillman's subsequent long incarceration by the Russians was borne with

dignity and steadfastness and his final move to the American Zone was on par with his previous work. He has been a credit to the British Army and to his own country, which is Austria.[24]

The infamous Captain Kennedy

Now that Leo Hillman's mission was complete, SOE officers discussed what to do with him: his 'disposal'. He wanted to stay in the British Army, but the rather callous suggestion that he return to the Pioneer Corps was quickly squashed. He would have had to relinquish his commission and reapply as a private soldier. The SOE unit in Austria, now calling itself 'No 6 Special Force Staff Section' and commanded by Lieutenant-Colonel Charles Villiers, took him on. No 6 SFSS planned to arrange a counter-intelligence job for him in Austria, which was approved by London.

His commission had been awarded in his real name, so it was 'Lieutenant Leo Hillman' who was formally posted to the British occupation forces in Austria as a counter-intelligence officer, with effect from 1st October 1945.[25] What that meant in practice was hunting for hidden Nazi war criminals and carrying out interrogations. It was in this latter role that Captain Charles Kennedy, as some in Austria knew him, gained an unfortunate reputation.

The attitude of the Allies in conquered Germany and Austria, as information about mass murder spread and conditions in the liberated concentration camps were uncovered, was one of barely contained anger. There was a determination to bring the perpetrators to justice; Leo and his colleagues were the means of doing so. He worked at the former PoW camp, previously Stalag XVIIIA, near the Carinthian town of Wolfsberg. It had become a British internment camp for some 3,000 suspected war criminals and prominent Nazis. There he was tasked with investigating war crimes committed at the Mauthausen concentration camp near Linz.

As an investigator and witness, Leo appeared at the military tribunal in Klagenfurt in the autumn of 1947, which tried twelve of the camp personnel for war crimes. He had interrogated one of the main defendants, Walter Briezke. Two of the accused were acquitted, Briezke and one other sentenced to death and hanged in March 1948, the rest given sentences ranging from three years to life. Most of those imprisoned were released in 1951; the camp doctor, sentenced to life imprisonment, was freed in March 1954.[26]

In the post-war years, right-wing voices in Austria, and particularly in Carinthia, became more confident. Newspapers characterised the British camp at Wolfsberg as an 'Allied concentration camp' and the suspected Nazis as martyrs.

Meanwhile, Leo Hillman had married a girl from Carinthia in 1946 and in later years returned there on leave and family visits. The local newspaper built up his role at Wolfsberg, highlighted his background as a Jewish emigrant from Vienna who had fought on the British side and published front-page articles saying 'You are not wanted here!'. The Austrian security service feared for his safety. In Carinthia at least, he was 'the most hated man in the land'.[27]

SOE and Austria

The story of Operation *Electra* in 1945, and others like it, show how the years of painstaking preparation by SOE led to relatively minor successes. Thus it would be wrong to overstate the importance of SOE's efforts to undermine Nazi domination of Austria. The repression and counter-espionage measures of the *Gestapo* were brutally effective and getting access to Austria was beset with difficulty.

Yet SOE persevered. The tiny Austrian sub-section in 'X Section'—the part of SOE responsible for subversion and sabotage in the German Reich—was at the forefront of the change in British and Allied policy on Austria's status: from an indistinguishable part of Nazi Germany to its 'first victim'. SOE set about recruiting and training Austrian exiles for an eventual paramilitary role in their homeland and worked in more subtle ways to undermine the German Reich. Independence for Austria was a goal for SOE from the outset, while British policy still treated Austria as the integral part of Germany that Hitler asserted it to be. Thus SOE spearheaded what eventually became British and Allied policy: the eventual restoration of Austrian sovereignty.

Operating into the German *Reich* itself was a much more challenging proposition than supporting resistance movements in lands conquered by the Nazis. There more than anywhere, SOE recognised the danger of provoking severe reprisals that would crush any uprising before it could achieve anything. Planners would have to bide their time, training and preparing for action at just the right time, most likely in support of regular forces.

Hundreds of other books about resistance to Nazi control of Europe in general, and about SOE in particular, are in print. Some of them mention Austria. The doyen of SOE historians, the late M R D Foot, devoted just one page to SOE's Austrian work in his book *Resistance*. I had already written books to fill two gaps in the story of SOE—on the crucial role of keeping undercover agents secure and on SOE's part in the Allied Mediterranean campaign—and I knew I had found another gap to fill. In SOE's Austrian efforts, a story remained to be told.

So this book tells the stories of the men and women of the Special Operations Executive who helped Austria oppose Hitler. Many were Austrians themselves. Most had fled Nazi persecution. In telling these stories, I hope not to duplicate other work, and I aim to cover the ground accurately, making full use of archives opened up in recent years. The book is of necessity selective. I focus on SOE, but the American Office of Strategic Services, the Soviet People's Commissariat for Internal Affairs and Britain's Secret Intelligence Service—respectively the OSS, NKVD and SIS (better known as MI6)—also deployed agents into Austria.[28] Although often described as such for dramatic effect, SOE agents were not 'spies'. Only rarely was their work espionage, although they did pass on intelligence acquired in the course of their undercover operations.[29]

The book is also selective in a different sense. Even within SOE, it would not be possible to tell the story of every officer and agent, many of which have in any case appeared elsewhere. Also, the book's vantage point is the SOE headquarters in Baker Street rather than Vienna, looking through a British lens rather than an Austrian one. I would not have the temerity to go into Austrian politics in any great depth. Nor do I claim to equal the comprehensiveness of works like the in-depth academic study (in German) of SOE in Austria by Dr Peter Pirker. For more detail, that is the place to look.[30] To duplicate Dr Pirker's academic depth and rigour is not my purpose. Instead, I aim to bring the stories of courageous Austrian and British agents to a new audience. But the back story begins in the Austria of the 1930s.

---

[1] Brigadier H W Wynter, 2001, pp.359-370. See also Ben Macintyre, *SAS Rogue Heroes: the authorized wartime history* (London: Viking, 2016), on which the recent BBC Television series of the same name is loosely based.

[2] Antony Beevor, *The Second World War* (London: Weidenfeld & Nicolson, 2012), pp.487-505.

[3] It is unclear from primary sources whether Hillman completed his training at Thame Park (STS 52) in Oxfordshire or at Mount Carmel (STS 102) in Palestine. The latter seems more likely.

[4] M R D Foot, *SOE: an outline history of the Special Operations Executive 1940-1946* (London: The Bodley Head, 2014), pp.71-72, Peter Dixon, *Guardians of Churchill's Secret Army: men of the Intelligence Corps in the Special Operations Executive* (London: Cloudshill Press, 2018), pp.116-117.

[5] Training in Palestine is mentioned briefly in M R D Foot, 2014, p.71. On *Massingham*, see Peter Dixon, *Setting the Med Ablaze: Churchill's Secret North African Base* (London: Cloudshill Press, 2020).

[6] A brief description of SOE training is in Peter Dixon, *Guardians*, 2018, pp.89-91, a more comprehensive one in M R D Foot, 2014, pp.51-74.

[7] Eric Sanders, *Emigration ins Leben: Wien-London und nicht mehr retour* (Vienna: Czernin, 2008), p.227.

[8] TNA HS 8/885, Report by DH/160 dated 20th April 1944.

[9] Fred Warner, 1985. 'Villa Rossa' may be the Villa Rosato in Selva di Fasano, where SOE requisitioned several villas and apartments.

[10] See Peter Dixon, *Guardians*, 2018.

[11] David Stafford, *Mission Accomplished: SOE and Italy 1943-1945* (London: Bodley Head, 2011), p.58.

[12] TNA HS 6/17, 25th November and 23rd December 1944.

[13] TNA HS 6/17, 22nd February 1945.

[14] TNA HS 6/20, 13th April 1945.

[15] Details are in TNA HS 9/711/2. The suggestion in various publications that Hillman had a false identity as a Gestapo officer cannot be verified.

[16] Letter from Hillman to Walter Hacker, quoted in Peter Pirker, 'a credit to ...', 2014.

[17] Hillman had also been briefed to contact another radio operator in Vienna, code name *Maus*, but he had already been betrayed (see Chapter 6).

[18] Hillman's reports on his mission are in TNA HS 9/711/2, FO 371/46603 and HS 7/146.
[19] Peter Pirker, 'a credit to ...', 2014, Note 43.
[20] Letter from Hillman to Walter Hacker, quoted in *ibid*, p.252.
[21] TNA HS 9/711/2, Brief for Operation *Electra*, 29th January 1945. The Hotel Metropole was on the Morzinplatz; a monument commemorating victims of Nazi terror now stands on the site. The 2020 film *Schachnovelle* tells the story of a debonair Vienna lawyer who has been helping Jewish clients to smuggle their savings abroad. He is arrested and taken to the Hotel Metropole, kept in solitary confinement and psychologically tortured to make him give up account numbers. The dramatic but surreal story revolves around the game of chess (no spoilers here) but gives a good impression of the atmosphere of fear and vulnerability in post-*Anschluss* Vienna.
[22] TNA FO 371/46603, 3rd September 1945.
[23] This and the following four quotes are from TNA HS 9/711/2.
[24] MC promulgated in The London Gazette, 15th November 1945. Citation at TNA WO 373/100/142.
[25] Posting was to GSI(B) in No 5 Corps. TNA HS 9/711/2, 22nd October 1945.
[26] Sources: K Kocjancic, 'Klagenfurt Trial (Sept.-Nov. 1947)', 2007, Axis History Forum, https://forum.axishistory.com/viewtopic.php?t=120852 (accessed 27th June 2021); Lisa Rettl and Peter Pirker, *"Ich war mit Freuden dabei!": der KZ-Arzt Sigbert Ramsauer: eine österreichische Geschichte* (Wien: Milena, 2010), reviewed by Rainer Mayerhofer in the *Wiener Zeitung*, 3rd December 2010. A previous US military tribunal in March 1946 had tried over sixty former camp personnel and prisoners from Mauthausen (https://www.jewishvirtuallibrary.org/mauthausen-trial).
[27] *Unterkärntner Nachrichten*, 12th July 1957, cited in Peter Pirker, *Subversion deutscher Herrschaft*, 2012, pp.507-510.
[28] Also known under the anodyne name Inter-Services Liaison Department. The better-known term MI6 will be used hereafter.
[29] Gathering intelligence was a role specifically not included in SOE's charter, so as not to step on the toes of MI6.
[30] Peter Pirker, *Subversion deutscher Herrschaft*, 2012. Based on Dr Pirker's prize-winning PhD dissertation, which he defended at the University of Vienna in October 2009.

CHAPTER 3

Approaching Storm

Prince, King, Duke

IN THE TUMULTUOUS YEARS OF 1935 AND 1936, His Royal Highness the Prince of Wales, His Majesty King Edward VIII and His Royal Highness the Duke of Windsor all visited Austria. All three were, of course, the same person. The visits came at a time of uncertain British policy regarding Austria. Edward was far from being the voice of British foreign policy—often the opposite—but attitudes to his visits are an indicator of Anglo-Austrian relations.

As the heir to the British throne, Edward, Prince of Wales, was expected to hold his tongue on political issues. Privately, though, he made his views clear. In 1933, without the benefit of today's hindsight, he thought that the growing strength of the Nazis in Germany was no bad thing. It was an internal matter for the Germans and an important bulwark against Soviet Communism. The German Nazis avidly courted his sympathy, and he encouraged British-German connections, partly in order to head off war but also because he favoured powerful government and saw value in many of Germany's claims. He was far from alone in Britain in holding these views. But Austrians saw his visit in 1935 as an encouragement to resist pressure from Germany. And he did not conform to the stereotype. Despite his privileged status, he preferred to visit model workers' houses in

Vienna rather than the Fascist-dominated city hall. Edward's reason for the Austrian visit was a skiing holiday in the Alpine resort of Kitzbühel. The central issue about the trip was not his political outlook but the fact that his American lover, Mrs Wallis Simpson, was with him.[1]

The death of King George V on 20th January 1936 brought Edward to the throne as King Edward VIII. Following a summer Mediterranean cruise, he made a private trip through Eastern Europe, with Wallis at his side. In Austria, he met the President and Chancellor Kurt von Schuschnigg. According to Sir Walford Selby, the British Envoy in Vienna, the King's five days in the capital had been invaluable from the viewpoint of Britain's position in Austria. Those who opposed union with Germany saw the visit as support against Hitler's pressure.

The King had 'caught the imagination of the Austrians to a quite remarkable degree', Selby reported to Foreign Secretary Anthony Eden. For the King's send-off 'the Ringstrasse was a seething crowd and he was cheered again and again', with cries of 'Come back again!'. Chancellor von Schuschnigg 'had received numerous letters, especially from the working classes, congratulating him on his success in bringing the King again to Austria'.[2]

When Edward next visited Austria, his status had changed again, this time not for the better. On 10th December 1936, the King abdicated the throne in order to marry Mrs Simpson. Edward, Duke of Windsor, made a hurried departure from England and arrived by train in Vienna three days later, at 10.05 pm on 13th December.

His friend Baron Eugene de Rothschild had invited him to occupy a secluded forty-room hunting lodge on the Baron's estate at Enzesfeld, 'among woods in the foothills of the mountains' twenty-five miles from the city. Sixty journalists had travelled on the train, hoping for an interview. Along with a police escort, Walford Selby was there to greet the controversial ex-King. The Duke, attired in a fur-collared winter coat, red woollen scarf and bowler hat, sped off in the Baron's car to the initial location of his exile. Angry and depressed, he spent almost four months there, while Wallis stayed in France. For

Walford Selby, it had been 'difficult to explain to the Austrian aristocracy why the Duke was staying with a Jew'. In April 1937, Edward and Mrs Simpson were married in France, but returned to Austria that summer to spend their honeymoon in a borrowed castle in Carinthia.[3]

Duke and Duchess of Windsor with Adolf Hitler, Berchtesgaden 1937

Later he accepted an invitation for an official tour of Germany, during which the Nazis orchestrated a meeting with Adolf Hitler. For the British Government, even in Austria he was no longer a foreign policy asset.

Britain and Austria

Austria, and Britain's policy towards it, were at the mercy of higher-level geopolitics. Famously, the policy of British Prime Minister Neville Chamberlain was to appease Hitler hoping he could be persuaded to settle issues peacefully. British military strength was insufficiently developed to challenge Germany.

The concept of collective security, developed after the 1914-18 War in the form of the League of Nations and ostensibly made concrete by the Locarno Pact in 1925, had unravelled by the mid-1930s. The Japanese invasion of Manchuria in 1931, Mussolini's attack on Abyssinia in 1935 and Germany's unchallenged re-militarisation of the Rhineland in 1936 all showed that a military response to aggressive action was at least for the present out of the question. German and Italian involvement in the Spanish Civil War was an added complication.

Balancing Italy against Germany was a key goal of British foreign policy in 1937, for 'no matter how unreliable Mussolini might be, France and Britain now desperately needed his support to keep Hitler at bay'. Britain, Italy and France had met at Stresa in the Italian Lakes in the spring of 1935, when 'the two black clouds over Europe' were 'Hitler's threats to Austria' and 'Mussolini's intention to attack Abyssinia'.

Italy had joined France and Britain in recognising 'the necessity of maintaining the independence of Austria'. Yet the British Foreign Office did not see the threat of *Anschluss* as a serious problem, although it would outflank the defences of Czechoslovakia. According to historian Richard Lamb, 'it was because British leaders completely underestimated the Abyssinian crisis that mistakes were made that drove Mussolini into the arms of Hitler'.[4]

A month before German troops rolled across the Austrian border, the instinct of Anthony Eden's close advisor was:

> Not to take Hitler's demands on von Schuschnigg too tragically; the prohibition on the *Anschluss* has been wrong from the start ... One way or another an Austrian majority has always been in favour of *Anschluss*: Catholics, Socialists, Nazis, according to the ruling colour in Germany. *Anschluss* or at least a satellite Austria is probably inevitable, and to stop it from outside is impossible and indefensible, ... I can't believe the absorption of Austria will strengthen Germany; it should put water in the Nazi wine.[5]

Any hope of rebuilding what had been called the 'Stresa Front' of Anglo-Franco-Italian solidarity against German expansion was extinguished in September 1937. On a state visit to Germany, Mussolini made a bargain with Hitler: Germany could annex Austria and Italy would have a free hand in the Mediterranean.[6]

The way was open for *Anschluss*.

Roots of Anschluss

The road to German annexation of Austria stretches back to the end of the First World War in 1918, which brought about the dissolution of the Austro-Hungarian Empire and the formation of the Republic of Austria. The Republic's founding document stated that 'German Austria is a part of the German Republic' (*'Deutschösterreich ist ein Bestandteil der Deutschen Republik'*). A majority of the population, particularly in Salzburg and the Tyrol, wanted to join Germany. But the victorious Allies would not allow the two defeated states to combine, and banned the word *Deutschösterreich*.

During the years following the First World War, in an atmosphere of mistrust, violence, unemployment and even starvation, a 'cold civil war' in Austria occasionally became hot. The country was 'in the throes of political unrest owing to the collision of various political forces ... in opposition to one another long before the Nazis came to power in Germany'.[7] Economic hardship led to socialist ascendancy in politics and the capital became known as '*Rotes Wien*'. It was in this 'Red Vienna' in 1933 that Kim Philby met Austrians who shared his Communist convictions and started his career as an undercover Soviet agent. Long before the Cold War, this was the genesis of the Cambridge spy ring, which served the Soviet cause with devastating effect for the next two decades.[8]

In Austria, not least for economic reasons, many continued to favour some kind of partnership with Germany. For some, though, the desire for amalgamation of the two states rather cooled after 1933 as the repression in Hitler's National Socialist rule in Germany became more obvious. In particular, the Christian Social party seemed to want to 'rescue the great German tradition from National Socialism'. On the German side, Hitler saw Austria as a military and economic springboard for expansion into central and eastern Europe. Meanwhile, the Austrian Nazis gained ground. Using skilled propaganda techniques, they mounted populist political campaigns from their base in Munich, with support from the German Nazis and alongside their banned paramilitary arms, the *Sturmabteilung* and *Schutzstaffel:* the SA and SS.[9]

The Nazis attempted a violent coup in July 1934. Chancellor Engelbert Dollfuss, himself leading an authoritarian regime but at least outwardly a defender of Austrian independence who had banned the Nazi Party, was shot and killed. The putsch failed, though, as loyal troops took back control. Kurt von Schuschnigg became Chancellor and continued to defend Austrian sovereignty. Nevertheless, the National Socialists, financed and egged on by Berlin, had stepped up their campaign of terror. Bombings took place nearly every day in some part of the country. In the mountain provinces, massive and often violent Nazi demonstrations weakened the government's position. Meanwhile, the external pressure from Germany intensified. The western powers, including Britain, lacked the military strength to do much more than provide verbal support for Austrian independence.

Given this weak position, Schuschnigg could do little. He tried to walk a tightrope between drawing closer to Germany and keeping Austria independent. In a July 1936 agreement, Germany undertook to respect Austrian sovereignty, while von Schuschnigg agreed independent Austria would consider itself German in character and would encourage cultural, economic and touristic contacts with Germany. Hitler's surprising acceptance of von Schuschnigg's proposal may have been linked to fears of a restored Hapsburg monarchy in Austria, a live issue at the time.[10]

The relaxation of travel restrictions between the two countries made it easier for Austrian Nazis to connect with their comrades across the border and for Germany to infiltrate agents into Austria. Although deeply divided and still banned, the Austrian National Socialist Party remained a significant threat. Hitler had already forced von Schuschnigg to appoint Nazi-leaning politicians to his cabinet, but when the two leaders met in February 1938 at Berchtesgaden he went further. Going beyond the published agreement, he issued a secret ultimatum whose demands amounted to a takeover by the Austrian Nazis. Schuschnigg must release and reinstate Nazi prisoners, appoint further Nazis in key ministerial posts, and forge links between the two armies. He had to sign on the spot. Back in Vienna, his cabinet reluctantly agreed to the changes. Outside help was unlikely. Answering a question from Winston Churchill about Britain's 'duties and responsibilities … in respect of the independence and integrity of Austria' in the House of Commons in London, Foreign Secretary Anthony Eden said, 'we do not think it lies with us to take the initiative'.[11]

In a two-hour speech broadcast on 24th February 1938, von Schuschnigg made a 'dramatic affirmation of Austria's independence'. He reported on his talks at Berchtesgaden and emphasised that Hitler had undertaken to respect Austrian sovereignty. The loyal Austrian, he said, 'wants to co-operate in the common destiny of all Germans, but within our own frontiers'. 'We realise that we have gone to the limit', he continued defiantly, 'beyond which is written 'Thus far and no further'. … Austria will remain free, and for this we will fight to the death. Because we are resolved, there is no doubt about our victory'. Referring to the Austrian national colours, he continued defiantly, 'Till death, the red-white-and-red![12]'. These were stirring words, and a direct challenge to Hitler, listening to the broadcast in Munich. The German press found the speech 'disturbing'.[13] British diplomats, unable from a distance to challenge German power, wished the 'Austrian Question' would simply go away. Nazis in Austria put pressure on von Schuschnigg through 'people's uprisings' in many parts of the country. Bizarrely, the extremely rare appearance in Austria in February 1938 of the *aurora borealis*, the Northern Lights, convinced some that momentous events were looming. In that at least, they were right.

Referendum poster, 13th March 1938

To build popular support for his position, von Schuschnigg announced a referendum on Austrian independence, to be held on 13th March. The plans included manipulation of the voting rules, such as the wording of the question and the minimum voting age. Von Schuschnigg may not have realised how powerful a genie he had let out of the bottle.

Furious, and concerned that the tactic would succeed, Hitler demanded that the referendum be cancelled. Arthur Seyss-Inquart, Minister of the Interior in the Austrian cabinet but a Nazi sympathiser and in close touch with Hermann Göring in Berlin, challenged von Schuschnigg on Friday, 11th March: delay the vote by a month or resign. A few hours later, von Schuschnigg, seeing no further chance of compromise, stepped down as Austrian Chancellor. Seyss-Inquart took his place and allegedly invited Hitler to send in his troops.[14] They were already on the way.[15] In the early hours of Saturday morning, William Shirer—the American journalist based in Berlin—wrote in his diary, 'The *Reichswehr* is invading Austria. Hitler has broken a dozen solemn promises, pledges, treaties. And Austria is finished. Beautiful, tragic, civilised Austria! Gone'.[16]

Occupation

German troops crossed the Austrian border on 12th March 1938, still uncertain whether they would be opposed by Italy and the Austrian Army. They had heard reports of political change in Vienna on the preceding day, but they did not know if that would translate into orders for the Austrian troops. They were ready for battle.

The reality was different. The detailed plans made in Rome for an Italian intervention in the event of Austrian civil war were not activated. And most people in western Austria welcomed the German units. German officers described the entry into Austria as an 'unforgettable moment', as 'the light in the eyes of the soldiers and the elated population showed that all knew this was a great historic moment'. The people 'ran from their workplaces with indescribable enthusiasm to greet the German soldiers, who had freed them from the difficult years of oppression'. It was 'a sign that the people of

Greater Germany belong together'.[17] The arrival of German troops in Vienna was soon followed by the occupation of the whole of Austria. The German High Command (*Oberkommando der Wehrmacht, OKW*) summarised the operation as a 'classic example of policy being carried out with modern methods, through heavy application of military and propagandistic means'.[18]

Jews forced to scrub pavements, Vienna 1938

Accompanied by military staff, his press officer and personal photographer, Adolf Hitler arrived by air in Linz on the evening of 12th March. The enthusiastic welcome of the crowds, together with the assumption by the foreign press that *Anschluss* was a foregone conclusion, convinced Hitler to implement it immediately. He had a love-hate relationship with the land of his birth, but he reserved his particular dislike for Vienna, where he had been an art school failure.[19] He wanted no half-measures. The new '*Ostmark*' region quickly came into legal existence as part of the *Grossdeutsches Reich* and Austria's fate was sealed. Three days later, a *Luftwaffe* flypast marked the start of a parade through the city streets by German troops. Offices and shops in Vienna were required to close, to assure Hitler of an appropriate welcome.

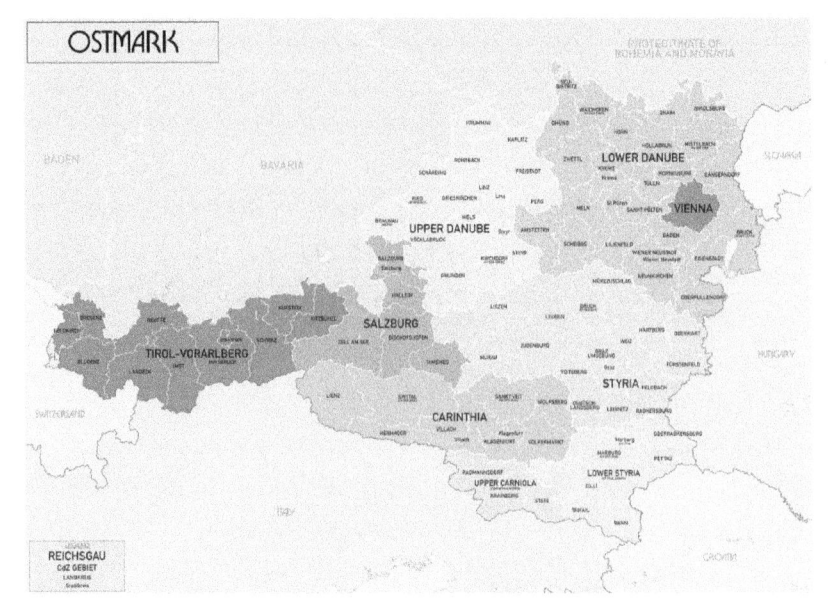

Post- Anschluss Austria: the Ostmark 1941

As well as the ubiquitous swastikas, other signs of Nazi domination quickly became evident. Increasingly, stores owned by Jews attracted special attention. Signs stating 'Jewish firm' appeared in shop windows and potential customers were discouraged from entering. But this was the tip of a much larger iceberg: the systematic persecution of Jews and anyone who opposed the new regime.[20] The Nazi newspapers called it 'the great spring cleaning': the 'wholesale dismissal of Jews from various employments, their exclusion from various professions and occupations and the taking over from them of big businesses'.

Theatres and music halls were completely 'cleansed' of Jews; those owned by Jews were 'placed under Aryan commissars'. Seventeen judges were 'dismissed because they have Jewish blood in their veins'. Black-uniformed SS guards were rounding up 'supporters of the former Government, including prominent members of the Catholic and Jewish bourgeoisie, the Freemasons, Socialists and Communists' and 'constantly discharging loads of prisoners in the various prison yards'. Jews who were not rounded up went into hiding. G E R (Eric) Gedye, the *Daily Telegraph* correspondent, reported these events five days after the Nazi takeover.[21] In a later book, he explained the 'acceptance of suicide as a perfectly normal and natural incident by every Jewish household'.[22]

Austrian Nazis at first welcomed the changes: what they had demonstrated for was coming to fruition at last. But they quickly realised that this was less a realisation of their National Socialist goals, and more a wholesale takeover by the German Nazi machine.[23] The Austrian Nazi movement had always been filled with contradictions. Its members 'proudly asserted their allegiance to one large German *Volk*, but jealously guarded the autonomy of the Austrian Nazi party and the Austrian state, viewing Germans from the *Altreich* as outsiders'.[24]

A day after the Telegraph report, Gedye was 'invited' by Austrian police to leave Vienna within three days, on orders from Berlin. Nazi bureaucratic squabbling led to the order being cancelled by the *Gestapo* and then reinstated. At last, though, the time for Eric's departure came. Journalists who had not yet been expelled brought apricot brandy, a chocolate cake and a red carnation to the railway station for an impromptu farewell party on the platform. It was a hint of the Vienna Eric Gedye had known in previous years, where 'cheerful crowds engaged in that leisurely saunter which is the Viennese equivalent for hurrying about one's business'. The city of art, music and culture would not be the same for many years to come. Despite the bravado, Gedye was not sorry to leave. He left a Vienna from which, as he later put it, the glory had departed.[25]

'The greatest inter-war foreign correspondent'

During his thirteen years in Vienna, Eric Gedye had variously represented the *Daily Express*, the London *Times*, the *New York Times* and the *Daily Telegraph*, often several of them at once. As a prominent correspondent for American and British newspapers, he seemed to know everyone and be known by all. A convinced social democrat, he did not flinch from pointing out the threats to Austrian independence and highlighting the dangers of the growing Fascist influence in the country. A particular target of his criticism was the Austrian Social Democrat Party. Despite being politically strong and well-organised, the Party did not, as Gedye saw it, have a coherent strategy to combat Fascism. Disillusioned by the failure of Western liberal powers to confront the dangers, he saw the Soviet Union as the only viable challenge to the Nazi threat. Only much later, when Ribbentrop and Molotov signed the Nazi-Soviet Non-Aggression Pact in August 1939, were his expectations dashed.

Eric Gedye was born in 1890 in Clevedon, Somerset, to George Gedye, a provisions merchant with a business in the busy port city of Bristol, and his wife, Lillian. As a member of the London University Officers' Training Corps, Eric took up a commission in the Gloucestershire Regiment when war broke out in 1914. Wounded on the Somme in September 1916, he joined the Intelligence Corps in May 1918 and served after the Armistice in the multinational force administering the Rhineland. His marriage in 1922 to a German girl, Elisabeth Bremer, meant that he had to resign his commission. But it worked to his advantage. While Eric was in Cologne, Lord Northcliffe, owner of *The Times* and the *Daily Mail*, met him and offered him the position of local correspondent for both papers. 'Being there' is said to be the key to successful journalism, and Gedye's incisive local reports on the French extension of their occupation of the coal-rich Ruhr gained him promotion to 'Special Correspondent'. Professionally, he never looked back.[26]

Eric Gedye arrived in Vienna in 1925 to cover central Europe for various newspapers (and for MI6).[27] He soon got used to the Viennese atmosphere, enjoying coffee topped with whipped cream and a *Wiener Frühstück* in the sunshine on the Café Heinrichhof terrace. As Gedye put it, 'Of all the ingenious devices invented by this ingenious race for consuming time, the café habit is certainly the most insidious'.[28]

The coffee came from the stores of Julius Meinl II, a coffee merchant with a long history under the Austro-Hungarian Empire but also an Austrian patriot and Anglophile with close connections to the Austrian capital's British community. Falling for Vienna's charm, Eric soon wrote the almost obligatory article for the London *Times* extolling the delights of the city's *Gemütlichkeit* and the tolerance of the sentimental, easy-going Viennese. By unhappy coincidence, though, the paper printed on the same day a later piece he had written more urgently, entitled 'Rioting in Vienna. An Anti-Zionist Outbreak'.[29]

For Gedye, Austrian politics of the mid-1920s was a stagnant deadlock. On one side were the dominant forces of social democracy, on the other the still-powerful reactionary elites who hankered after restoration of the Austro-Hungarian monarchy. For the latter, and for the influential Catholic Church, the workers should be kept in their place; the 'red threat' was the greatest danger. It was the fear of socialism, thought Gedye, that destroyed Austrian democracy and paved the way for the rise of fascism.[30]

This is of course a highly simplified view of inter-war Austrian politics. The left-wing Social Democrats were indeed at times the strongest party, but—lacking an overall majority—they ruled in coalition with smaller 'bourgeois' parties. Their policies were therefore less extreme than conservatives had feared. The 'Christian Socials', in opposition, 'were not socially homogeneous, consisting instead of genuine democrats, monarchists, capitalists, small shop owners, pan-Germans and, above all, peasants'. However Gedye may have simplified it, Austrian democracy was 'born in an atmosphere of military defeat, political catastrophe and patriotic humiliation', not to mention the Great Depression.[31]

It was certainly fragile, and fragile democracy can leave the field open for a repressive alternative. Journalist William Shirer recorded in his diary in February 1934 that 'Dollfuss has struck at the Social Democrats in Austria, the only organised group (forty percent of the population) which can save him from being swallowed up by the Nazis'.[32]

Slim and full of energy, with brown hair and grey eyes, Eric became well known in Vienna's British community. But he kept his distance from the fashionable social set, preferring to mix with 'ordinary' Austrians, or with the Anglo-American Press community in Vienna's bars and cafés. Even then, he often held back. He gained the nickname 'Lone Wolf', but other foreign correspondents liked and respected the work of 'G E R Gedye' and saw him as one of the finest of their number.

Eric Gedye

He travelled widely in Austria and the region, taking time to write a well-received guide book to the country he had come to love.[33] He interviewed increasingly polarised political leaders, warning readers of the trouble to come from the region. After his expulsion from Austria, Gedye wrote a hard-hitting book, *Fallen Bastions*, harshly condemning Chamberlain's policy of appeasing Adolf Hitler. He refused to remove contentious passages to which Lord Camrose, the proprietor of the *Daily Telegraph,* objected. As a result, Gedye left the paper, according to the editor 'by mutual consent'. 'That is correct', commented Gedye, 'It is equally correct that Herr Hitler invaded Czechoslovakia by "mutual arrangement" with President Hácha'.[34]

---

[1] Philip Ziegler, *King Edward VIII: the official biography* (London: Collins, 1990), pp.206-209.
[2] TNA FO 954/1A/91. Sir Walford Selby, *Diplomatic Twilight, 1930-1940* (London: John Murray, 1953), p.66.

[3] Philip Ziegler, 1990, pp.338-367, Deborah Cadbury, *Princes at War: the British Royal Family's private battle in the Second World War* (London: Bloomsbury, 2015).

[4] Richard Lamb, *The Ghosts of Peace, 1935-1945* (Salisbury, Wiltshire: M Russell, 1987), pp.1, 50-56.

[5] Edward Harvey diary, 16th February 1938, quoted in *ibid*, p.56.

[6] Paul Baxa, 'Capturing the Fascist Moment: Hitler's Visit to Italy in 1938 and the Radicalization of Fascist Italy', *Journal of Contemporary History* 42, no. 2 (2016).

[7] G E R Gedye, "Austria's Dark Outlook", *The Fortnightly* (1934).

[8] Philby had developed his political beliefs as a student at Trinity College, Cambridge. He helped Austrian Communists to oppose Chancellor Engelbert Dollfuss's Fascist crackdown in early 1934. Among them was Litzi Friedmann, whom he later married in order that she could escape with him to England. In London, she introduced him to Soviet agent-handler Arnold Deutsch, code name *Otto* (Christopher Andrew, *The Defence of the Realm: the authorized history of MI5* (London: Allen Lane, 2009), pp.167-172). See also Phillip Knightley, *Philby: the life and views of the KGB masterspy* (London: Deutsch, 1988); Ben Macintyre, *A Spy among Friends: Kim Philby and the great betrayal* (London: Bloomsbury, 2014).

[9] Erwin A. Schmidl, *Der 'Anschluss' Österreichs: der deutsche Einmarsch im März 1938* (Bonn: Bernard & Graefe, 1994), pp.13-17. On the development of the Austrian Nazi movement see Bruce F Pauley, 'From Splinter Party to Mass Movement: The Austrian Nazi Breakthrough', *German Studies* 2, no. 1 (1973). On the Nazi Bavarian roots see Geoffrey Pridham, *Hitler's Rise to Power: the Nazi movement in Bavaria, 1923-1933* (St Albans: Hart-Davis MacGibbon, 1973).

[10] Erwin A. Schmidl, 1994, p.20. TNA FO 954/1A/88.

[11] Hansard, 17th February 1938, Col. 2074.

[12] Daily Telegraph, London, 25th February 1938.

[13] The Times, London, 28th February 1938.

[14] Many sources reported that copies of the telegram allegedly sent by Seyss-Inquart, and published in German newspapers, were actually concocted afterwards in Berlin (e.g. in William L. Shirer, *The Rise and Fall of the Third Reich: a history of Nazi Germany* (New York, Simon and Schuster, 1960)).

[15] A very detailed account (in German) of the events immediately before the *Anschluss* is in Erwin A. Schmidl, 1994, pp.71-134. American journalist William L Shirer was based in Vienna in 1937-38; his chapter on the *Anschluss* is effectively an eyewitness account (William L. Shirer, 1960, pp.322-352), as is G E R Gedye, *Fallen Bastions: the Central European tragedy* (London: Gollancz, 1939). Although it would strictly be correct to refer to the 'former Austria' after the *Anschluss*, I will continue simply to refer to 'Austria'.

[16] William L Shirer, *Berlin Diary: the journal of a foreign correspondent, 1934-1941* (New York: A A Knopf, 1941), 4am, 12th March 1938.

[17] War Diary of 10th Anti-Tank Battalion, quoted in Erwin A. Schmidl, 1994, p.165.
[18] *Übersicht 65*, Berlin, 24th March 1938, quoted in *ibid*, p.207. British political reactions are well illustrated in David Dilks, *The Diaries of Sir Alexander Cadogan, OM, 1938-1945* (London: Cassell, 1971), pp.60-63.
[19] M R D Foot, *Resistance: European resistance to the Nazis, 1940-1945* (London: Biteback Publishing, 2016), p.328.
[20] Oral history interviews regarding the *Anschluss* are at https://www.doew.at/erinnern/biographien/erzaehlte-geschichte/anschluss-maerz-april-1938 (in German), accessed 1st July 2021.
[21] Daily Telegraph, London, 18th March 1938.
[22] G E R Gedye, *Fallen Bastions*, 1939, p.305.
[23] Further detail on the system of Nazi control is for instance in Wolfgang Neugebauer, 'Zur Struktur, Tätigkeit und Effizienz des NS-Terrorsystems in Österreich,' in *Krieg im Äther: Widerstand und Spionage im Zweiten Weltkrieg*, ed. Hans Schafranek and Johannes Tuchel (Vienna: Picus Verlag, 2004) (in German) and Wolfgang Neugebauer, *The Austrian Resistance 1938-1945*, trans., John Nicholson and Eric Canepa (Vienna: Edition Steinbauer, 2014), pp.28-51.
[24] Bruce F Pauley, 1973: pp.xiii-xiv.
[25] G E R Gedye, *Fallen Bastions*, 1939, pp.238, 346. Anna Goldenberg and Alta L Price, *I belong to Vienna: A Jewish family's story of exile and return* (New York: New Vessel Press, 2020) brings to life the experiences of Jewish families in Vienna after the *Anschluss*.
[26] Oxford Dictionary of National Biography, www oxforddnb.com, accessed 6th July 2021.
[27] Helen Fry, *Spymaster: the man who saved MI6* (New Haven: Yale University Press, 2021), pp.41,50.
[28] G E R Gedye, *A wayfarer in Austria* (London: Methuen, 1928), p.18.
[29] The Times, London, 18th August 1925.
[30] G E R Gedye, *Fallen Bastions*, 1939, pp.11-12.
[31] Bruce F Pauley, 1973: p.15.
[32] William L Shirer, 1941, 12th February 1934.
[33] G E R Gedye, *Wayfarer*, 1928.
[34] Obituary of Litzi Gedye, Daily Telegraph, London, 3rd September 2005, and Oxford Dictionary of National Biography.

CHAPTER 4

Espionage and Sabotage

Intelligence

ON 19TH AUGUST 1938, five months after Eric Gedye had left Austria, the London Times reported that the *Gestapo* had arrested Captain Thomas Kendrick near Salzburg. Kendrick, the Passport Control Officer at the British Consulate in Vienna, had actually been on the way back to Britain by car, with his wife and a driver. He was being held in the former Hotel Metropole, now *Gestapo* headquarters and the place where former Chancellor von Schuschnigg was incarcerated. In Berlin, the German Propaganda Ministry said that Kendrick was 'heavily under suspicion'.[1]

There was more to this than meets the eye. Immediately after the First World War, the military travel control system had been transformed into a network of Passport Control Officers attached to British embassies. The Secret Intelligence Service, MI6, eventually used these positions as cover for its station chiefs. Since being 'blown' in a 1932 memoir, the actual role of the PCOs was far from secure. Knowing this, MI6 Deputy Director Claude Dansey had formed the 'Z Organisation', an informal intelligence network. Eric Gedye was one of his agents.[2]

Three days after his arrest, Thomas Kendrick was expelled from the *Reich* as a spy. The German newspapers claimed Kendrick had confessed to espionage, which he later denied. The *Gestapo* were in any case well aware of the PCOs' activities.

Ironically, the 'day job' of the passport control staff often got in the way of spying. As the number of refugees wishing to leave Austria and requiring visas increased, the pressure on Kendrick and his small staff exploded. He reported that his staff were 'so overwrought that they will burst into tears at the slightest provocation'.[3]

The comment was a little unfair. Kendrick left most of the passport control work to his staff. They spent long hours trying to help desperate men, women and children, as the Nazi authorities placed constant obstacles in their path out of Austria: a distressing situation for all. A Jewish family wanting to leave the country had to leap many hurdles.

Each individual had to stand in a long line to get an exit permit, then to queue for a certificate to prove he or she was a Jew. They spent hours waiting at the Finance Ministry for a certificate showing that they owed no taxes; for Jews, 'tax' was about seizure of assets. Next came the wait in line for the issue of a passport. At each place, the first queue was for the right form, to be taken away and returned, completed and countersigned, after another long wait. At the British Consulate, there was yet more waiting. But it was the final hurdle.[4]

Among Kendrick's people were his MI6 deputy, Kenneth Benton, and three women also working in intelligence: Evelyn Stamper, Clara Holmes and Betty Hodgson.[5] In their passport control role, they were on the front line. Tensions ran high in the Consulate as a flood of refugees pleaded for the speedy issue of visas.

Individual family stories were heartbreaking. Clara was often willing to interpret the British entry requirements flexibly—she 'broke every law she could in order to give as many people as possible a visa'—Evelyn perhaps less so.[6]

Because of some vague and unwise remarks under the constant pressure, Evelyn faced a formal complaint alleging anti-Semitism. Tommy Kendrick, though, vigorously rebuffed the accusation, and it was probably Evelyn whom Eric Gedye meant, when he described an official distressed after seeing violent and demeaning treatment of

Jews on the street. Just the same, Evelyn was posted back to England soon thereafter.[7]

Clara 'Midge' Holmes with daughter Prudence, Vienna c. 1934

Clara Holmes had joined MI6's Vienna Station from Switzerland in the early 1920s, having already worked in Prague. She was born Clara Marguerite Bates in 1895 in Playden, Sussex, the eldest child of Guy Lockington Bates, a clergyman. Her mother, Clara Louisa, died when Clara was five years old, but Guy married again in the following year. Clara grew up in the large family house with her father, stepmother, brother and two sisters. In the days before labour-saving household appliances, Victorian families who could afford it had servants. With a governess, a cook, a nurse and two domestic maids, the Bates household was no exception.[8] By the time she was fifteen years old, Clara was away at boarding school. Six years later, she was engaged in First World War intelligence work with MI6, focusing on Germany and Austria.[9]

Clara was of average height and had grey eyes. Friends knew her as 'Midge'. One of them, the then popular novelist Phyllis Bottome—who herself married an MI6 'Passport Control Officer'—had a high opinion of Clara. She thought her counter-espionage work 'skilled and responsible' and reported that Clara had gained the nickname 'Sergeant-Major Bill' on account of her 'great personal efficiency'.

Not only that, Clara dealt with 'complicated individuals' and 'sharp feuds' so that office relationships 'immediately became as smooth as cream'. The novelist based one of her fictional characters on Clara. While Phyllis was more at home with Austrian social democrats, Midge and her colleagues circulated in the world of diplomats, government officials and Viennese society.[10]

In 1926, Clara had returned to England to marry Reginald 'Rex' Holmes, a big game hunter; their daughter, Prudence, was born two years later in Nairobi, Kenya. In January 1929, Rex died in Africa from Sleeping Sickness after being bitten by a Tsetse fly. 'Midge' was widowed, a single mother with a nine-month-old baby. Her daughter, Prudence, grew up in Vienna, becoming fluent in German and excelling in all subjects at school.[11]

Elizabeth 'Betty' Hodgson was two years older than Clara. After working for MI5 in the 1920s, she had joined MI6 and eventually arrived in Vienna.[12] Like Clara, both Betty and Evelyn were fluent in German. The pair were well-versed in Austrian and German literature, enjoying the rich cultural life of inter-war Vienna. They published English translations of works by well-known Austrian authors.

For all three colleagues, the time in Vienna came to an abrupt end. As soon as Kendrick's arrest became known, MI6 evacuated Betty and Clara. Evelyn had already left. Prudence Holmes, then ten years old, transferred to a school in Paris.

Clara Holmes, Betty Hodgson and Evelyn Stamper all loved Austria. Like Eric Gedye, they would together form a crucial element of the Austrian efforts of the Special Operations Executive. They would also shape SOE's thinking about the place of Austria in Greater Germany.

Subversion

Intelligence-gathering was always a 'sideline' for the Special Operations Executive. Its principal business was sabotage and subversion. The idea of irregular warfare struck a chord in the romantic mind of Winston Churchill. After he became Prime Minister in the summer of 1940, he famously chose the ambitious Labour politician Hugh Dalton to lead a new organisation that was to 'set Europe ablaze'.

Like many apparently simple decisions, the formation of SOE had a back story.[13] Before SOE was formed, the seeds were sown for this disreputable activity. Austria was one target.

In 1938, a tiny room in the depths of the War Office housed Royal Engineers officer Major Jo Holland and a typist. Together, they formed the sum total of a research section in the intelligence staff known as Military Intelligence (Research), or MI(R).[14] Holland was free to research almost anything, but his particular interest was guerrilla operations.

Meanwhile, Admiral Hugh Sinclair (or 'C', as Britain's intelligence chief is to this day traditionally known) had been looking since 1935 at clandestine ways to fight Germany that would go beyond MI6's intelligence brief. Not much came of it for some years. Few recognised the urgency. As one politician commented 'Probably the reason that sabotage has never been organised is that it is nobody's particular job'.[15]

In the first week of March 1938, as Hitler was piling up the pressure on von Schuschnigg that culminated in the *Anschluss*, the urgency was more acute. Sinclair called in the flamboyant Major Laurence Grand and invited him to 'cogitate on the possibilities of sabotage'. Grand started work on 1st April and reported back in May with some very ungentlemanly proposals. Not only did he propose the sabotage of railways, docks, airfields and other infrastructure with military potential; he also wanted to attack Germany's economic resources and agriculture. 'C' approved, formed 'Section D' of MI6 in June 1938 and appointed Grand its head. Its cover name was the

'Statistical Research Department' of the War Office. Its task would be 'sabotage and propaganda in neutral countries'.[16]

Grand quickly assembled friends and personal contacts from the financial world of the City of London. The process of catching up from Britain's unprepared pre-war situation was fast-moving. It accelerated when Winston Churchill became Prime Minister in May 1940. One result was the merging of Section D, MI(R) and the propaganda organisation at Electra House known as EH, to form the Special Operations Executive.

Laurence Grand was a snappy dresser who smoked constantly through a long cigarette holder. He was a tall and good-looking forty-year-old, sporting a red carnation, dark glasses, a confident air and a black Homburg hat to match his heavy moustache. He was secretive, but rarely bothered to exercise tact with officials, and he was full of schemes.[17] Kim Philby, a Soviet 'mole' in MI6, saw Grand as 'never shrinking from an idea, however big and wild'.[18]

Jo Holland was a quieter, more sombre individual but just as creative. On Holland's team in MI(R) was Colin Gubbins, then a lieutenant-colonel but eventually to become the head of SOE as a major-general. Gubbins enjoyed working with Holland, but had mixed feelings about MI6's Section D. He was often 'aghast at the amateurishness and sheer extravagance of some of its wilder projects', but 'enjoyed the company of enterprising young businessmen used to cutting corners and taking risks'. It was a far cry from the 'ponderous hierarchy and financial stringency of the pre-war War Office'.[19]

Perhaps unusually for units reporting to different bureaucratic masters, MI(R) and Section D were in touch with each other, working closely in offices at No 2 Caxton Street. A secret passage led to St Ermin's Hotel, a hub for London's undercover pre-war activities. They forged an informal agreement: MI(R) would concentrate on actions carried out in uniform that would be secret but could be acknowledged if necessary; Section D would focus on more clandestine activities. Until war was declared, Grand had more freedom of action in the field than did the military group. Section D got to work.[20]

Balkan Action

Laurence Grand's freedom to act was far from total. His military priority in central Europe was to disrupt barge traffic on the busy River Danube and to interrupt Germany's supply of oil from Romania. But cautious diplomats were breathing down his neck. Even after war was declared in September 1939, the Foreign Office kept the diplomatic brakes on military action. Neville Chamberlain and his Cabinet colleagues instructed the military commanders in May 1940 that: 'No action must be taken which was likely to precipitate the armed occupation of the river or an early invasion of the Balkan States by Germany'.[21] As well as constraints on disrupting Danube shipping, the Cabinet limited early subversive action on the southern borders of Greater Germany, particularly if it had a political element. Not provoking further German expansion was a key part of British foreign policy.

In London, Laurence Grand was dreaming up ideas for sabotage and destruction. Meanwhile, his people on the spot were becoming embroiled in Balkan politics. Subversion was inherently political. It was a harbinger of the future frustration in the Foreign Office at SOE's tendency to fashion its own 'British foreign policy'. Nowhere was this more so than in the Balkans, and particularly in Yugoslavia, where Julius Hanau, codename *Caesar,* represented Section D.

Hanau was a South African Jewish convert to the Christian faith, a businessman who had lived in Belgrade since 1930. He was 'a man of exceptional energy, quite fearless and determined to carry through anything to which he set his hand'.[22] Already working for MI6 as an intelligence agent, he joined Section D in mid-1939 and intensified his 'own private war with German agents in Yugoslavia', with tacit support from within the Yugoslav security services. He and his colleagues built up supplies of arms and ammunition in the country, to the annoyance of the diplomats in whose buildings they were stored.

As well as undermining German economic efforts and hijacking railway wagons carrying Messerschmitt fighter planes, or disabling them by seizing up the wheel bearings, Hanau organised demonstrations and distributed leaflets denouncing Nazi representatives in Belgrade.[23] Thus political propaganda was a key part of Section D's work in the Balkans and Central Europe.

Part of this campaign was to encourage the nationalist aspirations of ethnic Slovenians on both sides of the Yugoslav-Austrian border. Sabotage of railway traffic was a particular bugbear to the Nazis, attacks often taking place inside Austria, within the newly expanded *Reich*.

With British support under university lecturer Alex Lawrenson, primarily Catholic and social democrat Slovenian groups stepped up their campaign. Apart from the sabotage, Section D printed and smuggled vast quantities of anti-Nazi and nationalist Slovenian and Croatian propaganda leaflets into Austria. Austrian historian Dr Peter Pirker has written a comprehensive account of Section D's action in Yugoslavia and its impact on his homeland.[24] Pirker suggests that the growth of Slovenian separatism depended heavily on British encouragement and practical support. In turn, Section D's network of contacts within post-*Anschluss* Austria could not have been developed without the Slovenians, and the Slovenian anti-Nazi contribution has been undervalued.

Section D's activity in Yugoslavia and Austria may not have been significant in military terms, but it was a thorn in the flesh for the Nazis in Austria. Long before Germany invaded Yugoslavia in April 1941, German intelligence services, the *Sicherheitsdienst* and the *Abwehr*, had redoubled their efforts to stamp out Section D. Through double agents, assassinations, loss of Yugoslav government support and continued criticism by British diplomats, it became progressively harder for British agents to operate.

In the subsequent years, opposition to Nazi rule in Slovenia would come from a new direction and in a different context. Following Hitler's invasion of Russia, Joseph Stalin was now allied with Churchill and Roosevelt. The Soviet Union would come to the aid of Tito's Communist partisan army, against both Germany and the alternative royalist opposition, and Britain would have to decide which of the rival anti-Nazi Yugoslav rebels to support.[25]

Black, White and Grey

When the *Gestapo* arrested Tommy Kendrick in August 1938, Evelyn Stamper had already left Austria. But MI6 immediately took the precaution of recalling Clara Holmes and Betty Hodgson to London. The danger was too great to ignore. And Clara was responsible for her ten-year-old daughter, Prudence. After a comprehensive debrief at the MI6 headquarters in Broadway Buildings, all three started working on the best way they could contribute to combating the Nazis: propaganda.

That autumn, Betty Hodgson joined the Joint Broadcasting Committee. Sounding innocuous, the committee was a brainchild of Laurence Grand, made up of his personal contacts. As its secretary, Betty was on the MI6 payroll and a member of Section D[26]. The committee's role was to spread propaganda by radio broadcasts to the German and Austrian populations.[27] Guy Burgess, another Soviet spy, would later coordinate its activities with those of the Ministry of Information and Electra House, the new organisation within the Foreign Office responsible for propaganda to enemy countries once the war started.

So when Hugh Sinclair instructed Grand 'to form immediately a section for the dissemination through all channels outside this country of material to enemy and neutral countries', Section D was already on the case. Within a few days, they arranged for Radio Luxembourg to transmit a translation of the British position in the September 1938 Czechoslovakia crisis directly to the German people, to Hitler's annoyance.[28] It did not help the ultimate outcome at Munich, but this was a classic example of 'white' propaganda: material whose source is disclosed. In contrast, 'black' propaganda falsifies where it comes from and 'grey' propaganda does not identify its source.[29]

Section D did all three. As Grand explained it, his people would work on broadcasting through foreign radio stations, providing material to foreign journalists, distributing leaflets 'by any and every means' and running 'whispering campaigns of the type that had been effective in the First World War'.[30]

The Joint Broadcasting Committee was like an iceberg, with a public element above the surface distributing cultural material about Britain, camouflaging Section D's undercover distribution of propaganda. The hidden capability grew rapidly. Various parts of Section D wrote, designed and secretly printed pamphlets. They recorded programmes for broadcast by foreign radio stations and distributed other recordings on four-inch flexible miniature gramophone records, easily smuggled in rolled newspapers.

For journalists in neutral countries, Section D provided articles, news bulletins and photographs, either by mail or wire. Up to the outbreak of war in September 1939, the Section distributed over a million leaflets in 'Greater Germany', including Austria. Grand's people considered Austria a tough target for propaganda, because of the 'multiplicity of parties, ideas and ideals'. Even so, the Section distributed posters explaining the necessity for Austrian independence. The influence of the 'three ladies' can be detected.

Betty Hodgson was fully engaged in the higher-level organisation of the propaganda effort. Meanwhile, Evelyn Stamper and Clara Holmes had moved across from the intelligence side of MI6 in May 1939 to help Laurence Grand set up Section D. They became one half of the German department of the new organisation. Boundaries were fluid, but their focus, not surprisingly, was on Austria, while the other two officers worked mostly on the *Altreich*—the 'Old *Reich*'—the Germany that existed before the *Anschluss*.

As soon as they had arrived back in London, Evelyn and Clara had established contact with Austrian émigré organisations. They were both convinced that encouraging Austrian separatism was a key element of breaking up Greater Germany.[31] Not all émigrés agreed. The idea of union with Germany had plenty of supporters among Austrians in Britain, but the sense of Austrian identity was strong. With encouragement, they thought, it could become stronger, both in Britain and the home country.

Evelyn and Clara set to work collecting material, editing, printing and distributing leaflets to the *Reich*. Many were destined for Germany, but the pair made sure that they included titles like *Austrian*

News, *A Magazine for Austrian Women* and *Letters to Austrian Railwaymen*. They took the printed pamphlets to Clara's home at 46, Lexham Gardens in South Kensington, where they packed them into authentic envelopes, mostly obtained from abroad. From the contacts they had built up during the Vienna years and since arriving in London, they had developed a massive card index—no computers then—of Austrian and German individuals who might distribute the leaflets. The refugees in London who helped them collect the names also addressed the envelopes in different hands, all with a convincing Germanic script.

Then came the problem of distribution. Couriers from Switzerland smuggled some of the material into Austria. But the most practical route until the fall of France in May 1940 was through Paris, where Section D had representatives. 'Midge' Holmes acted as courier. She struggled with heavy suitcases, full of the stamped and addressed envelopes, by train to Paris. There she carried them up to the top floor of an apartment building, above a baker's shop. There was no elevator.[32]

On one visit to Paris in July 1939, Clara delivered 2,000 propaganda sheets. The primary contact in Paris, who undertook to get the pamphlets into Austria and Germany, was Karl Groehl of the anti-Nazi *Lex* organisation.[33] Groehl was a small man of East Prussian origin who was deaf and mild-mannered, characteristics that worried him. He thought them inappropriate for someone engaged in espionage and subversion.[34]

Karl Otten, his partner in the organisation, had been introduced to Laurence Grand just before Christmas 1938. Otten had been born in Oberkrüchten in the Rhineland, but he and his Berlin-born wife had lived in Vienna, where their son was born in 1919. Otten looked professorial, was partially sighted and eventually became blind. He claimed to have almost fifty workers dropping up to 25,000 leaflets into the German mail each month.

Grand arranged for a clergyman in Brighton to invite Groehl to visit Britain, as cover for a planning meeting, and the system got going. Groehl was as usual full of plans, some impractical, others fictitious.

When war broke out in September 1939, the French arrested him, accusing him of being a Stalinist agent. For three weeks, the French *Deuxième Bureau* would not reveal to the British where he was being held. It seemed likely, thought Section D, that the French were teaching him a lesson on 'the inadvisability of working for the British without their knowledge'.

'London Karl' and 'Paris Karl' were inseparable friends, but 'lived in an atmosphere of continual mutual recriminations which generally ended in a particularly violent outburst of one against the other, after which they met and all was forgiven'. Clara Holmes acted as 'general confessor, mediator and instructor'.

Otten and Groehl had first come to the attention of MI6 in 1936 in Paris, where Groehl was reported to be a 'well known German Communist who played a prominent part in the Communist movement in Munich', and he was mentioned in letters intercepted by MI5, the Security Service.[35] His wife, in Germany, was trying to get a permit to move to England and to get their nine-year-old child into an English school. Groehl was said to be a Trotskyist, rabidly anti-Nazi and a quarrelsome individual.

Before the war and until Hitler invaded Russia in June 1941, the Soviet Union was allied with Nazi Germany and a serious worry to Britain. Even after 1941, the USSR was not much less of concern as an ally. Soviet spies remained active in the United Kingdom. MI5 kept an eye on possible foreign agents and had files on the two Karls. Groehl's name, in particular, came up often. He had frequent contact with a suspected spy who was being watched, his phone tapped and his mail opened. At meetings, MI5 reported, the indiscreet Groehl spoke openly about working for a British undercover agency and about delivering propaganda into Germany and Austria. Evelyn Stamper and Clara Holmes received regular reports from the watchers. When 'Paris Karl' arrived at Bristol (Whitchurch) Airport on 9th October 1940 in a British Overseas Airways Corporation DC-3 Dakota from Lisbon, he produced documents identifying him as a Pole by the name of Stanislaw Retzlaw. His inability to speak Polish and his perfect Berlin-accented German made the Special Branch officers suspicious.

Eventually, he admitted his real name. At MI5 request, the police escorted him to Lexham Gardens, where Clara Holmes was waiting for him.[36]

Otten and Groehl did not realise that their correspondence was being monitored by the British. In one letter, Groehl complains to Otten about 50,000 copies of a propaganda postcard he has just received. But he does not want Clara to know. 'You must keep this from Madame,' he writes.[37]

SOE

When Winston Churchill became Prime Minister on 10th May 1940, Britain's situation could not have been much worse. The Norway campaign had been a disastrous failure. German armies were storming across the Low Countries and advancing into France. Within weeks, the remnants of the retreating British Expeditionary Force would be evacuated from the beaches of Dunkirk. The rescue of 327,000 British and French soldiers was miraculous, but it was no victory. German forces built up in France, preparing for the invasion of Britain, *Unternehmen Seelöwe* (Operation Sealion).[38]

Churchill's immediate focus had to be on defence, but he hankered after ways to take the fight to the enemy. One of the few options was irregular warfare, dear to Winston's heart. The War Office's Military Intelligence (Research) section, MI6's Section D and the Foreign Office's unit at Electra House offered possibilities for offensive action.[39] With some overlap, they had been developing and carrying out sabotage, subversion and propaganda operations, as the British military and intelligence 'communities' belatedly transitioned from peace to war. Section D and MI(R), in particular, were already reservoirs of knowledge and experience of undercover operations. A new organisation was needed, decided Churchill's new coalition War Cabinet on 27th May 1940. Thus was born the Special Operations Executive. Inevitably, the War Office and MI6 disagreed as to which of them should control it. 'Neither' was the answer. Churchill gave Labour Minister Hugh Dalton the responsibility, in his Ministry of Economic Warfare. As ever, the context is important. Opinion was widespread in the Britain of 1940 that prior Nazi subversion had been a key factor in the success of the German advance through Europe. Surely powerful European resistance would rise against Nazi domination and food shortage would undermine Hitler's war machine.[40] Dalton and his Labour Party colleagues were at the centre of this thinking.

During the summer and autumn of 1940, MI(R), Section D and EH were progressively subsumed into SOE.[41] The difference of approach between Dalton's favoured political subversion—'revolution' by left-wing political movements—and the soldiers' preference, clandestine paramilitary operations, would be a source of tension within SOE for the rest of the war. Other tensions existed with some of the governments-in-exile in London, with which SOE took over the responsibility of liaison.

The formation of SOE from Section D and MI(R) was messy and acrimonious. Hugh Dalton's dismissal of Laurence Grand, as Grand fought a rearguard action against the dissolution of his empire, was curt. Yet we should not underestimate the contribution of the two earlier organisations. They 'laid the foundations for SOE in doctrine, training, equipment and experience of clandestine warfare', as Mark Seaman put it, and 'there can be no doubting that without their ground-breaking endeavours, SOE would have struggled to make its contribution to the Allied victory in the Second World War'.[42] One of SOE's assets, gained from Section D, was the knowledge, contacts and passionate commitment to Austria of the three women. Evelyn Stamper, Clara Holmes and Betty Hodgson kept their jobs and became SOE officers.

---

[1] On the intelligence work of Thomas Kendrick, his arrest and the escape of his staff, see Kenneth Benton, 'The ISOS Years: Madrid 1941-3', *Journal of Contemporary History* 30, no. 3 (1995), Peter Pirker, *Gegen das 'Dritte Reich': Sabotage und transnationaler Widerstand in Österreich und Slowenien 1938-1940* (Klagenfurt: Kitab, 2010), pp.28-33 and Helen Fry, 2021.

[2] *The Times*, London, 18th, 19th, 22nd and 24th August 1938. Now 'blown', Kendrick went on to serve in MI6 in Britain, leading the successful bugging of senior German prisoners at the Combined Services Detailed Interrogation

Centre; Helen Fry's biography has recently been republished (Helen Fry, 2021). The memoir was *Greek Memories* by Compton Mackenzie. The decreased value of the 'official' SIS network under PCO cover led to the development from 1936 of the 'Z Organisation' by Dansey, built on the foundation of the business contacts he had developed as PCO in Rome. Dansey's primary agent in Vienna was Frederick Voight, Central European correspondent of the Manchester Guardian, but Eric Gedye was another. Also, Sir Robert Vansittart, the senior civil servant in the British Foreign Office and a strong advocate of rearmament, developed his own private intelligence agency. His most effective agent was Group Captain Malcolm Christie, who had been at university with Hermann Goering in Aachen and had excellent connections with senior Nazis. Christie gave warning of Hitler's remilitarisation of the Rhineland and was told by Goering of the Nazi intention to invade Austria and Czechoslovakia. (Christopher Andrew, *Secret Service: the making of the British intelligence community* (London: Heinemann, 1985), pp.240, 380, 391, Keith Jeffery, *MI6: the history of the Secret Intelligence Service, 1909-1949* (London: Bloomsbury, 2010), p.301, Nigel West, *MI6: British Secret Intelligence Service Operations 1909-1945* (London: Weidenfeld & Nicolson, 1983), pp.58, 115.)

[3] Christopher Andrew, *Secret Service*, 1985, p.379, Keith Jeffery, 2010, p.301.

[4] Eric Sanders Oral History, Imperial War Museum Collections (29954).

[5] Evelyn Stamper signed herself in this way, but was formally known as Miss Graham-Stamper (TNA HS 9/1329/6, HS 7/145).

[6] Eric Sanders Oral History.

[7] Peter Pirker, *Subversion deutscher Herrschaft*, 2012, pp.66-67, G E R Gedye, *Fallen Bastions*, 1939, pp.309-10.

[8] Public Records Office Census: 1901, RG13/860; 1911, 14 Humphreys Cross, Playden, Sussex.

[9] Malcolm Atkin, *Section D for Destruction: forerunner of SOE* (Barnsley, South Yorkshire: Pen & Sword Military, 2017), Appendix 2.

[10] Phyllis describes Clara as Miss Margery (after Marguerite) Bates (Phyllis Bottome, *The Goal* (London: Faber & Faber, 1962), pp.65, 73, 98, Peter Pirker, *Subversion deutscher Herrschaft*, 2012, p.57. Kenneth Benton also knew her as 'Bill Holmes' (Kenneth Benton, 1995). The 'secretaries' kept contact with Kendrick's agents around Europe, using invisible ink to conceal messages in innocuous correspondence. According to her daughter, Prudence, Clara Holmes also had an active intelligence role: during the 1935 Abyssinian war, Kendrick sent her to 'befriend' an Italian officer and elicit naval secrets (Helen Fry, 2021, pp.71, 76).

[11] Information from family archives, courtesy of Adrian Hopkinson.

[12] While SIS/MI6 is Britain's spy agency, gaining intelligence in support of national policy, the Security Service, MI5, is responsible for protecting Britain against foreign and domestic threats. For more, see Christopher Andrew, *Defence of the Realm*, 2009 and Keith Jeffery, 2010.

[13] Peter Dixon, *Guardians*, 2018, pp.39-43.
[14] Simon Anglim, 'MI(R), G(R) and British Covert Operations, 1939–42', *Intelligence and National Security* 20, no. 4 (2005).
[15] Mark Seaman, *Special Operations Executive: a new instrument of war* (London: Routledge, 2006), p.8.
[16] *Ibid*, Malcolm Atkin, 2017, p.28. The Section's formal title within SIS/MI6 was 'Section IX'.
[17] Bickham Sweet-Escott, *Baker Street Irregular* (London, Methuen, 1965), p.20; M R D Foot, *SOE 1940-1946*, 2014, pp.4-6; W J M Mackenzie, *The Secret History of SOE: the Special Operations Executive, 1940-1945* (London: St Ermin's, 2000), pp.12-37; and Malcolm Atkin, 2017, p.25.
[18] Kim Philby, *My Silent War* (London: Grafton, 1968), p.27.
[19] Peter Wilkinson and Joan Bright Astley, *Gubbins and SOE* (Barnsley: Pen & Sword Military, 1993).
[20] TNA HS 7/3, *SOE Early History to September 1940*.
[21] Meeting 15th May 1940, quoted in W J M Mackenzie, 2000, p.27.
[22] TNA HS 7/3, *Early History*.
[23] Malcolm Atkin, 2017, pp.137-141.
[24] Peter Pirker, 'Transnational Resistance in the Alps-Adriatic Area in 1939/40: On Subversive Border Crossers, Historical Interpretations and National Politics of the Past', *Acta Histriae* 20, no. 4 (2012).
[25] Antony Beevor, 2012, pp.421-3.
[26] TNA HS 7/5, 'Special Achievements'; Malcolm Atkin, 2017, Appendix 2.
[27] TNA ED 121/195, HS 7/3, *Early History*.
[28] Malcolm Atkin, 2017, p.30.
[29] Collins English Dictionary.
[30] TNA FO 898/1, quoted in Malcolm Atkin, 2017, p.31.
[31] Austrian separatism was not the only way in which the cohesion of the Reich could be challenged. In October 1943, Winston Churchill latched on to an intelligence report drawing attention to 'separatist tendencies in Bavaria, Wurtenburg (sic) and Baden where there was deep-rooted hostility to the Prussians'. The Prime Minister 'assumed that SOE would be taking all possible steps to play upon the local anti-Prussian feeling described' (TNA HS 7/253, p.26).
[32] Here and next four paragraphs: TNA HS 7/3 SOE *Early History*.
[33] Also going under the code name *Probst*. Described in his MI5 file as 'a mixture of a conceited Prima Donna and a dyspectic misanthrope' (TNA KV 2/2172, 10th March 1942).
[34] TNA KV 2/2172, 10th March 1942.
[35] TNA KV 2/2171, 14th December 1936 and following. He had apparently been police chief in Munich for ten days during the short-lived Communist Republic (*Münchner Räterepublik*) in 1919.
[36] TNA KV 2/2171, Special Branch report, 10th October 1940. The airport, three miles south of the city, was replaced in 1957 by the present Bristol

(Lulsgate) Airport (https://www.bristolpost.co.uk/news/history/how-time-flies-bristol-airport-43390, accessed 24th July 2021). On the same Lisbon-Bristol route on 1st June 1943, the same civilian DC-3, registration G-AGBB, was attacked by eight Luftwaffe Junkers Ju88 fighters. All on board were killed, including actor Leslie Howard. The Germans may have believed that Winston Churchill was on board (https://aviation-safety.net/database/record.php?id=19430601-0, accessed 24th July 2021).

[37] TNA KV 2/2171, 17th December 1936 and 18th November 1939.

[38] Anthony McCarten, *Darkest Hour: how Churchill brought us back from the brink* (London: Viking, 2017); Harold Macmillan, *The Blast of War, 1939-1945* (London: MacMillan, 1967), pp.65-78; Antony Beevor, 2012, pp.79-92; and Deborah Cadbury, 2015.

[39] Electra House was known either as 'EH' after its location or 'CS' after its director, Canadian newspaperman Sir Campbell Stuart.

[40] David Stafford, *Britain and European Resistance, 1940-1945: a survey of the Special Operations Executive, with documents* (Toronto: University of Toronto Press, 1980), pp.14-17.

[41] M R D Foot, *SOE 1940-1946*, 2014, p.6. Responsibility for propaganda was removed from SOE and given in August 1941 to the newly formed Political Warfare Executive. See David Garnett, *The Secret History of PWE: the Political Warfare Executive, 1939-1945* (London: St Ermin's Press, 2002).

[42] Mark Seaman, 2006, pp.19-20.

CHAPTER 5

Early Days

A timber merchant and his assistant

AN IMAGE OF A TYPICAL SOE AGENT springs to mind: young, fit, courageous, resourceful, ready for anything.[1] Theodor Schuhbauer was probably resourceful and certainly brave, but otherwise he did not fit the bill. At the age of fifty, the Vienna-born Schuhbauer could not easily learn the skills for undercover paramilitary action. But that was not his purpose. A social democrat connected with the London-based 'Austria Office' of Austrian refugees, he volunteered in late 1940 to return to his homeland. He would have to travel via the Middle East and Yugoslavia. This roundabout route to the Balkans gave the only feasible access to Austria in 1941, with the whole of Europe under Axis control. Theodor's mission would be to revive former contacts and try to build up a network of anti-Nazi activists.[2]

Of the several groups of Austrian exiles in Britain, the Austria Office was the one that most suited the purposes of Evelyn Stamper and Clara Holmes. Their plan was to build up a movement, in exile and in the home country, working towards Austria's independence from Nazi Germany. They had helped Austrian social democrats in London, prominent among them Heinrich Allina, to found the Austria Office. With modest funds, SOE supported it in October 1940 to publish a monthly magazine, *Free Austria*. It was 'a non-political publication intended to acquaint the British public with Austrian affairs'.[3] To keep it free of political dispute but in line with Allied war aims and the 'idea' of Austria, Evelyn and Clara edited the magazine, wrote some articles and vetted others. They also maintained the list of subscribers to the magazine, a useful source of intelligence about those in Britain with an interest in Austria. The Office itself also provided recruits for the operations that SOE's tiny Austrian sub-section had in mind. Among them was Theodor Schuhbauer.

Schuhbauer received limited training, while SOE concocted a false identity for him. His birth date and first name remained the same, to give him less to memorise. It made sense. At least for the journey to Yugoslavia, he would be Thomas Shearer, a timber merchant born in Rorschach, Switzerland, of British parents. The timber idea had originated as a plan to ask an Austrian-American timber merchant living in Portugal to smuggle propaganda into Austria on lumber transports. That came to nought, but the idea stuck.

The first choice to be Schuhbauer's travel companion, and his assistant when they reached Austria, contracted bronchial pneumonia. To replace him, Evelyn Stamper identified a candidate currently working in Wales. She sent a telegram, inviting eighteen-year-old Franz Preiss to London for an interview. He proved extremely suitable.

Franz was not Austrian, though. He was born in the spa town of Teplitz-Schoenau, today's Teplice, in Moravia. The town had been part of Austria-Hungary until the Empire was dissolved after the 1914-18 War, when it became part of the new state of Czechoslovakia. Like the other residents of the town, the nationality of Franz's family had shifted over the years. But his mother tongue was German, and he probably felt as Austrian as did Theodor. A refugee from the Nazi takeover of Czechoslovakia, Franz was 'a young tough, famous for shooting Nazis on sight'.[4] He had been working in the forests near Llangollen in North Wales. While there, he had learnt English with a distinct Welsh accent, so part of his 'legend' under his alias of 'Frank Pryce' was that he had been born in Llangollen. Like Theodor, he kept his real birth date. His knowledge of forestry and the timber trade would help both him and Theodor maintain their cover during the journey.[5]

When the armed cargo ship SS *Jonathan Holt* sailed from Liverpool on 19th February 1941 and joined up with Convoy OB289, four of the twelve passengers on board were SOE operatives. Thomas Schuhbauer and Franz Preiss were two of them.[6] 'I saw your husband off last night', wrote Clara Holmes to Theodor's wife, Valerie. 'He asked me to send you this £1,[7] which he did not want to take with him', she wrote, and she promised to send Valerie £4 per week during Theodor's absence. Theodor had said, wrote Clara, that Valerie 'would hear from him through me in two to three weeks' time'. She never did.

On the night of Sunday 23rd February 1941, four German U-boats launched an attack on Convoy OB289, midway between Iceland and the northern extremities of Scotland. In the early morning hours of Monday 24th, two torpedoes from the German submarine U-97, commanded by *Kapitänleutnant* Udo Heilmann, hit the *Jonathan Holt*. She sank in two minutes. There was no time to launch lifeboats, but nearby ships rescued three fortunate survivors. Theodor and Franz were not among them.[8]

For Clara and Evelyn, this was a devastating blow to their early plans for Austrian operations. They also had to find a way to support Theodor's lonely widow, Valerie. For several months, she did not know of her husband's fate. Until his death could be confirmed, all they could do was continue to provide some money each week and help her gain some other income. They tried to get the Home Office to rescind its ban on her earning money, as an 'enemy alien', through giving private piano lessons. They eventually succeeded in this, and in time could give her the sad news of her husband's death. For the next four years, Clara kept up a sympathetic correspondence with Valerie: trying to regularise a widow's pension; politely declining Valerie's invitation to a concert she and a Viennese singer were giving in Guildford, Surrey; trying to help her get her two Jewish nephews out of Vichy France to safety in England; thanking her for a gift of Earl Grey tea and lavender sachets.[9] From time to time, Valerie visited Evelyn and Clara in London, taking tea with them at 50, Hans

Crescent. On one such occasion, Evelyn handed over a £500 settlement—in cash—instead of a pension.[10] Then Clara became her financial advisor as Valerie agonised about where to invest the money. She was worried that the assets of an 'enemy alien' might be confiscated. The nationality itself was a political issue. The Guildford police had registered Theodor and Valerie as German, on the basis of the passports issued by the Nazi authorities in Vienna. Valerie wished to correct this 'unpleasant error'. Commander John Senter, SOE's Director of Security, had a word with the Chief Constable of Surrey to have this put right. And the question arose of providing her husband's death certificate, complicated by the fact that he had died under the name of 'Thomas Shearer, timber merchant'. When the Austrian social democrat Heinrich Allina wanted to commemorate Theodor in a pamphlet, Evelyn begged Valerie 'not to permit him to do anything of the kind'. Her husband's name would be properly honoured in Austria after the war and 'it would be most inadvisable to have any publicity given to him or the manner of his death at the present moment'.[11]

These were all part of the normal duties of SOE country sections. Clara and Evelyn fulfilled them with tact, sympathy and dogged determination.

Uphill struggle

The failure of the first operation into Austria was a serious setback for the small Austrian sub-section of SOE, 'X/Aus' or 'X/A'. Like those focusing on Germany, they grappled with the problem of encouraging opposition to the Nazis. The issue in the *Reich* differed from that in occupied countries like France or the Netherlands and was much more difficult. Even in those countries, most people 'turned their backs on the war' and got on with their lives as best they could.[12] In the 1930s in Germany and from 1938 in Austria, the Nazi party had seized control of all areas of society, including the security forces and education. Those who opposed it were treated as traitors. They faced imprisonment in a concentration camp or worse. Many fled to safety. Undercover opposition to Hitler existed, but SOE had instructions from the Foreign Office to treat such people with suspicion.[13] Peace feelers from within Germany were not to be encouraged.[14] The same applied to Austria.

In principle, Austria was a better prospect than Germany. But Austria was not an occupied country in the same way as France or The Netherlands. The events of March 1938—the collapse of Schuschnigg's government under pressure from Hitler, the seizure of power by Austrian Nazis and the German military occupation—had led to a situation where 'Austrian National Socialism coexisted with foreign German domination'. Resisters belonged to two primary groups: the left-wing social democrats, Communists and trade unionists; and the right-wing monarchists, Catholics, Christian Socials and nationalists. Armed resistance on the southern borders of Austria, particularly in Slovenia, had a particular nationalist flavour. Those who resisted the regime were not simply opposing occupation out of national honour. Instead, their reasons were more complex: 'political, ideological, religious, social, moral, humanistic or patriotic'. And they were faced with 'a hostile social environment in which informers and fanatical supporters of the regime were ubiquitous'.[15]

Evelyn Stamper and Clara Holmes were determined to hasten Germany's defeat by exploiting the underlying desire for Austrian autonomy that they believed still existed.[16] Having left Vienna in early 1938, they probably underestimated most Austrians' passive acceptance of Nazi and 'Prussian' domination.[17] Intelligence reports from Austria only partly supported their view: a snapshot of Austrian opinion in January 1943 concluded that 'The Austrians desire nothing so much as the end of the war', and 'Those who were pro-Nazi before 1938 are disillusioned, those who were anti-Nazi are confirmed in their hatred of the *Reichsdeutschen*; all are disgruntled'.[18]

Evelyn and Clara's primary aim from the beginning was to 'assist in the disintegration of the Third Reich by fostering a revolutionary and separatist uprising in Austria, fully supported by propagandist, political and military action'. As a secondary goal, they hoped to 'bring about the restoration of Austria as a national unit, possibly within the framework of a federation or economic bloc'.[19] They stuck to these aims with remarkable consistency throughout the war. At first, though, their aspirations did not quite match the foreign policy of the British Government. The Foreign Office doubted how viable the small, landlocked country could be. It envisaged forming a federation of Danubian states if Germany was defeated, countering any future German expansion. Experts advising the US State Department took a similar line.[20] At first, SOE was careful not to oppose the FO directly.[21] In its own 'foreign policy', it recognised a Danubian federation as a possibility but focused more on using Austrian autonomy to undermine the *Reich*. It was a key tool in political warfare.[22]

A perhaps unlikely ally of SOE in this debate was the British Prime Minister. To the dismay of some within the Foreign Office, Winston Churchill took a romantic view of Austria, grounded in his historical perspective of the Austro-Hungarian Empire. Official British foreign policy in late 1941 was that the future of Austria should be determined according to the wishes of the Austrians, but an independent Austria was 'not at present an official war aim of His Majesty's Government'. For Churchill, though, Austria had been 'trampled down under the Nazi and Prussian yoke'. He was 'not without deep emotion', remembering 'the charm, beauty and historic splendour of Vienna, the grace of life, the dignity of the individual'. 'The people of Britain will never desert the cause of the freedom of Austria', he proclaimed. 'We shall go forward'.[23] Three months earlier, he had said that Austria was 'one of the countries for which we have drawn the sword and for whom our victory will supply liberation'.[24]

Evelyn and Clara were realistic about early prospects of success. Military intervention would have to wait for the right moment. They planned to train 'a special elite corps of saboteurs, parachutists and leaders', but they did not expect to introduce them into Austria until 'twenty-four hours before the crack comes'.[25] Even so, 'X/Aus' had a steep hill to climb.

'X/Aus'

The Germany/Austria specialists from Laurence Grand's Section D of MI6 were brought over to SOE as a unit in November 1940 to form the German, or 'X', Section. Evelyn Stamper led the Austrian work, assisted by Clara Holmes, who had a particular responsibility for coded communications.[26] They reported at first to Lieutenant-Colonel Brien Clarke, designated 'X', but he soon moved to Gibraltar and took over Iberian operations, to be replaced by Major Ronald Thornley.

Thornley, the son of a Yorkshire doctor, had won scholarships to the prestigious Winchester College and then to Clare College, Cambridge, where he studied Modern European History and Modern Languages.[27] He was six feet tall, with grey-blue eyes and a pragmatic and even cynical approach to his task. An accomplished linguist, he spoke French and German fluently and had a working knowledge of Italian, Spanish, Dutch and Swedish.

Like many Cambridge students with language ability, Thornley was recruited by an MI6 talent-spotter for intelligence work. After graduation, he took a job as cover with an American company at its Paris headquarters, travelling widely and sending back reports to London on the German *Luftwaffe*. The atmosphere in Germany became more threatening for foreign residents as war loomed, and Thornley had to come back to Britain in 1939. On his return, Laurence Grand recruited him into Section D, where he was commissioned as a major. He was based in London, but—after his father died in December 1939—he felt a keen responsibility to support his widowed mother back in Scarborough.

Lieutenant-Colonel Ronald Thornley

Thornley migrated in December 1940 to SOE, just a few weeks after Brigadier Colin Gubbins joined it as Director of Training and Operations. Gubbins had been a member of MI(R) but had in the meantime commanded *Scissorsforce*, the group of four 'Independent Companies' formed in May 1940 to harass German forces in Norway. The Norway campaign ended disastrously, but Gubbins operated with great effectiveness. He moved on to form and command another MI(R) creation: the 'Auxiliary Units', a secret guerrilla force that would resist Nazi occupiers of Britain should the worst happen.[28] Mercifully, it did not.

As Thornley's boss, Colin Gubbins recognised both his ability and the depth of his knowledge of Germany and Austria. He gave Thornley considerable freedom of action, but made it clear that X Section's area was not a great priority for SOE. In February 1941, Thornley attended the first course for SOE staff at Station XVII, the sabotage and irregular operations school at Brickendonbury Manor. He scored the highest marks in the examination and proved himself 'keen and intelligent', with 'plenty of guts'.[29]

As well as the staff officers, two former NCOs from SOE's own Field Security Sections—Lieutenants Russell and Keir—became 'conducting officers', accompanying German-speaking agents through training.[30] Russell's background is unknown, but Allan Keir hailed from Glasgow and had a wife and baby daughter. He spoke German fluently, having travelled throughout Germany, Holland and Scandinavia promoting export sales of oilskin clothing. He became an expert in railway sabotage, passing on his skills to trainee agents.

X Section's task was to 'establish channels of communication into Germany and Austria for subversive activities' and to build a 'network of agents suitable for these activities'. Working from a standing start, it was a 'stupendous task'. Not only was the Nazi police state against them; so was MI6. 'It's pointless for you to have a German Section', said MI6 Deputy Director Claude Dansey to Thornley in early 1941, 'and we certainly won't be sharing any of our contacts there or channels of communication'.[31]

Ronald Thornley and his colleagues realised that trying to build a resistance movement in Germany itself was a forlorn hope. Most of the so-called anti-Nazi elements were neither willing nor able to undertake any subversive activities. The most X Section could expect to achieve was subversion through propaganda, sporadic sabotage—itself potentially counter-productive—to alarm the *Gestapo* and encourage any genuine subversive elements, and 'administrative sabotage'.

This last initiative involved undermining the Nazi administration by flooding the country with, for example, forged ration coupons. This, thought Thornley, was a 'most valuable weapon against the methodically minded Germans'. Through experiencing Nazi effectiveness during his travels, he was also a convert to the power of propaganda.

The lack of contacts in Germany and Austria forced Thornley to consider other channels of communications. Thousands of foreign workers, shipped to the *Reich* from Nazi-occupied countries, were a potential source of subversive contacts. But SOE sections like F Section (France) and N Section (The Netherlands) were far too busy trying to build their own resistance networks. They had neither time nor resources to help X Section contact French or Dutch slave workers. What remained were the neutral countries bordering Germany and Austria, and wherever émigré communities existed. Thornley decided to establish X Section representatives with the SOE stations in Sweden, Switzerland and Turkey and to exploit contacts in Britain.

The constraints affecting Germany applied to Austria too. The Nazis enjoyed vigorous support, especially outside Vienna. Dissent had been ruthlessly suppressed. Fear reigned. Yet there was a glimmer of hope that the distinctive Austrian identity might help to drive a wedge between the two German-speaking countries. This was the ember that Evelyn and Clara hoped to fan into flame, and the best place to look was the Austrian community in London.

Austrians Abroad

Although Evelyn Stamper and Clara Holmes had gained plenty of contacts in Austria during their time there, they had no practical way of contacting them. In the early months, their only access was to Austrian refugees and émigrés in Britain, some in internment camps as enemy aliens, others living freely in London and elsewhere. Of these there were many, with a spectrum of political colours and a confusing range of titles. What mattered to Evelyn and Clara was their attitude to Austrian separatism.

The organisation that seemed at the time least 'useful' to SOE was the Revolutionary Socialist group. This was 'largely composed of internationalists forced to leave Austria for racial reasons, but who have no quarrel with Germany'. Its ultimate aim was 'not an independent Austria, but an Austria incorporated in a Greater German bloc'.[32] Ronald Thornley had been instructed to refuse categorically the political conditions attached to offers of potential agents by their representative, Oscar Pollak.[33] The essentially non-political but social democrat-leaning 'Austria Office' was a much better prospect; Thornley vigorously defended SOE's support of it.

The bewildering collection of other groups, who were often squabbling with each other and engaging in mutual accusation, ranged between Communists at one extreme and Monarchists at the other. Between the two ends of the spectrum stood various social democrat groups, but even so the Austrian diaspora did not represent a political cross-section of Austria. The Christian socials, for example, what Evelyn called the 'Catholic peasant party', were barely represented in Britain. There was, reported Evelyn, a 'disproportionate number of internationalists (Communists and Radical Socialists) owing to the preponderance of the Jewish element'.[34] Unsurprisingly, most of those who had been forced to flee were Jewish.

The two ladies of X/Aus kept a close eye on the different Austrian factions, but they reserved their greatest support for social democrats and especially for the Austria Office in Eaton Place, a social hub for this group, and its *Free Austria* magazine. With a confusingly similar name, the 'Austrian Centre' had been formed in 1939 to aid Austrian refugees, but gradually became dominated by Communists. After the USSR and Germany signed the Molotov-Ribbentrop Pact in August 1939, the Centre used the money of unwitting donors for anti-British propaganda. When Hitler invaded Russia, the message became pro-British again. MI5 carefully watched the Centre, and particularly its dynamic 'presiding genius', Eva Kolmer. She had been well known to the police in Vienna as a committee member of the illegal Austrian Communist Party.[35]

In late 1941, eleven groups joined to form the 'Free Austrian Movement', claiming to represent ninety per cent of Austrians in Britain and aiming to secure the right of self-determination for their homeland. The British Foreign Office was sceptical, and gave the group a lukewarm response.[36] Thornley, Stamper and Holmes, who wished the Austrian exiles would set aside their internal differences and act against the common foe, at first took a more positive approach. From July 1943, social democrats and monarchists left the Movement, and SOE commented that Communists had acquired all the key positions in it.[37]

The lack of unity and cohesion among Austrian political organisations in Britain was mirrored around the world. In the USA, five entities represented the political spectrum.[38] One key figure was Dr Gregor Sebba, who had been a close associate of the British community in Vienna and editor of the Meinl coffee concern's in-house magazine. He was secretly working for SOE in New York from January 1941 and helped to found 'Austrian Action', described as a 'military non-partisan organisation'.[39] The machinations in the USA by monarchists like Archduke Otto von Hapsburg caused consternation in SOE. 'Any suspicion of HM Government supporting Hapsburg will throw Austrian workmen into the arms of the Nazis', wrote Eric Gedye from his new post in Istanbul.[40]

Organisations with various political leanings also existed in Canada, Latin America and South Africa[41]. In Palestine and Egypt, both British-administered, Zionist Jewish movements dominated. Yet an 'Austrian Society in Palestine' and an affiliated organisation in Egypt had been set up.

Dr Peter Pirker suggests that Evelyn Stamper had an 'almost arrogant certainty' regarding her own interpretation of Austrian politics. He also examines whether prejudice against Jews coloured SOE's judgement in selecting agents for deployment and in its relations with Austrian exile groups.[42] Thornley, Stamper and Holmes were certainly far from politically correct, to use the modern term, in their decision-making. Their focus was on defeating the Nazi regime. Whether agents could keep a low profile in a hostile Aryanised society was a key issue, but SOE recruited plenty of Jewish volunteers for action in Austria. On the political front, it was clear that the mainly socialist and Jewish exiles could not speak for Austria.

One diplomat, resident in Britain but with links to many of the organisations in the USA, was recognised by the British Government as influential. Sir George Franckenstein had been Austrian Envoy in London from 1920 to 1938, holding dual nationality, 'representing his country admirably' and 'keeping Austria in the forefront of public interest'. He was 'a man of great integrity', but 'too nervous to take any decisive action'. Politically conservative and knighted by the King in 1938, he did not ally himself with any party, but desired above all an independent Austria.[43]

Franckenstein was a respected representative of Austria internationally, so when he visited 10 Downing Street in November 1942 to meet Desmond Morton, representing Winston Churchill, he was given a hearing. In inviting SOE to send a representative to the meeting, Morton could not resist speaking of 'the Franckenstein monster'. Ronald Thornley attended, using the name of 'Major Thurston' and described as 'an officer from the War Office interested in Austrian affairs and in the Underground Movement in particular'.[44] Later, in discussions between 10 Downing Street, SOE and Franckenstein, SOE helped Sir George develop a broadcast appeal to the Austrian people. Franckenstein also mooted the idea of an Austrian Committee or Trustee Group to represent Austria to the Allies, rather like the occupied countries' governments-in-exile. Given the disunity among Austrian exiles, this second idea never came to fruition. SOE's Austrian Section turned to operations.

Exploring options

In 1940, the Austrian Section consisted only of Evelyn Stamper and Clara 'Midge' Holmes. Living with Midge was her daughter Prudence, now twelve. As the danger from German bombing became more acute, Clara arranged for Prudence to be evacuated to safety in Canada. 'Prue' departed from Liverpool in the RMS *Duchess of Athol* on 19th July 1940, bound for St Michael's School in Vernon, British Columbia. However exciting this adventure may have been, when the danger of German invasion receded Prue pleaded to be allowed back. She sailed in 1943 to Portugal and flew from there to Britain in a Sunderland flying boat. Her first destination was Lowther College, a girls' boarding school in a Welsh castle, but after a few terms she again prevailed on Midge to bring her back to London. From then on she lived at home with her mother, who juggled SOE duties with looking after her daughter. One Austrian agent recalled arriving at a secret location in London to find the door opened by a young girl, who politely welcomed them in German and asked them to wait in the living room for 'Frau Holmes'.[45]

To fulfil the objectives of undermining the Third Reich and restoring Austria as a national unit, X Section had three tools at its disposal: politics, propaganda and military action. At least this is how they saw it in early 1941. From the outset, they had recognised that the political liberators of Austria were not to be found in England among the émigrés. Within Austria, any active opponents of the regime were already in concentration camps. Political progress might be made by contacting potential resisters among the population. But the disastrous failure of Theodor Schuhbauer's mission (see 'A timber merchant' above) to do just that, as well as the lack of progress in unifying the Austrian diaspora, had weakened X Section's confidence in influencing politics within Austria. Their faith in the political weapon had been dented. Influencing British policy was more feasible. They would continue to chip away at the Foreign Office's reluctance to come out clearly in favour of Austrian independence.[46]

SOE was sceptical about early military action. Evelyn Stamper believed that sporadic sabotage would lead to reprisals and 'give the

Gestapo an excuse for rigid controls', making future action more difficult. What was needed, she thought, was 'to lull the *Gestapo* into a false sense of security'.[47] Irregular military operations would be most effective in support of an eventual major campaign. Most would be saved until then.

What remained was propaganda.

Seditious messages

Laurence Grand's Section D at MI6 had included propaganda in its repertoire. Betty Hodgson at the Joint Broadcasting Committee was working mostly on 'white propaganda', coming openly from Britain. In SOE's new X/Aus Section, though, Evelyn Stamper and Clara Holmes focused on the 'black' kind: source concealed.[48]

Black propaganda could take many forms, but its overall aim was to undermine enemy morale and will to fight. SOE and the Political Warfare Executive worked together to pass subtly subversive messages: through leaflets dropped—reluctantly, it must be admitted—by the Royal Air Force; through radio broadcasts; and through printed material sent through the post or rumours passed by word of mouth.[49] In all cases, they hoped to undermine military discipline and reduce popular support for the war.

For the military, PWE and SOE tried to develop discord between soldiers and the Nazi Party. The material encouraged requests for leave, incited 'malingering' through feigned sickness and even suggested desertion. Expert forgers prepared subtly worded military instructions and proclamations that would destroy soldiers' trust in the leadership and stickers with the increasingly popular slogan '*Schluss*', a concise way of saying 'let's put an end to this war'. They printed clandestine newspapers such as *Nachrichten für die Truppe* for soldiers that looked authentic but brought accurate reports of Axis defeats, resistance successes and the impact of the war on relatives back home. SOE agents distributed detailed instructions, hidden inside packets of cigarette papers or lottery tickets, on how to simulate illness or injury. Concealed messages reassured potential deserters of the way they would be treated in neutral Switzerland or showed them how to avoid being sent back by Spanish authorities. Ronald Thornley was quick to share any evidence of impact on the Nazi regime of the black propaganda: what he called 'come-backs'. It was 'eloquent testimony ... right from the horse's mouth' of the high quality of the material and the successful efforts of SOE agents in getting it to its target audiences'.[50]

Propaganda aimed at the general population had the broader goals of increasing confusion and reducing trust in the claims of the Nazi leadership: themselves coordinated by the master of propaganda, Joseph Goebbels. Distribution was the hardest problem. Paris was now an occupied city, so Clara's earlier route was closed. Dropping leaflets from an aircraft was a scatter-gun solution and very obvious to the Nazi authorities. SOE couriers and agents were potentially much more effective. They could surreptitiously place official-looking posters, leave subversive leaflets or apply seditious stickers in public places like cafés, bus shelters or railway stations. Agents in Switzerland or Sweden could hide material in packing cases being shipped by rail to Austria or Germany. SOE distributed millions of leaflets, booklets and posters.

Feedback on whether these blows hit home was scarce. But the arrival of actual deserters, questioning of captured soldiers and evidence from neutral countries provided some proof. Some projects involved infiltrating forged postage stamps into the German postal system. The 6-pfennig 'Himmler stamp' of 1943 showed Heinrich Himmler's head instead of Hitler's, encouraging speculation that the ruthless SS leader was planning a coup. Some of the stamps leaked out and philatelists around the world were excited by the appearance of these rarities.

For Austria, Evelyn and Clara had the added purpose of building anti-German feeling, while also weakening Axis capability more directly. One widely circulated leaflet on red-white-red paper encouraged Austrians to prevent Germany from stealing Austrian oil. Also popular was a red-white-red sticker saying *'Kehrt um die Flinten: der Feind steht hinten'* ('Turn your guns around: the enemy is behind you').

Playing the long game

Propaganda was a key tool, but the Austrian Section also planned more direct action to build Austrian opposition to the German war machine. For that they needed to recruit agents. But where from?

Thousands of Austrians were in Britain, some free, but many interned as enemy aliens on the Isle of Man. Others had been shipped to internment camps in Australia, Canada or Mauritius. Some had found their way to the USA or South America. The British Army had only allowed young men wanting to fight the Nazis to join the Pioneer Corps, its non-combatant labour force. But among those who had fled Nazi persecution were men like Leo Hillman who hankered after a more active role. A large proportion of them were Jews.

To expand the number of possible recruits from those identified by the Austrian émigré community, X Section needed to spread the net. Recruiters quietly travelled to internment camps to find likely candidates. Britain's undercover representatives in the Americas, based in New York under Canadian millionaire Sir William Stephenson and calling themselves 'British Security Coordination', worked with Austrian exiles there to find volunteers.[51] Another early idea was to intercept German and Austrian prisoners-of-war who might be recruited as agents, while they were being processed but before being registered as PoWs. They would later be known as Bonzos.[52] But the most promising source was probably the Pioneer Corps, in which many Austrian men were serving.

Poster for Auxiliary Military Pioneer Corps

Very early in X Section's existence, Clara Holmes helped the Austria Office set up a social club at Eaton Place where Austrian members of the Pioneer Corps could meet. It opened on 22nd February 1941, providing an additional way of finding prospective recruits and a good way of informally assessing potential agents.[53] More formal assessment followed for any promising prospects. Unlike SOE country sections like the French Section, where women served as wireless operators, as couriers and sometimes as resistance network leaders, the Austrian agents were all men.

SOE 'trawled' the Pioneer Corps more directly. A representative of X Section called Hartmann toured the Pioneer units seeking likely individuals. Although older and more 'distinguished' than the other Pioneers, he would mingle with the men, working alongside them as they chopped wood in the Welsh forests. When he found likely candidates, he would sidle up to them and drop a hint.[54] 'Some of the boys in 87 Company have gone off to join the Commandos', Eric Sanders remembered Hartmann whispering. 'That sounds interesting', said Eric, a young Viennese Jew whose original name had been Ignaz Erich Schwarz, 'Tell me more!'. 'That's all I can say', replied Hartmann, and he disappeared.

A few weeks later he reappeared and told Eric about a unit that would operate behind enemy lines ahead of the Allied invasion. Eventually, Eric was summoned to London and asked if he would volunteer for an undefined special duty. This was his introduction to SOE.[55]

Training an agent

One of those earlier 'boys' had been Friedrich Franz Reitlinger.[56] 'Freddy' Reitlinger was the son of a prominent industrialist in the Tyrol, also named Friedrich, who was a well-connected local dignitary and a Jewish convert to Catholicism. He had been the 'principal financier of the Tyrolean *Heimwehr*', an Austrian nationalist paramilitary group. Together with Freddy's sister Johanna, he allegedly committed suicide in March 1938 while under Nazi arrest.[57]

Friedrich Reitlinger

Not surprisingly, Freddy was a vehement anti-Nazi. In Vienna, he had been pursuing doctoral studies in law and had completed officer training at the Austrian Military Academy. When the *Anschluss* came, his Jewish origins meant that he had to resign his commission. He dropped out of sight, hiding in a convent hospital for several months. Somehow, he found his way to Britain and in January 1940 joined Auxiliary Military Pioneer Corps. By the time the SOE recruiter came round in mid-1941, Friedrich was established in No 87 Company of the Pioneer Corps in Llandysul, Wales.

His ability and former officer status soon gained him the rank of corporal, and the recruiter thought he was a 'splendid fellow'. MI5 had interviewed him on his arrival in Britain and responded to SOE's request for security vetting, putting him 'through the cards': 'Nothing Recorded Against'. Unlike the unfortunate Theo Schuhbauer, Friedrich entered a comprehensive and well-organised training process, rapidly built up in SOE's first months.

By late 1941, SOE had developed a structured system for turning volunteers into trained agents. Although 'X/Aus' Section recruited Austrians, its potential agents trained alongside Germans. It was not feasible or necessary to separate the two. After interviews and security clearance, Friedrich Reitlinger reported on 10th November 1941, with a dozen others, to Special Training School No 1. STS 1 was at Brock Hall in Northamptonshire, one of many country houses requisitioned by SOE.

The students built up their physical fitness and learned weapon handling, demolition, navigation and living off the land. But a hidden purpose was to sift through the group and ensure that only those likely to succeed as agents went on to the next phase of training. Each group was observed by the German-speaking conducting officer and field security NCO—Lieutenant Keir and Corporal Sinclair—who would accompany them through each stage of their training. Allan Keir's business travel in Europe before the war had given him a sound understanding of German and Austrian culture.[58] Those students who were thought unsuitable, unreliable or insecure were sent back to their units with little idea of what they had been training for.

Friedrich Reitlinger was a popular member of the group, keen and earnest. He offered to give up his corporal's pay so as to be equal to his comrades, conscious that his background seemed to put him a cut above the others. That social difference led to teasing from the rest of the party, who dubbed him 'Agnes', but he fought back with suitable retorts. His lack of physical strength proved a disadvantage, but he was determined to progress, had 'lots of guts' and would tackle anything. Progressively, he improved physically and gained a more aggressive outlook. Although not quick on the uptake and still needing to gain self-confidence, he was among about half of his party who progressed to the next stage.

The group travelled in December 1941 by rail to Glasgow and then onward in a closed train compartment to Inverness-shire in Scotland. Here, at one of the 'Group A' schools, at houses in the area and commanded from Arisaig House, the serious paramilitary training commenced. Well-fed despite wartime rationing, they built up their strength, confidence and ability to fight. They learned to navigate undetected in darkness, to sabotage railways, to set an ambush, to fight without weapons and to handle a range of British and enemy firearms. The role for which they were training soon became clear to them.

Under the increased pressure of the training in Scotland and as the instructors got to know him better, Friedrich's progress became more uncertain. He was committed and trustworthy, but did not take instruction easily and lacked the confidence that would help him survive tough situations. The trainers still thought him 'eminently suitable for special work' but his training would take longer than others. On the other hand, he picked up Morse code quickly. A student who did not reach the standard, or who decided that serving undercover in enemy territory was not for them, would be sent to the 'Cooler' at Inverlair Lodge in the depths of Scotland.[59] They would stay there for several months, returning to their original units only when the knowledge they had gained could not harm ongoing operations. Friedrich Reitlinger, though, had enough potential to be allowed to continue.

The next phase of training was in the parachuting school at Royal Air Force Ringway, today better known as Manchester Airport. Friedrich did his five jumps, at first from a static balloon and then dropping from a hole in the bottom of an aircraft. By the turn of the year, the party had moved on to STS 44 at Gumley Hall, a 'holding school'.[60] The name suggests a boring wait, but this is misleading. Potential agents were certainly waiting while the operational sections worked out the details of their employment, but they received tailored training focused on their projected missions. Friedrich Reitlinger, though, learned that he would not be included with the rest of his party as they moved on. He was dismayed. But Corporal Sinclair had reported that the highly motivated Friedrich did not have the attention to detail he would need. He would undertake a major task but forget a small but crucial point. Also, he was becoming nervous and temperamental. He would fly into a rage when frustrated and just as quickly calm down again. The grief of losing his father and sister was still present. In a party led by Allan Keir, Friedrich set off by ship in March 1942 for the Middle East, the best area from which to get into the Balkans and Austria. As he travelled, X Section was still working out what to do with this valuable but perplexing asset.

[1] The BBC immersive history television series *Secret Agent Selection: WW2* (2018, aka *Churchill's Secret Agents: The New Recruits*) gives an authentic if simplified view of what was expected of SOE agents. Fourteen modern-day volunteers undertake 'SOE selection'; not all reach the finish line.

[2] The Schuhbauer story in this section is based on his personal file (where his name is given as Schubauer), TNA HS 9/1329/6.

[3] TNA HS 6/2.

[4] TNA HS 6/692, 5th December 1940.

[5] TNA HS 9/1209/1.

[6] The other two were David Crichton and John Gabriel. The Oxford-educated Second Lieutenant Crichton had been recruited by MI(R) and progressed into SOE. His interest was Albania and he claimed to be a friend of ex-King Zog. He was on his way to join the British legation at Belgrade. John Gabriel had lived at The Old Vicarage in the village of Grantchester, near Cambridge, made famous by the poet Rupert Brooke. A national-level athlete and a skilled photographer, he became an Intelligence Corps officer soon after the outbreak of war. He joined SOE, which planned to use his knowledge of Yugoslavia and Hungary. In February 1941, he embarked in the same ship as Schuhbauer and Preiss, posted to Cairo with responsibility for the Balkans. Neither Crichton nor Gabriel arrived. Eight months later, Gabriel's widow Clothilde gave birth to a son. In 1944, she joined SOE's German Directorate as a secretary.

[7] Equivalent to about £40 in 2023.

[8] Brendan Keelan, *Eric Redmond and the Secret History of the SS Jonathan Holt*, unpublished article.

[9] The nephews had fled in 1940 from Belgium to unoccupied France during the German advance. Later, presumably when the Germans occupied the whole of France in November 1942, they fled to Spain, leaving their documents behind.

[10] Equivalent to about £20,000 in 2023.

[11] TNA HS 9/1329/6, 5th June 1944.

[12] Neville Wylie, 'SOE and the Neutrals,' in *Special Operations Executive: a new instrument of war*, ed. Mark Seaman (London: Routledge, 2006), p.157.

[13] Further detail on anti-Nazi movements in Germany and Austrian is in Paddy Ashdown, *Nein!: standing up to Hitler 1935-1944* (London: William Collins, 2018) and Hans Mommsen, *Germans against Hitler: the Stauffenberg plot and resistance under the Third Reich*, trans., Angus McGeoch (London: I B Tauris, 2009).

[14] An account of British attitudes to anti-Nazi Germans is in Richard Lamb, 1987.

[15] Wolfgang Neugebauer, *Austrian Resistance*, 2014, pp.23, 53.

[16] An account of the Austrian Resistance is in *ibid* and comprehensive archives on the subject are held by the Documentation Centre of Austrian Resistance (*Dokumentationsarchiv des österreichischen Widerstandes*, https://www.doew.at).

[17] Peter Pirker, *Subversion deutscher Herrschaft*, 2012, p.69.

[18] TNA 6/3, Opinion and Morale in Austria, 25th January 1943.

[19] TNA HS 6/3, 21st January 1941.

[20] Robert H Keyserlingk, *Austria in World War II: an Anglo-American dilemma* (Kingston: McGill-Queen's University Press, 1988), pp.98-101, 115-117.

[21] TNA HS 6/3, 7th February 1941.

[22] Robert H Keyserlingk, 1988, pp.123-135.

[23] Speech on the occasion of the presentation of a trailer canteen by Austrians to the Women's Volunteer Service, 18th February 1942, quoted in TNA HS 6/3, 21st September 1942.

[24] Speech at the Mansion House, 9th November 1940, quoted by Anthony Eden (Hansard, 9th September 1942).

[25] TNA HS 6/3, 21st January 1941.

[26] Stamper was designated X/Aus or X/A, Holmes as X/A.1. They were later joined as X/A.4 by Captain David Dobell and even later Captain James Joll (HS 9/806/2, Personal File, James Bysse Joll; Obituary, The Times, 15th July 1994). Alan Ogden has kindly provided information on Dobell, a former actor who, after being injured in a parachute accident in India, joined the German Directorate in November 1944. He was killed in action in February 1945 (HS 9/436/8).

[27] TNA HS 9/1465/8 and HS 9/1643. See also Malcolm Atkin, 2017, Appendix 2.

[28] Peter Wilkinson and Joan Bright Astley, 1993; Malcolm Atkin, *Fighting Nazi Occupation: British resistance 1939-1945* (2015).

[29] TNA HS 9/1643.

[30] See Peter Dixon, *Guardians*, 2018

[31] Here and following paragraph: TNA HS 7/145.

[32] TNA HS 6/4, 4th February 1943.

[33] TNA HS 6/3, 26th March 1942.

[34] TNA HS 6/2, 7th February 1942 and HS 6/3, 25th February 1942. See also William S Stephenson, *British Security Coordination: the secret history of British intelligence in the Americas, 1940-1945*, (New York: Fromm International, 1999), pp.407-410. The groups included the Monarchist (or 'legitimist') 'Austrian League', the pan-German Revolutionary Socialists (Otto Bauer, Oskar Pollak, Club of the Austrian Socialists on England, later the London Bureau of Austrian Socialists), the social democrat groups ('Association of Austrian Social Democrats in Great Britain' (Heinrich Allina), 'Austrian Democratic Union' (Julius Meinl III)), the 'Association of Austrian Christian Socialists in Great Britain' and the Communist-dominated 'Austrian Centre' (under whose umbrella were the 'Council of Austrians in Great Britain',

'Young Austria' and *'Kommendes Oesterreich'*). Smaller groups, with various purposes, included the cultural 'Austrian Circle for Arts and Sciences' under Baron Guido Fuchs, the 'Austrian Women Voluntary Workers' and the Jewish organisations *'Beth Am'* and the 'Jakob Ehrlich Society'. The most comprehensive account of these groups is probably Helene Maimann, *Politik im Wartesaal: österreichische Exilpolitik in Grossbrittanien 1938-1945* (Vienna: Hermann Boehlhaus Nachfolger, 1975), but Dr Peter Pirker has had access to more recent sources in Peter Pirker, *Subversion deutscher Herrschaft*, 2012.

[35] TNA HS 6/2, 7th February 1942, and KV 2/2517-2523. As Helene Maimann pointed out, 'whatever the political implications of the Austrian Centre's activities, its work with refugees did a great deal to improve the difficult lives of Jewish migrants, especially in the early years' (Helene Maimann, 1975, p.232, author's loose translation).

[36] TNA HS 6/2, 11th March 1942.

[37] TNA HS 7/148.

[38] As described by X Section in February 1942 as the overseas contacts of the Free Austria Movement, these were the 'Austrian Labor Committee' (social democrats, under Fritz Adler), 'Austrian Action' (liberal, under Count Ferdinand Czernin), the 'Assembly for a Democratic Austrian Republic' (socialist and liberal, under Fritz Rager), the 'Free Austrian Youth Committee' (cooperating with the previous two) and the 'Free Austrian Movement (Monarchist, under Hans Rott). An attempt to form an Austrian National Committee stalled, being seen as Monarchist-dominated. TNA HS 6/2 and HS 6/692, 12th April 1942.

[39] TNA HS 7/145, 1st October 1945. New York Times, 2nd and 10th April 1941. Dr Peter Pirker gives more detail on Sebba, who went on to an illustrious academic career in the USA, in Peter Pirker, *Subversion deutscher Herrschaft*, 2012, pp.58-63.

[40] TNA HS 6/3, 21st February 1942.

[41] Specifically Argentina, Chile, Mexico, Venezuela, Costa Rica, Colombia, Brazil and South Africa. TNA HS 6/2.

[42] Peter Pirker, *Subversion deutscher Herrschaft*, 2012, pp.89, 124-134.

[43] TNA HS 6/4, 10th November 1942.

[44] HS 6/4, 13th November 1942.

[45] IWM Oral History 29954, Eric Sanders, Reel 2. The address was 1 De Vere Cottages, Canning Street, London W8 (TNA HS 6/19, letter 3rd January 1945).

[46] In a paper for the Chiefs of Staff, Thornley bemoaned 'the complete lack of a clear statement of policy towards Austria from [His Majesty's Government], for which we had pressed in vain'. Reference XF/22 of 11th October 1943, cited in TNA HS 7/145.

[47] TNA HS 6/3, 21st January 1941.

[48] The pre-war situation had been 'out of hand'. The roles of Laurence Grand's Section D, the Ministry of Information, Electra House, the War Office, the Admiralty and the BBC all overlapped. Under the July 1940 reorganisation,

Section D and MI(R) became part of SOE as 'SO2', while Electra House became 'SO1'. In the summer of 1941, SO1 was detached from SOE to become the Political Warfare Executive (PWE). PWE operated under cover of the Political Intelligence Department of the Foreign Office. Details are in *The Major Developments in Political Warfare Throughout the War 1938—1945*, by Y M Streatfield (TNA CAB 101/131), courtesy of Lee Richards. See also David Garnett, 2002.

[49] Here and throughout this section: TNA HS 7/145, *SOE History: 'Black' Propaganda Activities*.

[50] TNA HS 7/145, X (Thornley) to AD/E (Mockler-Ferryman), 1st July 1944.

[51] W J M Mackenzie, 2000, p.328, M R D Foot, *SOE 1940-1946*, 2014, p.45.

[52] TNA HS 6/692, 27th February 1941.

[53] TNA HS 6/692, 19th December 1940.

[54] TNA HS 6/692, Progress Report 23rd July 1941. Research by Dr Peter Pirker suggests that this was probably Major Albert Hartmann, a former instructor at the Austrian Military Academy (Peter Pirker, *Subversion deutscher Herrschaft*, 2012, p.95).

[55] Eric Sanders Oral History.

[56] Friedrich Reitlinger, "Als Tiroler in der britischen Armee," in *Österreich und die Sieger*, ed. Anton Pelinka and Rolf Steininger (Vienna: Wilhelm Braumueller, 1986).

[57] Daily Telegraph, 17th March 1938. Wolfgang Meixner, .Engineer Friedrich Reitlinger (1877-1938). Industrialist and economic functionary in the Tyrol between *Heimwehr* and National Socialism', *Zeitgeschichte* 29, no. 4 (2002).

[58] TNA HS 9/825/9, Personal File Keir A.

[59] Peter Dixon, *Guardians*, 2018, p.92.

[60] The holding schools were renumbered some time in 1942 and Gorse Hill near Godalming in Surrey became STS 44, but at the time this party was there the location would have been Gumley Hall (TNA HS 8/435 p50).

CHAPTER 6

Working from Outside

Into Tyrol?

RONALD THORNLEY AND EVELYN STAMPER considered various options for Friedrich Reitlinger's employment. Messages bounced to and from Allan Keir in Cairo about what to do with '*AH288*', or '*Freddy*'. After arriving in Egypt, Friedrich had been sent to the Signals School in Palestine to learn the skills of a wireless operator, a W/Op.[1] He had been in the Middle East for five months when Thornley thought of infiltrating him from Switzerland. 'We have available and trained as wireless operator', he wrote in September 1942 to Betty Hodgson, 'a young man of good family, fanatically Austrian, Catholic and anti-Nazi'.

Betty was no longer in London pushing out propaganda with the Joint Broadcasting Committee, but established in Switzerland as the X Section representative. She was to ask her contacts in Austria to investigate preparing a safe house for Friedrich Reitlinger in a monastery. Friedrich was willing to 'become a monk' for the purpose.[2] This plan came to nothing and 'Freddy' remained in Egypt for a further eighteen months, but at the time insertion from one of Nazi Europe's neutral neighbours was almost the only possibility for X Section.

No alternative

The difficulty of SOE operations into Austria was obvious to Evelyn Stamper and Clara 'Midge' Holmes from the start. It had been no different when they had been in Laurence Grand's Section D at MI6. Since then, though, it had got worse. The Nazis had brutally crushed any open challenge to their rule. Political opponents were hauled off to concentration camps or apparently committed suicide. Many Austrians wholeheartedly supported Hitler's war, encouraged by Nazi propaganda to hate the Jews and fear the Russians.

The goals of those who had the courage to go underground and resist Nazi domination were many and varied, and not necessarily aimed at Austrian independence. The strongest military challenge to the *Wehrmacht* was in the Carinthian region in Austria's southeast, where Slovenian separatists were fighting for a free Slovenia.[3] Regional aspirations also inspired a less powerful movement in the Tyrol, the western region straddling Austria and Italy, particularly through the *Patria* group under Wilhelm Bruckner.[4]

Resistance that was not connected to territorial claims had broader political goals. But the *Gestapo* still had its finger on the resistance pulse. Thousands of Austrian Communists had been rounded up in 1938-9 and either executed or incarcerated in concentration camps. Others continued to print propaganda and plot insurrection, but the *Gestapo* had infiltrated most groups. Soviet agents, given limited training in Russia and parachuted into Austria to contact local Communists, were arrested.[5] At the other extreme, apart from the Nazis themselves, right-wing activists were aligned with the so-called 'legitimist' movement, whose goal was to restore the Austro-Hungarian monarchy. Between the two were the social democrat groups. SOE saw the latter as its most likely partners. After all, they, like the Communists, had opposed the Dollfuss regime in the early 1930s.[6] But, crushed by Dollfuss and then by the Nazis, they had limited presence inside the country. Most socialists were in exile or in concentration camps.

The powerful Roman Catholic church in Austria at first adjusted passively to the new situation after the 1938 *Anschluss*, but tension between the Church and the Nazi regime quickly escalated. In October 1938, Archbishop Theodor Innitzer spoke before a crowd of ten thousand at a youth meeting in St Stephen's Cathedral, Vienna. *'Unser Führer ist Christus. Christus ist unser Führer'* he said.[7] Courageous Catholic priests and lay people performed individual acts of self-sacrifice, some laying down their lives on behalf of victims belonging to all faiths and backgrounds.[8]

The bonds uniting other resistance groups were less party-political or religious. Their modest growth arose late in the war, when the tide had turned and Austria's cleaving to Nazi Germany held little attraction. Again, though, resisting the police state was far from easy. The members of a small 'Free Austria' group, which had distributed leaflets advocating Austrian independence, were arrested in late 1944. The larger all-party 'O5' organisation crossed political and social boundaries, from workers to aristocrats, and claimed adherents across the country. SOE was more sceptical of the group's claims than was its American ally, the OSS.[9]

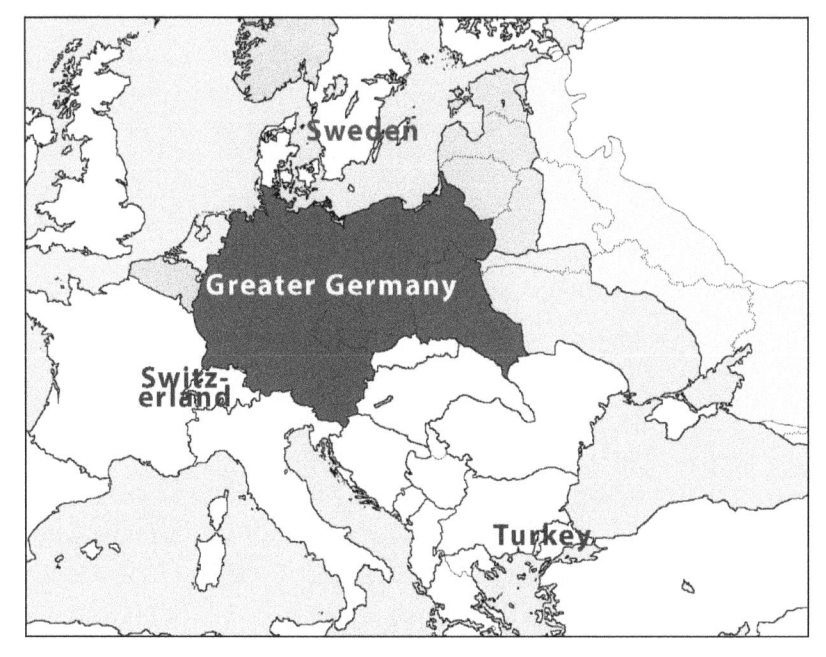

Greater Germany 1942

Despite the many examples of courage and determination, there was no significant resistance organisation in Austria to which SOE could send agents as organisers. M R D Foot suggests that subversion comprises four elements: sabotage, attacks, propaganda and insurrection.[10] But timing is critical. A repressive regime will brutally suppress insurrection unless some outside force is ready to back it. Even focused attacks on leaders, military units or security forces at the wrong time can lead to reprisals that turn the population against the resistance cause. Evelyn and Clara had few options. Until the 'eleventh hour' before the Allied invasion that must someday come, only two tactics existed: propaganda to raise a spirit of Austrian independence and sabotage to damage the Axis war machine. The obvious places from which to launch either of these were the neutral countries bordering Nazi-occupied Europe: Sweden, Switzerland and Turkey.

The Stockholm link

Looking at the geography, one might imagine that SOE in Sweden had nothing to do with Austria, and that is a fair assumption. But Austrian émigrés in Britain, the USA and elsewhere formed a network, in touch with friends and socialist comrades in Austria. The network extended to Sweden, where the revolutionary socialist Oscar Pollak had two prominent socialist contacts; Franz Novy and Bruno Kreisky were in regular contact with British representatives.[11] Their reports from contacts in Vienna claimed that the socialist underground movement was growing and anti-German feeling increasing.[12]

The first SOE organiser in Sweden with responsibility for Germany and Austria was Major Henry Threlfall, who arrived in Stockholm in January 1942. His stay was brief, though, as the Swedes accused him of planning railway sabotage. The Swedish security service, 'largely German-trained and working according to German methods with an enthusiasm, but fortunately not an efficiency, which the *Gestapo* have hardly surpassed', expelled him in August of the same year.[13] His eventual replacement in August 1943, Lieutenant-Colonel Euan Butler, received and forwarded reports from Novy and Kreisky about conditions in Austria, but SOE in Stockholm naturally focused on propaganda and subversion in northern Europe and Scandinavia.[14]

Nevertheless, Kreisky's continued presence in Sweden impacted Austria's war even after the European war was over. Sixty men of a *Wehrmacht* artillery battery in Norway, most of them Austrians, defied their Nazi commander's order to fight on after Germany had surrendered. Kreisky helped some of the men, who had escaped into Sweden, to avoid extradition. Four who had not made it into neutral territory were tried in a German military court and executed.[15] Bruno Kreisky served for seven years as Austria's Foreign Minister and became Chancellor in 1970 for a record term of thirteen years.

Escape from Switzerland

Betty Hodgson's time in Switzerland as the SOE representative came to an abrupt end in late 1943 when she had to flee the country. It was an unexpected adventure. Suddenly, she was a fugitive from the Swiss police. The sensitivity of prosecuting the secret war in a genuinely neutral country applied just as much in Switzerland as in Sweden. But Betty was extremely fit, an expert skier and a well-trained SOE operative.[16]

Betty had been based in Zurich for over two years when the efficient Swiss security services caught up with her and her network of anti-Nazi saboteurs. Fortunately, she was visiting the Swiss capital, Bern, when the news came that her main contacts in the *Lex* group, German socialist Karl Gerold and Swiss schoolteacher Elsa Hersberger, had been arrested with a dozen of their collaborators. Betty quickly went to ground in a safe apartment in Bern and awaited developments. She had always realised the danger to her operations from the Swiss, at that stage of the war enthusiastically protecting their neutrality. She took careful precautions. She would often meet Gerold or Hersberger at night in the woods outside Zurich. Sometimes she would set off on a skiing expedition and meet Gerold in a remote area of the Swiss mountains, both arriving separately on skis. Gerold was a romantic; he was stubborn, not easily directed, and thought himself something of a poet. Betty had to listen to his long compositions as they sat together on the rocks, before she could move on to discussing sabotage.

The arrests in the autumn of 1943 were a shock. The police at working level may well have been aware of the group's activities but took action when the scale became greater than the Swiss Government could tolerate. Karl Gerold and Elsa Herberger gave away little under interrogation, but Karl appears to have talked about his activities to his mistress, Elsa Lang, 'whom he had promised to marry, a promise which he had been reluctant to implement'.[17] His indiscretion and her disappointment may be how the police learned enough to close down the network, discover a radio set, and cause Betty to flee.

When Elsa Herberger was released after interrogation, she lost no time in sending a warning message to Betty in Bern. The Swiss issued a warrant for Betty's arrest. She agreed with Ronald Thornley in London that her position in Switzerland was untenable. Betty quietly crossed the border into German-occupied France, an escape that was usually made in the opposite direction. With help from SOE escape lines, she made her way across southern France, crossed the Pyrenees on foot and stayed only a short time in Spanish internment before being repatriated to Britain. But the *Lex* group folded; she had called it 'the family' and nurtured it for two years. A Swiss court sentenced her *in absentia* to a prison term, putting a definitive end to her involvement in X Section's Swiss operations. Her training for it had been extensive.

Betty Hodgson had grown up in Germany, and spoke German and Italian. To prepare for her Swiss assignment, she had completed a tailored course at the SOE 'finishing school' at Beaulieu in August 1941.[18] The Foreign Office had agreed to diplomatic cover for her and she spent time with members of the *Lex* group in London, plotting their new Swiss operations. Back in 1940, when the fall of France made Clara Holmes' deliveries of propaganda to Paris impossible, Karl Groehl had joined his *Lex* colleague Karl Otten in the UK.[19] 'Paris Karl' made several clandestine journeys to deliver material to Karl Gerold in Switzerland. The three Karls formed the core of the *Lex* group, which had worked with Laurence Grand's Section D of MI6 and was now working with SOE. Betty Hodgson became their controller in Switzerland.

In early September 1941, Betty travelled by air via Lisbon to Zurich. She contacted *Lex* agent Karl Gerold within a few weeks and soon reported that getting into Austria from Switzerland was extremely difficult, even for *bona fide* travellers. They would have to rely on skiers crossing the frontier illegally.[20]

Betty and Karl Gerold progressively built up the volume of black propaganda material and sabotage supplies smuggled into Switzerland through southern France and onward into the *Reich*. The route through southern France, at first the collaborationist 'Unoccupied Zone' and from November 1942 occupied by the Germans, was far from easy. But gaining access to Germany and Austria held a different scale of difficulty.

Sympathetic Swiss railway workers, led by Swiss railwaymen '*Albert*' and '*Buddy*' in Basel and elsewhere, carried out 'delayed-action' sabotage in Switzerland itself. Deep in Austria or Germany, a train would inexplicably break down: air brake hoses leaking, valves gummed up with a mysterious substance, axle-boxes empty of lubricant. Although Nazi railway officials suspected sabotage, Betty's cautious security measures kept the arrests in Zurich from damaging this undercover work. *Albert* and *Buddy* remained successful in concealing the origin of the mischief until the end of the war.[21]

More direct contact for sabotage or propaganda needed couriers. Courageous men and women took the material and instructions forward into the *Reich*. Some were arrested, as were their contacts in Austria.[22] As in other SOE areas, Betty Hodgson wished to establish radio contact between Austria and London. A wireless set, code name *Aquavit*, was prepared and tested in Switzerland, but the Zurich arrests occurred before it could be put into operational use.[23]

Sketchy reports had been trickling back of sabotage attacks on railways. As Clara Holmes recognised, it was difficult to confirm the reports and almost impossible to ascribe them to the Swiss connection rather than some other group. *Gestapo* posters offered rewards for information about railway saboteurs, but in general the Nazi authorities preferred to hush up such 'accidents'. That said, Clara identified several cases that she believed should be attributed to *Lex*: an explosion in a munitions train near Steyr in Upper Austria in August 1942; damage to a Vienna locomotive works in December 1942; sabotage in the Innsbruck-Brenner area in September 1943.[24]

For her Swiss work and her courageous escape, Betty Hodgson was secretly awarded the MBE.

The Zurich Connection

In the early part of the war, successes in gaining access to Austria from Switzerland were few. Sabotage by the *Lex* group and its partners was primarily focused on Germany—the *Altreich*—and collapsed after Betty Hodgson's flight. Propaganda was certainly delivered into Austria, including copies of *Der Freie Österreicher*, 'The Free Austrian', written by Dr Hans Hollitscher, code name 'No 8'. Hollitscher was a seventy-year-old Catholic with many connections in Vienna with 'leading Austrian statesmen' from the Hapsburg and Dollfuss eras, indefatigably active and with a passion for intrigue. He claimed to have been a member of the Austrian secret police. He frequently 'slipped across the border into Liechtenstein, to confer with members of the Austrian aristocracy'. At retreats in a monastery in Fribourg, he would meet prominent Austrian Catholics.[25] Betty Hodgson had started working with Hollitscher in early 1942, but when she fled she handed him over to Robert Jellinek, known as 'Peter', whose view was more jaundiced. Most of Hollitscher's contacts, he thought, were 'paralysed if not by imprisonment then by age'.[26]

'Peter' Jellinek was British, but from a Viennese family. Before the war, he had been an executive of the Bally shoe company in the USA and Switzerland, where SOE's representative, John McCaffery, had taken Peter on as his assistant in December 1941. For Jellinek, the autumn of 1943 brought a perfect storm. The *Lex* arrests in Zurich came when SOE's Bern post was reeling from an Italian shock. Along with the good news—Italy had changed sides and joined the Allies— came a revelation: The Italian counter-espionage service had been 'playing' SOE Bern with radio messages from imaginary Italian resistance movements and fictitious sabotage attacks for over two years.[27] As they came to terms with this disaster, McCaffery was in a Lugano clinic recovering from 'nervous exhaustion and cerebral commotion'.[28]

Rebuilding a capability to operate into Austria from Switzerland would take new impetus, a clear shift in the direction of the war and a change of attitude from the Swiss security services. That would be part of SOE's final push and would come much later. Meanwhile, the former journalist Eric Gedye was pressing home an SOE campaign from Turkey and the Middle East.

Intrigue in Istanbul

Eric Gedye was totally committed to Austria during his time there, which ended abruptly in 1938. Then a convinced socialist, he was sympathetic to the Austrian left-wing perspective. Forced to leave Vienna soon after German troops marched in, he fought in his own way for the rebirth of the country he loved. In his 1939 book *Fallen Bastions: the Central European tragedy*, he had written a scathing rebuke to Neville Chamberlain's British Government for its betrayal of Austria.

Evelyn Stamper and 'Midge' Holmes knew Gedye well from their time together in Vienna. When they invited him to join SOE's Austrian Section and move to Istanbul as its organiser for the Middle East, Eric 'took up his new task with enthusiasm and unflagging energy'.[29] But getting him established in Turkey proved difficult. Eric's predecessor, Harriman, had been respected in Istanbul as a genuinely successful businessman. He had industriously prepared his organisation and had several couriers carrying microfilmed messages into the *Reich*. Eric, though, had already been in trouble with the Turkish authorities. The British Ambassador was reluctant to give him cover. As in many cases, SOE's aggressive approach was at odds with the Foreign Office's caution about launching subversive activity from a neutral country. Even more sensitive were SOE's potential operations within Turkey. Getting Turkey to join the Allies and preventing a German invasion of the country were key objectives for Winston Churchill. And the Turks did not want to provoke the Germans.[30]

It was indeed Eric Gedye's activities in Turkey itself, rather than using it as a base for operations into the *Reich,* that enraged the Ambassador, Sir Hughe Knatchbull-Hagessen.[31] Eric had established good relations with the Austrian community in Istanbul. Many of them were scientists and intellectuals who had been invited by Kemal Atatürk as part of his reform of Turkish higher education and research, others opposition politicians. Especially for the Jews among them, life in Austria had become increasingly uncomfortable. In the early stages of the war, they had presented a petition to the British Embassy in Ankara, asking to be treated separately from the German émigrés. Prominent among these 'Free Austrians' was Erich Weinzinger, who nominated others to work with Gedye, including Oskar Behron, Josef Dobretsberger and Herbert Feuerlöscher.[32] Gedye moved many of the group to safety in Palestine in mid-1941 when a German invasion of Turkey seemed likely.[33] While they were there, political infighting led to the group's collapse. Dobretsberger denounced Weinzinger to the British authorities in Mandate Palestine and succeeded in having him interned.[34] Eric Gedye could do nothing about it; he was still in Istanbul, carrying on with black propaganda.

Eric's task, under the direction of the then SOE representative, Colonel W S Bailey, was to counter the effective Nazi propaganda in Turkey with messages of his own. The Ambassador was unimpressed. 'I can imagine nothing more fatal to our interests', he wrote to the Foreign Office.[35] One can imagine Eric's frustration. As one SOE staff officer wrote about trying to get operations in Turkey off the ground, 'At present we are wasting money and much hard work begetting and nourishing schemes which are doomed to be stillborn'.[36]

The last straw for Ambassador Hagessen was an audacious leafleting stunt In February 1942. Clouds of anti-Nazi leaflets fluttered down from the rooftop of one of the tall buildings lining the bustling *Grande rue de Pera*, today the *İstiklal Caddesi* in the fashionable *Beyoğlu* district. The Turkish police lost little time in arresting thirty-two suspects and in interrogating Eric Gedye along with them. Nothing could be proved against him, but the Turks complained bitterly to the Embassy and the Ambassador insisted that Eric leave Turkey. One of those arrested was Gedye's assistant, Alice Lepper, who had followed him from Vienna and now travelled with him to Jerusalem. Known as 'Litzi', she eventually became Eric's wife. 'He married his secretary' is a common enough cliché, but her story is more interesting than that.

Litzi Gedye, Vienna 1959

Back in 1938, Litzi had been in danger when the Germans marched into Vienna. As the Jewish secretary of prominent British journalist Eric Gedye, she was unlikely to evade the *Gestapo*'s attention. When Eric was forced to leave Austria, Litzi had to find a way out for herself. Her two brothers escaped to the USA; Robert became a New York lawyer, Stephen established optician practices in Philadelphia. Litzi refused her siblings' entreaties to flee with them, deciding to continue her secret anti-Nazi work in Europe.[37] To leave Austria, she found a different solution. A generous British diplomat, John Harper Lepper, agreed a marriage of convenience and Litzi became Mrs Lepper. She escaped with her new husband to Prague, where she acquired a brand-new British passport. In March 1941, SOE took her on as Eric Gedye's assistant in Istanbul.[38] Marriage to him came later.

Sitting in Jerusalem with responsibility for SOE's Middle East work, the frustrated Eric and Litzi had no way of influencing the Austrian situation in Turkey. Eric agreed with London to send an agent in his place. They chose the 35-year-old Herbert Feuerlöscher, originally from the Austrian region of Styria, and gave him the code name '*Sapeur*'. His cover would be to represent the Haifa construction firm Solel Boneh, buying Turkish timber. He did not use an alias, having traded timber in Turkey until June 1941 without falling under suspicion. His frequent visits to Eric Gedye's home in Istanbul in early 1941 were not thought to have drawn police attention. Eric instructed him to have nothing to do with SOE's controversial propaganda work in Turkey.

Gedye hoped that Feuerlöscher would be able to re-establish contact with his old socialist friends in Styria through couriers, students or businesspeople. In writing to London, Eric was vague about whether Herbert's party affiliation was 'socialist' or Communist. In a letter to Istanbul, Gedye passed on the names and descriptions of four possible contacts in Vienna, that could be given to Feuerlöscher at an opportune time. Clara Holmes had filed away names obtained from Theodor Schuhbauer in 1941. Before his fateful sea voyage, the unfortunate agent had provided the contacts and suitable greetings: '*Herzliche Grüsse von Theo und Vally*'.[39]

Herbert was also to feed back crucial information about travel restrictions, documents required—if possible with samples—and possible safe havens for undercover agents. Back in London, Evelyn and Clara were hoping to get agents under training into Austria as quickly as possible. The agents would need all the information they could get.

Despite Gedye's detailed preparations, he was far from confident of success. The chances were slender, but Feuerlöscher was 'determined, devoted, pertinacious and conspiratorially skilled'; he would 'leave nothing untried to make it work'.[40]

Feuerlöscher

Herbert Feuerlöscher left for Istanbul on 1st September 1942, taking the Taurus Express international train.[41] Once he had established his legitimate business activities, he prepared a courier to travel via the Balkans to Austria and started to report back snippets of intelligence from the Istanbul Austrian community, which were passed on to MI6. The Turkish police apparently left him alone, but the Germans took a close interest in him. Istanbul was a hotbed of intelligence activity, full of German agents. The news from Austria was mixed. In the highest Nazi circles, no trace of confidence in victory could still be found, but fear for the future held them together. 'We *must* be victorious', they said in despair. Overworked and undernourished workers were disillusioned, exhausted and apathetic. Minor sabotage was common, but the population felt that the defeat of Germany might lead to brutal Russian occupation of Austria. Without some Allied assurance that Austria would be treated differently than Germany, it was pointless for Austrian anti-Nazis—those who had not already been imprisoned or executed—to resist the regime. SOE in London had been making this argument to the Foreign Office for months, if not years.[42]

On his return to Palestine in early November, Herbert Feuerlöscher reported to Eric Gedye on two ingenious plans to infiltrate clandestine radio sets into Austria. The first required the contacts in Austria to follow instructions on how to build a transmitter from components sent in, hidden in separate packages. The second involved building a transmitter into a normal radio receiver and then sending it to Austria with an unsuspecting courier. If both risky schemes failed, instruction for receiving a wireless set by parachute would be sent. Over the ensuing months, the tortuous attempts to get these wireless, or W/T, sets into Austria continued. Ronald Thornley in London was doubtful, if not outright suspicious. 'This entire W/T project smells not a little', he wrote, 'but we cannot afford to ignore any possibilities'.

Meanwhile, an intelligence report from 'a very reliable source' made Herbert Feuerlöscher's position more complicated. Allegedly, he had been seen in the 'Elli Bar' in Istanbul in conversation with two 'well-known enemy agents' and the words 'Palestine' and 'Haifa' had been overheard.

Eric Gedye exploded. He pointed out the inaccuracies in the report, expressed doubts about the motives of the source, and criticised the threat to Herbert through the lax security in the report's transmission. It was another example of a political rival having a score to settle, he thought. He vigorously defended Feuerlöscher's integrity and loyalty, and threatened to resign. Ronald Thornley admonished him to be more objective. London's view of Feuerlöscher was in any case less positive. They recognised that his primary role was not to collect intelligence. Just the same, Thornley wrote about one of Herbert's reports of Nazi tittle-tattle, 'To my mind, this is tripe picked up in Istanbul and is quite valueless. I don't intend to pay [Feuerlöscher] one cent for such stuff'.[43]

From the start, Herbert Feuerlöscher had hoped to be trained for undercover deployment and dropped into Austria. But Evelyn Stamper had others, already in training, in mind for this role. Herbert served effectively as an organiser in Istanbul, running several sub-agents. In December 1944, he was sent back to Palestine and given £200 in full and final settlement for his work.[44]

'Wirl'

As 1943 dawned, Hagessen reluctantly allowed Eric Gedye to return to Istanbul for a short visit. By May, Eric had been able to persuade the Ambassador to allow him to stay on permanently, using his own well-known name but under cover as a freelance journalist for the New York Times and other papers.

Eric's primary partners in his new work were the Austrian revolutionary socialist group. As they had favoured a pan-German socialist state rather than Austrian independence, Evelyn and Clara in London had not actively built up the connection. Yet they were well organised inside Austria and Eric knew several of them well. And some of them were as devoted to Austria as he was.[45]

Thornley instructed Gedye to establish communications with reliable opposition groups in Germany and Austria, recruit potential workers, infiltrate subversive propaganda and stimulate passive resistance, sabotage and eventually mass strikes. The Nazi rail, road and sea networks were to be the primary targets. To stay at a secure arm's length from the undercover work, Eric needed a middleman. SOE invited the well-known socialist Karl Hans Sailer to join Gedye in Turkey to fulfil this role. Sailer had participated in the February 1934 revolt against the dictatorial Dollfuss regime, was sentenced to twenty months' hard labour, fled to France in 1938 and to the USA after the fall of France in 1940. 'His name will have a first-class appeal to Austrian socialists inside the country', mused Evelyn Stamper. Eric Gedye knew and respected him. Sailer accepted the job offer and arrived in Istanbul in February 1943.

But Eric soon came to the conclusion that 'four years of soft living in the USA had sapped whatever fire this man possessed and that he was useless for SOE work'. A harsh judgement, reinforced by Sailer's complaints that he could not have his wife and family with him. Based on his failure to recruit a single agent and his dangerous indiscretions, X Section decided to remove him. Sailer had asked for Stefan Wirlandner, a socialist who was already in SOE training, to be sent as his assistant. Instead, Ronald Thornley sent Wirlandner to replace Sailer in September 1943. Karl Hans Sailer returned to New York.

Stefan Wirlandner

Stefan Wirlandner was a different prospect than Sailer. He too had been arrested in Austria in the 1930s, and sentenced to fourteen months in prison for high treason. Arriving in England in January 1939 as a textile worker, he had been interned on the outbreak of war and despatched to Canada in July 1940, returned and released in early 1941. He worked during 1941 in the Political Intelligence Department of the Foreign Office and then joined the Pioneer Corps. Whether he had actually worked for MI6 is unclear, but by 1943 he had completed 'para-military and SIS finishing training'. According to Ronald Thornley, his appearance was 'darkish, inconspicuous, thin': very suitable for going undercover. He was intelligent, had a pleasant personality, spoke fluent English with an accent and was prepared to volunteer for 'specially dangerous work'.[46] Like Sailer and millions of soldiers, 'Wirl' too was separated from his family; he learned by telegram of the birth of his son in Glasgow on 16th February 1944.

As an excellent 'second' to Eric Gedye in Istanbul, wrote Evelyn Stamper later, he was 'an unqualified success from the outset', proving 'enthusiastic, energetic and skilful'. Gedye agreed: 'In him', he wrote later, 'you certainly sent me a jewel, even if in appearance a rough diamond'.[47] No surprise, as he had been very successful in SOE training. In a four-day 'scheme' in Cambridge, he had prepared his cover meticulously on the foundation of his real-life experiences. He carefully reconnoitred the city and held clandestine meetings with the field security NCO acting as his contact in the Fitzwilliam Museum and the swimming pool. Under four hours of interrogation by the Cambridge police after arrest, Wirlandner convincingly rearranged the chronology of his story to hide the times of his secret meetings. Overall, in this 'excellent scheme', he showed 'very great thoroughness, care, imagination and astuteness'.[48]

Betrayal in Vienna

The greatest success for Gedye and Wirlandner—code name *Whirlwind*—was in the distribution of black propaganda. Their aims were to encourage Austrian desertion from the German Army or at least faked illness, to increase Austrian resentment against Germany and to turn Austrians against going down with the sinking Nazi ship. Their methods of distribution were manifold: leaflets hidden in lottery ticket envelopes or slipped into soldiers' kit bags; posters on the doors of houses in Crete where *Wehrmacht* soldiers were billeted; sabotage instructions in waterproof bags hidden in tins of fish sent with food parcels.[49] The subsequent security crackdowns were as crucial to undermining morale and cohesion as the propaganda itself.

Less successful, although they did not think so at the time, were the attempts to contact underground socialists in Austria, *Whirlwind*'s primary mission. The socialists in exile in Britain, with Oscar Pollak at the fore, wanted 'their' people to be used by SOE only to support the long-term rebuilding of their political future: not for short-term operations like sabotage. Similarly, Stefan Wirlandner in Istanbul was hypersensitive about being seen as a paid agent of the British, rather than a political collaborator. Eric Gedye took care to treat him as the latter, but Ronald Thornley and Evelyn Stamper had little patience with these attitudes. They demanded unswerving commitment to the Allied cause. The tensions were often tangible.

Gedye and Wirlandner developed several courier lines into Austria, carefully keeping them isolated from each other. But the most promising means of contacting socialists in Vienna was a Swiss diplomat named Trumpe, already in contact with MI6, based in Istanbul and travelling freely to and from Zurich and Vienna. His security vetting by MI5 showed that he had been in contact with the Germans, but that was only to be expected for a neutral diplomat. Working through an MI6 intermediary in January 1944, Eric gave Trumpe a message to deliver in Vienna to a friend of Stefan Wirlandner by the name of Franz Mehlich. Trumpe reported back from his first visit that he had met Mehlich, who seemed nervous. In the process of a series of well-paid visits, Trumpe established a trusted channel of communications with Austria. The encouraging letter he brought back from his second visit was verified as being in Mehlich's handwriting and style. For the third visit, Gedye despatched Trumpe with a case containing a radio set and crystals with instructions and codes, propaganda material, microfilmed sabotage instructions and guidance for selecting parachute drop zones. This would establish an SOE radio in Vienna, code name *Maus*. The MI6 cut-out reported on 26th April 1944 that Trumpe had returned 'after safely delivering the goods'. Eric Gedye later met Trumpe, inviting him to dinner and listening to his descriptions of the meetings in Vienna. They were entirely fabricated.[50]

Franz Mehlich knew nothing of the 'authentic' handwritten message he had allegedly written. Trumpe appears to have betrayed his mission to the Germans at the first opportunity. The visitors to the Mehlich home, who met only his wife, had been sent by the *Gestapo*. The radio set never reached its destination and *Maus* never came on the air. Mehlich did receive a 'food parcel' from Turkey, but not until August 1944. The *Gestapo* had intercepted and examined it before forwarding it to him, but it still included microfilms hidden in a can of pickled fish. Mehlich was arrested in September, interrogated and tortured. When instructed later to give up the microfilms, he was able truthfully to report that there were none; his wife had already destroyed them. He was fortunate to escape alive, remaining useful to the *Gestapo* in writing letters to Istanbul, dictated by them, and as bait for any further SOE contacts.

A much more serious disaster was soon to come. One of the alternative lines into Austria was provided by an Austrian named Hochleitner, who was working for SOE in Istanbul on the technical task of concealing propaganda and secret messages in innocent-looking tinned food. His code name was *Thunder*. Not only did he have a half-Turkish mistress named Nowak who was expecting his child; he also had German papers.

Frau Nowak, code name *Blitz*, had obtained permission to travel to Vienna to get a divorce from her Austrian husband, return to Istanbul and marry Hochleitner before the birth.[51]

While dealing with (and financing) all of these domestic complexities, Gedye and Wirlandner started to train *Thunder* for a mission in Austria. As is often the case in war, though, the plan was 'OBE': overtaken by events. Turkey and Germany cut off diplomatic relations, and *Thunder* got permission to travel to Vienna among the many Germans and Austrians leaving Istanbul. He agreed to deliver clandestine letters, secret codes, propaganda and other material to SOE contacts. Included was a radio transmitter built into a bulky but normal-looking household radio receiver. *Blitz* was due to follow her new husband to Vienna. By making a scene at the German Consulate, she was able to get the radio transported as official baggage. The German Consul appeared to inspect the radio with little interest.[52]

The radio never arrived. And Agent *Thunder* disappeared.

Much later, after the Nazi surrender, Stefan Wirlandner returned to Austria, searched for Hochleitner and interviewed those to whom he had been sent.[53] A distasteful story emerged. The agent had made contact according to his instructions, but his attempts to be put in touch with senior opposition figures made his hosts distrustful. He had more success elsewhere. Wirlandner reported that his quarry had gained the confidence of a certain '*XX*' or '*No 20*', spinning him a story about being in communication with the comrades in London. Attempts to put *Thunder* in contact with Carinthian and Styrian partisans met with suspicion and went no further. In September/October 1944, the *Gestapo* arrested *No 20*—identified by Dr Peter Pirker as Heinrich Widmayer, a prominent social democrat politician both before and after the Nazi period—and subjected him to torture. Widmayer learned from his interrogators that Hochleitner had provided them with information about the underground opposition. But the contacts had been cautious, and the information was sparse. Later released, Widmayer was able to warn most of his contacts about the danger of talking to the man.[54]

The danger appears to have been far greater than Eric Gedye and his London colleagues realised at the time. Peter Pirker's research has unearthed claims made by *Gestapo* officers during their post-war interrogations and trials that Hochleitner was from the start a double agent. According to them, he had infiltrated the Austrian émigré community in Istanbul under instructions from German military intelligence, the *Abwehr*. He had gained Stefan Wirlandner's confidence and had been set to work packing secret messages into doctored canned food.[55] Soon he was an apparently loyal SOE agent.

Hochleitner's SOE mission to Austria was a counter-intelligence coup for the Germans, but the damage could have been much worse. Neither of the smuggled radio sets gave the Germans the opportunity to establish deceptive radio contact with SOE: the *Funkspiel* they had successfully deployed against SOE and MI6 in the Netherlands. And Eric Gedye's compartmentalised security arrangements in Istanbul were good; crossover between the Trumpe and Hochleitner lines into Austria was avoided.

Like Herbert Feuerlöscher, Stefan Wirlandner was keen to take on a more active role 'inside', building up left-wing Austrian resistance to the Nazis. He proposed infiltrating through Yugoslavia with socialist colleagues already under SOE training.[56] The partisans in Slovenia would help to smuggle the group into Austria, he thought. Ronald Thornley was sceptical. The distrustful and uncooperative attitude of the Communist partisans was already becoming obvious. Thornley scotched the idea.[57]

Nevertheless, X Section sent Wirlandner in September 1944 to the newly established SOE base at Monopoli in southern Italy. By 1944, the strategic situation in the war and the Allied attitude to Austria's political future had both changed dramatically. Istanbul was no longer the place to be.

Tipping points: Lisbon and Moscow

Since Benito Mussolini agreed 'spheres of influence' with Hitler in 1937, Italy had been a staunch—if not fully respected—ally of Nazi Germany. Within the Berlin-Rome Axis, Italy's main focus was the Mediterranean. But the Mediterranean war was not going well for Italy and Mussolini's political standing was deteriorating. By mid-August 1943, German and Italian troops had been driven from North Africa and Sicily was in Allied hands. King Victor Emmanuel III had removed Mussolini from power, taken personal control of the armed forces and appointed Marshal Pietro Badoglio as Prime Minister.

Allied intelligence had been receiving indications that some senior Italians wanted to change sides and join the Allies. SOE played an essential role in the negotiations that led to the Armistice of Cassibile on 3rd September 1943, when Italy became a 'co-belligerent' with the Allies.[58]

A fortnight earlier, Brigadier-General Giuseppe Castellano had arrived with a secret Italian delegation in Lisbon and met senior British and American officers and diplomats. After this initial meeting, SOE facilitated negotiations between the Allied Command and the Italian Government via a secure radio connection between its North African base, known as *Massingham*, and Lieutenant Dick Mallaby, an SOE wireless operator now in Rome. The subsequent long-range political and military negotiations led to Italy's changing sides under an armistice whose terms remain controversial today.[59] Lost days in coming to agreement allowed the Germans to reinforce defences. The Allied advance through mainland Italy would be prolonged and bloody, and Austria would remain under Nazi control for many more months.

The diplomatic process started in Lisbon had major strategic implications, but the events that took place in Moscow in October/November 1943 had a much more direct impact on Austria. As Allied victory became almost certain, what should happen to Austria after the war developed into an important issue. Was Austria Hitler's first victim, the first country to be occupied by Nazi Germany, or an integral part of the *Reich*? Most Western states had accepted the 1938 *Anschluss* both politically and legally 'with a mere shrug'.[60] When war came, officials treated individual Austrians as Germans, as enemy aliens. The inability of Austrian exiles to get on with each other did not help. On that evidence, American and British politicians could not envisage a cohesive Austrian identity. Despite Winston Churchill's romantic view of Austria, the accepted political view on both sides of the Atlantic was that the tiny country could only survive economically as part of a Danubian federation. In London, the Foreign Office suppressed any challenges to this policy.[61] After all, nationalism had contributed to the outbreak of the war.

Among the few voices calling for clearer encouragement for Austrians were Evelyn Stamper and 'Midge' Holmes. Through Ronald Thornley, they consistently pushed for a shift in the Foreign Office stance and an explicit statement of support for Austrian independence.[62] The military argument for this was obviously the need to drive a wedge between Austrians and Germans, as a contribution to winning the war. But for the two women it was an emotional commitment to a principle. Differences between the two points of view were irreconcilable and attempts to come to a compromise were essentially unsuccessful. Foreign Office scepticism prevailed, but the need to give a message of hope to anti-Nazi Austrians had sunk in. When Foreign Secretary Anthony Eden presented a potential political policy for Austria to Churchill's War Cabinet on 16th June 1943, he recognised that 'efforts to encourage resistance to Germany in Austria were hampered by the absence of a declared policy' on the future of Austria. 'As a first step', the re-creation of an independent Austrian state, given 'preferential treatment as compared with Germany' should be a priority, but the ultimate aim should be a Danubian federation centred on Vienna. The War Cabinet approved the policy.[63]

The policy paper did not go as far as SOE and its propaganda partner the Political Warfare Executive had hoped. But it was a basis for the British diplomats to work with Allies. The Foreign Office shared the policy paper with just the USA. The suggestion of a federation in southeast Europe might be a red rag to Stalin; indeed, for his own geopolitical reasons he favoured Austrian independence.[64] The two Western Allies worked together on a draft declaration originated by the 'political warriors' and shared it with the USSR. In the hands of the diplomats, it had been watered down. Potential independence came with conditions. The Austrians would have to 'work their passage'. The final text of the 'Moscow Declaration' required Austria, Hitler's 'first victim', to contribute to her own liberation.

> The governments of the United Kingdom, the Soviet Union and the United States of America are agreed that Austria, the first free country to fall a victim to Hitlerite aggression, shall be liberated from German domination.

They regard the annexation imposed on Austria by Germany on March 15, 1938, as null and void. They consider themselves as in no way bound by any changes effected in Austria since that date. They declare that they wish to see re-established a free and independent Austria and thereby to open the way for the Austrian people themselves, as well as those neighboring States which will be faced with similar problems, to find that political and economic security which is the only basis for lasting peace. Austria is reminded, however, that she has a responsibility, which she cannot evade, for participation in the war at the side of Hitlerite Germany, and that in the final settlement account will inevitably be taken of her own contribution to her liberation.[65]

The Declaration certainly encouraged SOE's Evelyn, Clara and their Austrian partners, even if it did not fully meet their expectations. It later became a pillar of the post-war Austrian Republic and a foundation for what some call the 'fiction' of Austria's victimhood.[66] Yet its impact on the liberation of Austria was limited.

In late 1943, it had seemed that—once the German defences in Italy had been overcome—Austria would lie on the path to invasion of the heart of the *Reich*. Striking Germany's 'soft underbelly' from the Mediterranean was Winston Churchill's dream. Roosevelt saw it as a sideshow, Stalin as a threat to Soviet influence in Eastern Europe.

By the time the gruelling Italy campaign had been won, the Western Allies had landed in Normandy, the campaign in Northwest Europe was well underway and Austria's military significance had diminished. But rumours spread that the Nazis would retreat to a final redoubt. They would make their last stand, ran the story, in Bavaria and the Austrian Alps.[67]

---

[1] The Signals School was part of STS 102 on Mount Carmel, in Haifa.
[2] TNA HS 9/1245/3, Reitlinger personal file, X to JQX, 4th September 1942.
[3] TNA FO 371/44255, report by Lieutenant-Colonel Wilkinson, 27th April 1944, reproduced in Thomas M Barker, *Social Revolutionaries and Secret Agents: the Carinthian Slovene partisans and Britain's Special Operations Executive* (New York: Columbia University Press, 1990).
[4] Gerald Steinacher, '*Der Einzige Österreicher in der Schweiz, der den Nazis Effektiv Widerstand Leistete: Wilhelm Bruckner und der österreichische*

Wehrverband Patria 1943-1946,' in *Jahrbuch 2001-2*, ed. Christine Schindler (Vienna: Dokumentationsarchiv des österreichischen Widerstandes, 2001).

[5] Wolfgang Neugebauer, *Austrian Resistance*, 2014, pp.79-114.

[6] M R D Foot, *Resistance*, 2016, pp.128, 331. Foot suggests that some 170,000 Austrians were imprisoned for resistance activity, of whom 35,300 were killed or worked to death.

[7] 'Our Führer is Christ. Christ is our Führer'. Interview with Erwin Ringel, www.doew.at/erinnern/biographien/erzaehlte-geschichte, accessed 12th September 2021.

[8] Wolfgang Neugebauer, *Austrian Resistance*, 2014, pp.124-144.

[9] The title represented a 'cryptic abbreviation for Oesterreich', with the '5' representing the 'e'. In December 1944 O5 formed the Provisional Austrian National Committee (*Provisorisches Österreichisches Nationalkomitee*, POEN) (*ibid*, pp.216-219). SOE was more sceptical of the group's claims than was its American equivalent, OSS.

[10] M R D Foot, *Resistance*, 2016, p.65.

[11] Kreisky had been allowed to emigrate rather than being imprisoned. Wolfgang Neugebauer, *Austrian Resistance*, 2014, p.65.

[12] TNA HS 6/692, Progress Report 17th September 1941.

[13] London Times, obituary, 4th February 1985.

[14] Until Threlfall arrived, the German/Austrian work was part of the duties of Peter Tennant, in Stockholm under cover as Press Attaché. On Threlfall's expulsion, Miss Janet Gow and 'Miss J Forte' filled the gap for a year until Butler's arrival. TNA HS 7/145, *German Section representation in Stockholm*, September 1945, W J M Mackenzie, 2000, pp.200, 687, and Sir Peter Tennant, *Touchlines of War* (Hull University Press, 1992).

[15] Wolfgang Neugebauer, *Austrian Resistance*, 2014, pp.210-211.

[16] TNA HS 6/692, Progress Report 9th July 1941.

[17] TNA HS 7/145, *'The History of the Lex Group'*, by Clara Holmes.

[18] On the Beaulieu schools, see Cyril Cunningham, *Beaulieu: the finishing school for secret agents 1941-1945* (London: Leo Cooper, 1998).

[19] See Chapter 2.

[20] TNA HS 6/669, Progress Reports 6th August, 10th September, 8th and 15th October 1941.

[21] In addition to 'remote' railway sabotage carried out in Switzerland, propaganda material and instructions for in-country sabotage were carried on trains. For example, drivers would carry such material in black packages disguised as coal briquettes (TNA HS 7/199). Germany was a greater focus than Austria for this work. The cooperation of the International Transport Workers' Federation with SOE was substantial. More detail can be found in Dieter Nelles, *Widerstand und internationale Solidarität: die Internationale Transportarbeiter-Föderation (ITF) im Widerstand gegen den Nationalsozialismus*, Veröffentlichungen des Instituts für Soziale Bewegungen Schriftenreihe A, Darstellungen (Essen: Klartext, 2001).

[22] TNA HS 6/692.
[23] TNA HS 6/692, Progress Report 10th September 1943.
[24] TNA HS 7/146, 'The History of the *Lex* Group'.
[25] TNA HS 7/253, pp. 38-39.
[26] TNA HS 7/146, 'Work into Austria', by R Jellinek.
[27] See Roderick Bailey, *Target Italy: the secret war against Mussolini, 1940-1943* (2014), pp.354-361.
[28] TNA HS 7/263 p. 249.
[29] Here and below in this section: TNA HS 7/146, *Work into Austria from Turkey.*
[30] On SOE operations to support Allied interests in Turkey itself and their political implications, see Süleyman Seydi, 'The Activities of Special Operations Executive in Turkey', *Middle Eastern Studies* 40, no. 4 (2004).
[31] In September 1943, Knatchbull-Hagessen, known in the Foreign Office as 'Snatch', hired Elyesa Bazna as a valet. While Bazna could not understand the documents the Ambassador brought home to read, he understood the phrase 'Top Secret' on them, recognised their commercial value, photographed them and sold them to the *Abwehr*. Bazna, as *Cicero*, became one of Germany's most valuable spies in Turkey (Anthony Cave Brown, *Bodyguard of Lies* (New York: Quill/William Morrow, 1991), pp.393-9; Keith Jeffery, 2010, pp.503-4).
[32] TNA HS 9/116/6, personal file Oskar Behron. For more detail on this group, see Peter Pirker, *Subversion deutscher Herrschaft*, 2012, pp.139-144.
[33] TNA HS 6/8, 7th July 1942. Gedye and Weinzinger recruited a committee of six Austrians to travel to the safety of Palestine and form a Middle Eastern Austrian section to mount Free Austrian radio broadcasts. An invasion scare in Turkey prompted others to 'clamour to be taken out of danger' and ask to move to Palestine. TNA HS 9/116/6, 6th December 1944. Separately, Allan Keir was sent from Britain to the Middle East by sea in March 1942 as Conducting Officer for a group of Austrian and Sudeten German trainee agents, with a view to inserting them via the Balkans. This attempt to drop agents into Austria eventually failed, but Keir stayed in the Middle East to represent the German Section. He recruited and trained agents in Egypt and Palestine, planned operations and despatched agents.
[34] TNA HS 6/8, 20th February 1943.
[35] TNA FO 371/30095, 1st August 1941, cited in Süleyman Seydi, 2004.
[36] TNA HS/3/222, 1st December 1943, quoted in Neville Wylie, 2006, p.169.
[37] Litzi's mother and aunt were arrested in Paris by the French police and were killed in Auschwitz. Information courtesy of Robin Gedye.
[38] TNA HS 9/915/2, personal file Alice Lepper; *The Times* 3rd September 2005, obituary Litzi Gedye.
[39] TNA HS 6/8, 7th July, 21st August 1942.
[40] TNA HS 6/8, 31st August 1942.

[41] The *Taurus* was the lesser-known extension of the Simplon Orient Express and featured in Agatha Christie's novel *Murder on the Orient Express*. (*Cook's Continental Timetable, 1939*)
[42] TNA HS 6/8, 16th September 1942.
[43] Here and previous two paragraphs: TNA HS 6/8, various dates, October-November 1942.
[44] TNA HS 7/146, *Work into Austria from Turkey*, Appendix A.
[45] Here and below: TNA HS 6/23, 19th May 1945, and HS 7/146, *Work into Austria from Turkey*.
[46] TNA HS 9/1612, 26th April 1943.
[47] TNA HS 9/1612, 2nd September 1944.
[48] TNA HS 9/1612, 5th June 1943. The FS NCO was Lance-corporal Manser.
[49] Reported, for instance, on 27th April 1943 from Crete by Captain Patrick Leigh-Fermor (TNA HS 7/146).
[50] TNA HS 7/146, *Work into Austria from Turkey*, pp. 9-19.
[51] TNA HS 7/146, *Work into Austria from Turkey*, Appendix A.
[52] TNA HS 9/1612, 17th August 1944.
[53] This was the *Bobby* mission, undertaken with Theo Neumann and Walter Hacker (TNA HS 9/1613, various dates).
[54] TNA HS 9/1613, *Bobby* Report, *Der Fall 'Fox'*. SOE also referred to Hochleitner as *Fox* or *Fuchs,* the code name of the radio set he was due to be operating.
[55] Testimony and interrogations of Johann Sanitzer and Adolf Anderle: TNA KV 2/2656, and references in Peter Pirker, *Subversion deutscher Herrschaft*, 2012, pp.266-271. Sanitzer's primary interest was in establishing fake contact with Allied agencies using captured radio sets—the *Funkspiele* or radio games—but most of these were with the Soviet NKVD. The only British case he mentioned in his July 1945 interrogation was that of an MI6 agent parachuted into Styria in the late summer of 1944. Although the agent committed suicide using cyanide hidden in a button on his uniform, Sanitzer's wireless operators were able to convince careless British operators in Italy that the transmissions were genuine and to elicit the name of the agent's companion. When *Gestapo* HQ in Vienna became too dangerous as a base for these operations, Sanitzer used the requisitioned villa of Franz Josef Messner, the General Manager of the Semperit rubber manufacturer, who had been shot as a suspected British spy. Gustav Riediger, Messner's unreliable and indiscreet representative in Istanbul, had offered to work for SOE, but Gedye later severed contact (TNA HS 7/146, *Work into Austria from Turkey*, Appendix A).
[56] See 'By the Left' below.
[57] TNA HS 9/1612, 26th July 1944.
[58] See Roderick Bailey, 2014, pp.296-324, Peter Dixon, *Setting the Med Ablaze*, 2020, pp.161-181 and Gianluca Barneschi, *An Englishman Abroad: SOE agent Dick Mallaby's Italian missions, 1943-45* (Oxford: Osprey Publishing, 2019).

On support by German *Abwehr* chief Wilhelm Canaris for the Italian *'volte-face'*, see Paddy Ashdown, 2018, pp.236-237, which cites TNA KV 32/173.

[59] Elena Aga Rossi, *L'Inganno Reciproco: l'armistizio tra l'Italia e gli Angloamericani del Settembre 1943 (Mutual Deception: the armistice between Italy and the anglo-americans of September 1943)* (Rome: Ministero per i Beni Culturali e Ambientali). Mallaby, code name *Olaf*, had been captured soon after parachuting into Lake Como. He was in San Donnino prison awaiting execution as a spy, when he was suddenly transported to Rome. He still expected to be executed. Instead, he was taken to the Italian Defence Ministry, provided with a familiar radio set and ordered to make contact with *Massingham*. The Italians were impressed when they were told the Allies could provide a trained wireless operator at the Rome end, 'a British officer who entered your country by parachute so as to be available for just such an emergency' (TNA HS 6/775, 11th Oct 43, *The Olaf Story*. Also TNA HS 7/264 and HS 6/872). They would find him in a prison in Como.

[60] Robert H Keyserlingk, 1988, p.3. Keyserlingck covers the diplomatic process leading to the Moscow Declaration both here and in Robert H Keyserlingk, 'Die Moskauer Deklaration: Die Alliierten, Österreich und der Zweite Weltkrieg,' in *Österreich im 20. Jahrhundert*, ed. Rolf Steininger and Michael Gehler (Vienna: Böhlau Verlag, 1997). Pirker (Peter Pirker, "British Subversive Politics towards Austria and Partisan Resistance in the Austrian-Slovene Borderland, 1938–45", *Journal of Contemporary History* 52, no. 2 (2017)), too, covers the inter-Allied politics involved but also details the process leading to a shift in British policy.

[61] Robert H Keyserlingk, *Austria in WW2*, 1988, pp.60, 115.

[62] For instance, in TNA HS 6/3, 1st November 1941.

[63] TNA CAB 65/34/40.

[64] Peter Pirker, *British Subversive Politics towards Austria and Partisan Resistance in the Austrian-Slovene Borderland, 1938–45*, 2017: p.326.

[65] Declaration on Austria, Moscow Conference, October 1943 (Source: Avalon Project, https://avalon.law.yale.edu/wwii/moscow.asp, accessed 15th December 2021).

[66] Oliver Rathkolb, *Fiktion "Opfer" Österreich und die langen Schatten des Nationalsozialismus und der Dollfuss-Diktatur* (Innsbruck: StudienVerlag, 2017).

[67] For instance, in the *New York Herald Tribune*, 19th April 1945, and *Evening Independent*, 13th December 1944. Heinrich Himmler's plans for an 'Alpenfestung' never came to fruition.

CHAPTER 7

The Slovenian Route

The 'soft underbelly'

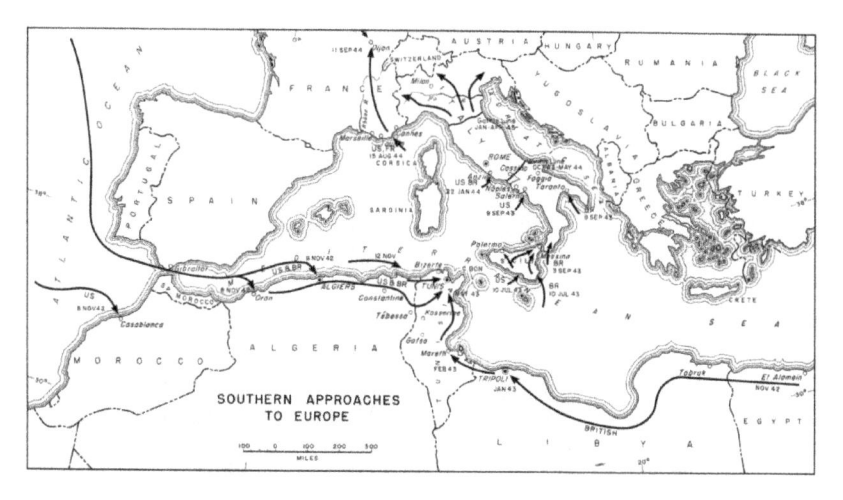

Map of Southern Approaches to Europe 1943-45

KING VICTOR EMMANUEL'S GOVERNMENT may have changed sides in September 1943, but thousands of Italian Fascists rejected the 'surrender' and continued to fight alongside the Germans. The 'soft underbelly' of Nazi Europe proved not to be so malleable after all. The Allies' firm grip on southern Italy, though, provided a reasonably secure base for SOE, from which it could support partisans in the Balkans and northern Italy. SOE staffs moved forward from

Massingham near Algiers and from Egypt and Palestine to locations in and around the Adriatic port city of Bari. The secret organisation established a base known as No 1 Special Force, code name *Maryland,* led by Commander Gerry Holdsworth and with its headquarters at Monopoli. The new forward base included paramilitary, parachute, clandestine operations and wireless schools—duplicating the UK training process in microcosm—supply depots and radio stations to contact agents in the field. In southern Italy, the airfields for launching parachute missions to Austria were now several hundred miles closer to their target.[1] The range of opportunities seemed to be expanding and Ronald Thornley deployed two officers to represent X Section at *Maryland*.

Major James Darton, a German speaker, had worked for the Bank of England in Central Europe before the war. He joined the Royal Artillery and was serving in Northern Ireland when his Commanding Officer said to him 'If you want to get out of here, which I gather you do, I suggest you learn Russian'. It was a curious suggestion, but Darton set about learning the language from a White Russian refugee. After an interview in London, conducted in Russian, he entered the arcane world of SOE.

His language training continued, as he handled and trained NKVD agents in the UK and Russia for the '*Pickaxe*' missions.[2] Many of these agents were Austrian social democrats who had ended up in Russia after fighting in the Spanish Civil War. In December 1943, X Section took him on and sent him for a reconnaissance to Italy, where he returned in February 1944 to set up the Germany/Austria country section at Monopoli and later in Siena.[3]

Jimmy Darton's deputy in Italy was Captain Betty Harvey of the First Aid Nursing Yeomanry, the FANY. But this was an alias. In reality, this was Betty Hodgson, who, after escaping from Switzerland as a wanted woman, had crossed the Pyrenees on foot and battled her way home to Britain. It did not take long for Ronald Thornley to find a new mission for Betty, a 'thoroughly stout-hearted and capable officer'.[4] Southern Italy was now SOE's European centre of gravity and new ways had to be found to crack the Austrian nut.

While Allied tanks, infantry and artillery forced their way northwards through Italy, the only opportunity to strike at Nazi control of Austria was through unconventional warfare. This meant backing any Austrians who were willing to resist. Not many were left; most were in concentration camps or dead. Supporting them depended on recruiting, training and deploying the Austrian agents who were X Section's hope. The focus for that would now be Italy.

Reitlinger and Greenleaves

Evelyn Stamper and 'Midge' Holmes had initially looked for Austrian recruits in Britain: in internment camps for 'enemy aliens' on the Isle of Man and elsewhere, in the Pioneer Corps and among Austrian refugees congregating around the Austria Office in Eaton Place. Training took place in the wilds of Scotland, at the undercover agent schools in southern England and at the RAF Ringway parachute school near Manchester. But after Allan Keir had delivered his party of trainees to Egypt in early 1942, his task was to recruit promising anti-Nazi Austrian and German soldiers from the PoW camps in North Africa and supervise their training in Egypt and Palestine. Once SOE was established in southern Italy, much of that training would take place there.

Friedrich *'Freddy'* Reitlinger reappears in the story. While languishing in the Middle East, as X Section decided what to do with him, he had shown an interest and aptitude for propaganda. He took courses in delivering it. But his fate became tied up with an unfortunate group of three Austrians: the *Greenleaves* party.[5] Because of the difficulties of gaining access to Austria, these three men—referred to in messages as *Gerhard*, *Peter* and *Charles*—were to parachute into Albania, where British Liaison Officers were fighting alongside local partisans. *Freddy* was to drop with them. The three were to try to reach Austria through Slovenia, but Friedrich's task was to help the British Liaison Officer find ways of distributing propaganda to *Wehrmacht* soldiers in Yugoslavia. From intelligence reports, it was known that the predominantly Austrian 100th *Jäger* Division was deployed there.

The operation did not go well. Allan Keir tried to keep the *Greenleaves* group sweet as the mission suffered delay after delay. SOE in London demanded that Cairo give the operation priority. They did, but the only aircraft with the range to reach Albania from the base at Derna in Libya was the Liberator. And only one machine was available. The RAF attempted the drop five times without success, because of problems with the aircraft, the weather or the reception party on the ground. Both *Freddy* and the *Greenleaves* party had been 'repeatedly over the target and under fire'.[6] That was when the Derna medical officer cried foul and sent the nerve-wracked men to Palestine for a week's leave.

While all this was going on, higher politics had intervened and Italy had become a 'co-belligerent' with the Allies. The men and women of SOE's *Massingham* base had helped to make this happen. Suddenly, the strategic situation had changed, and SOE's new bases in Italy brought it hundreds of miles closer to Albania, Yugoslavia and, of course, Austria.[7]

SOE's Balkans formation, known as *Force 133*, had moved from the Middle East to its advance base near Bari on the east coast of Italy and was now able to reach Albania by sea.[8] The *Greenleaves* party moved to Italy in January 1944 and its saga continued. A security breach caused by mismanagement in Italy led to one of them, *Gerhard*, being removed and sent back to a secure location in the Sudan until any knowledge he had picked up no longer mattered. The other two joined SOE's *Clowder* mission in Yugoslavia, led by Lieutenant-Colonel Peter Wilkinson, but faced continuing frustration and disappointment.[9]

Meanwhile, Friedrich Reitlinger followed on to Italy and pursued a different path, now using the name 'Roberts'. *Force 133* employed him in April 1944 for three trips across the Adriatic as a Conducting Officer, depositing agents on the inhospitable Albanian coast. But the 100th *Jäger* Division had moved away from Albania, so the opportunity to target propaganda at Austrian soldiers there no longer existed.[10] The Albanian Section could not use Friedrich as originally planned. 'Second Lieutenant Roberts' needed a new role. Ronald Thornley suggested he might join the *Molasses* group, but this was rejected.

Molasses, a Tyrolean agent, knew the Reitlinger family from their time together at the University of Innsbruck and was no friend of Friedrich. *Freddy* was a talented linguist and an asset for propaganda work, but he lacked the stability or resourcefulness needed in a high-threat environment. He was an individualist and not seen as prime operational material.

Friedrich did not see it this way. In a meeting with Major Jimmy Darton, X Section's representative in Italy, a suggestion of office work did not please him. He was still enthusiastic about going into the field. Meanwhile, he was 'kept on ice' in Italy, updating his knowledge of the situation in Austria and working in the censorship office checking German-language letters.[11] In July 1944, he joined the *Clowder* team and started training for its Operation *Castle*.[12]

It came to nought. By November 1944, the Germans had launched an offensive in Carinthia and the *Clowder* mission had to withdraw to safety. It had no further use for 'Roberts'. There was a suggestion that he had 'lost all incentive for operational duties' and was 'malingering'. He should relinquish his commission and return to the Pioneer Corps as a corporal.[13] But the discussions culminated in his return to the propaganda field through a posting to the Political Warfare Branch in February 1945. He became a civilian in April 1945, but continued to work for PWB.

Friedrich Reitlinger was one of the first Austrian potential agents to be recruited and trained. His story as the war developed was far from straightforward. He had left the Tyrol after the death of his father and sister, determined to strike back at the Nazis. SOE's Austrian Section saw him as a sound prospect and started his training, but he appeared temperamentally unsuited to the role of armed resistance. Ronald Thornley and Evelyn Stamp tried to find the right place for him, concerned for his and others' safety. Along the way, he fell victim to the uncertainties of war: aircraft limitations, weather, Army bureaucracy, enemy action and partisan group politics. His story shows how difficult it was to get the right people into Austria to support and encourage the far from dynamic resistance to Nazi domination. So too does the broader story of the *Clowder* mission.

Clowder

Lieutenant-Colonel Peter Wilkinson landed in an isolated Bosnian mountain valley in December 1943 to meet Tito. Wilkinson's idea was to enlist the help of Tito's partisans in getting SOE agents into Austria through Slovenia. With him were his fellow Royal Fusiliers officer, Major Alfgar Hesketh-Prichard, and their wireless operator, Company Sergeant-Major 'Ginger' Hughes.[14] Wilkinson had first proposed the *Clowder* Mission in July 1943, with an ambitious eye to opening up links via Yugoslavia into Poland, Hungary and Czechoslovakia.[15] Later, Colin Gubbins ordered the focus be limited to working with resistance movements in Austria. The Italian capitulation in September made the proposition a good deal more workable.

On the other hand, Ronald Thornley and the two women in his Austrian Section had their doubts. Would Austrian resistance erupt without long-term undercover preparation? And would *Clowder* find the necessary cooperation in Yugoslavia? The Slovenian partisans could well resent being used as a tool to help Austrians, with little benefit to themselves. And their political sympathies lay with Soviet Communism, not with the Austrian social democrats with whom X Section had forged close ties. Thornley kept options open, including the Swiss and Turkish connections. *Clowder* would be 'only <u>one facet</u> of X Section work into Austria', he wrote.[16] Later, he pointed out that only 'non-political' agents could be sent through Yugoslavia who would 'carry out work consistent with the partisans' creed and aspirations'.[17] Even though Wilkinson knew that the attempts in 1943 to infiltrate the *Greenleaves* party into Austria via Yugoslavia had fallen apart, he could not have imagined how difficult the much larger *Clowder* Mission would in fact be.[18]

Peter Wilkinson had been in at the birth of SOE. Before the war, he had been one of the young officers discreetly given tuition on irregular warfare at St Ermin's Hotel in London. When Colin Gubbins was appointed Chief of Staff to the British Military Mission to Poland in the summer of 1939, he took Wilkinson with him as his staff captain. The Mission arrived in the middle of the German invasion of Poland, hours after Neville Chamberlain had reluctantly declared war on Germany. It could offer little succour to the reeling Poles before escaping to Romania. Wilkinson accompanied Gubbins to Paris to assist the exiled Polish and Czech military, which had established themselves there. In the subsequent years, Wilkinson had become one of Gubbins' most effective senior officers.[19]

Alfgar Hesketh-Prichard was a tall, restless young man with striking eyes, a sallow complexion, a conspiratorial air and a broken nose gained in steeple-chasing. After reading mechanical sciences at Cambridge, where he was a member of Queens' College and joined the University Air Squadron, he had become the Assistant Director of a leading arms manufacturer in Czechoslovakia. He spoke fair German, having been an apprentice in several German firms, was a fully trained signals officer and an expert instructor in sniping and fieldcraft. As a result of riding accidents, he had been declared medically unfit for the Army but volunteered to teach sniping to guardsmen. With Peter Wilkinson's help, he found his way into SOE.[20]

Wilkinson's plan, after negotiating with Tito, was to travel the 400 miles on foot to the partisans' Slovenian headquarters, and to set up a base there for agents to be passed through to Austria. In return for their support, the partisans would receive further supplies of weapons and munitions. The partisans supposedly had contact with resistance groups in Austria, particularly the *Österreichische Freiheitsfront* (ÖFF, Austrian Freedom Front) in Upper Styria, claimed by Soviet propaganda to be a major force.[21]

Tito appeared to react positively and approved the plan. The small team's winter march over the Dalmatian mountains to Croatia, and onward through thick snow over the *Velika Kapella* ('Great Chapel') mountains into Slovenia, took ten days. Their suspicious and uncooperative reception at the Slovenian headquarters warned that the future would not be uncomplicated. And their marching was not finished. Communications with the Slovenian partisans in Carinthia, within Austria, were handled by Tito's No 9 Corps, at Ciapovano in the mountains north of Trieste and close to the Austrian border. This was a further two weeks' march away, through even deeper snow and with the added hazard of frequent patrols by German mountain troops. The 9 Corps commander was helpful, but the combination of heavy new snow and a German offensive foiled Wilkinson's attempt to travel north into Austria. Various other possibilities were tried, but by late February 1944 the prospect of better weather lay ahead. Wilkinson left Hesketh-Pritchard in Slovenia to establish the *Clowder* Advance HQ, with 'Ginger' Hughes to maintain communications with Italy. He himself set off on the long march back to Bosnia, flew to Italy and continued to London. He reported back to Gubbins at SOE, but his report was also seen at 10 Downing Street. One aspect made a deep impression on Desmond Morton, Churchill's personal assistant and intimate friend. The Slovenes were 'fighting Germans to the best of their limited ability' but doing so 'as a means to a well-defined end': a 'Slovene State run on left-wing lines incorporated in a Federated Yugoslavia'. Their 'single-minded fanaticism ... regards fighting the Germans as a mere incident, even though essential to its purpose'. Morton recognised the grievous error of underestimating the psychological difference between Yugoslav and British thinking.[22]

Slovenia and Carinthia

At the *Clowder* forward base in the Dolomite mountains in early 1944, Alfgar Hesketh-Pritchard prepared to receive Austrian agents and set up courier lines to infiltrate them into their homeland. Spring weather emerged and supply drops began; thirteen of seventeen attempted drops between January and June were successful. Radio communications from the field were difficult; having to report both to London and Monopoli, together with the range of codes and ciphers used, caused confusion.

Initially flown out from England to head the *Clowder* rear party in Italy, Grenadier Guards officer Major Charles Villiers moved forward to support Hesketh-Prichard. Villiers, who had worked in Germany for Glyn Mills Bank before the war, parachuted into the 9 Corps headquarters at Ciapovano on 15th May 1944. After helping to consolidate the *Clowder* forward base, Villiers was to move up to Carinthia, releasing Hesketh-Prichard for reconnaissance in Styria.[23] The challenge was acute; although Austrians in general were disenchanted about the post-*Anschluss* Nazi rule, these two provinces were 'probably the least disillusioned'.[24]

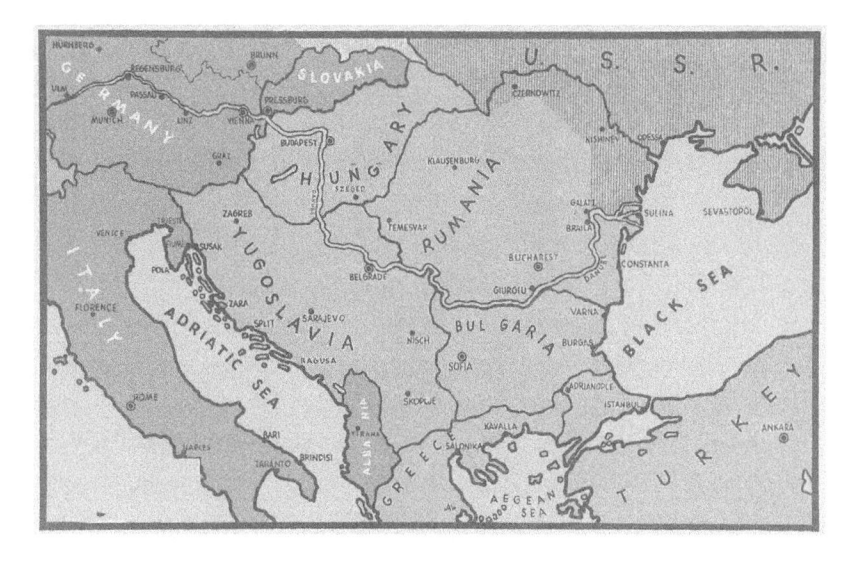

Map of the Balkans as seen from Germany, 1940

In early June, Villiers and a small party travelled with partisan guides into Carinthia. In classic understatement, he described the journey as 'unpleasant'. 'The weather was foul', he reported, 'the terrain mountainous (we seldom dropped below the 1,000-metre contour), and our route often followed tracks invisible to anyone except the courier. The Germans interrupted the courier stages almost daily, which ... often doubled the distance to be travelled'.[25]

The trek lasted ten to sixteen hours each day, on one occasion twenty-one hours. Of the four couriers, one was too small to carry any weight, another unable to keep up, and a third stole the party's stores. The partisans later executed him. As Villiers put it, 'the Red Queen has nothing on a partisan judge'.

Wilkinson's reconnaissance had shown good prospects in February 1944 for penetration of Austria. Unfortunately, the Germans saw the same picture, and in March smashed the main Slovenian partisan group (or *Odred*), which took some time to recover any strength. In charge of the combined western and eastern *Odreds* was Gasper, a 'fearless, simple, shrewd, uneducated farmer with a genius for partisan warfare'. He 'always boasted SS uniform and was a perambulating armoury'.[26] Working with the partisans was a challenge. Apart from the practical difficulties and the Communist bureaucratic approach, the Slovenes did not share the vision of subversive activity brought by the SOE officers. And that mattered. 'Almost nothing could be done without the approval and support of the partisans', recalled OSS officer Franklin Lindsay, who worked alongside SOE, 'We were literally never out of sight of our individual partisan couriers or bodyguards'.[27]

The partisans believed that nothing less than a paramilitary invasion of Austria would have any effect. Assisting the development of an Austrian Communist partisan movement would not conflict with their territorial ambitions for a Slovenian nation. The Soviet Union supported them in this, through secret arrangements unknown to the British officers. Based on a kernel of two dozen Austrian ex-POWs dropped to Yugoslavia from Russian aircraft, the Slovenes built up an 'Austrian Battalion' of several hundred men. However, its attempts in late 1944 to advance into Austria and develop partisan resistance were unsuccessful, and it returned to Slovenia before winter weather set in.[28] From the partisans' viewpoint, the SOE team's role was to coordinate supply drops in support of Slovene operations. Getting SOE agents into Austria was a low priority, and even something to be undermined.[29]

Murder most political

Into this tense situation had parachuted the two remaining members of the *Greenleaves* party. Gerhard Sanders (Sykora) had returned to the Sudan to protect operational security. His comrades *Peter* and *Charles*, though, were still in training in Italy and in principle willing to try to get through to Austria.[30] They joined *Clowder* in early April 1944, but were understandably willing only to go forward to a safe house or a definite resistance contact. Also, their forged identity documents lacked photographs. Villiers sent them to a local photographer, who photographed them in civilian clothes and German uniform. But the Germans arrested the photographer and seized his films. The *Greenleaves* pair were compromised and had to be evacuated.

Another team of agents destined for Austria parachuted to *Clowder* in Slovenia on 12th June 1944. This was the *Pyx* party, three men who had spent many months in the Middle East, had been given refresher courses at the paramilitary and parachute schools in Italy and had been briefed on current conditions in Austria. But cooperation with the partisans again proved less than perfect. When *Pyx* arrived with blank false documents, to be completed when cover stories were agreed in the field, the partisans could not or would not help. Charles Villiers signalled for completed documents to be prepared in London and sent via Italy. By the time these could be prepared, a German offensive against the partisans had made the move into Austria impossible. In mid-September 1944, the *Pyx* party returned to southern Italy.[31] Yet another setback.

Meanwhile, further disaster had struck on 13th July 1944, when two Austrian ex-PoWs working for MI6 were captured by a German patrol. One escaped, but the other was later seen talking in friendly terms with the Germans. He led his captors to the partisan base, which was overrun by over 1,000 German troops. Returning after four days on the run, Villiers found that the village had been destroyed and compromising material removed.

Major Alfgar Hesketh-Prichard

Hesketh-Prichard and Villiers concluded that the prospects of getting agents into Austria from Slovenia had more or less disappeared. The partisans would not provide the connections needed to get the agents in. They seemed determined to keep SOE out of the area beyond the Drava river (*Drau* in German), north of the Karawanken mountains. The few resistance contacts in that area, in and around the town of Klagenfurt, had been arrested or had fled, and the population lived in terror. Agreeing that the 'agent approach' had no future, the two British officers pinned their hopes on Hesketh-Prichard 'successfully crossing the Drava and forming there a nucleus of Austrian resistance'.[32] They still thought there may be some truth in the shaky information about the existence of the Austrian Freedom Front, the ÖFF. Villiers returned to Italy, suffering from typhoid fever, to be replaced in early August 1944 by Major Frank Pickering.[33]

Frank Pickering was a former member of one of SOE's field security sections, where his task had been to instil in agents the skills that could keep them alive in their undercover existence.[34] Speaking German, Italian, French and Spanish, he had become an interrogator of foreign arrivals in Britain, at the Royal Victoria Patriotic Schools in Wandsworth, London, before moving to Italy and being deployed to *Clowder*. His insightful report on Slovene attitudes was well received, but his determined attempts to find ways of stimulating Austrian resistance in Styria were of no avail.[35]

Hesketh-Prichard saw his proposed river crossing as the only option, even though it involved substantial risk. But SOE officers were not risk-averse, 'running outrageous risks was the heart of the matter'.[36]

In early October 1944, Hesketh-Prichard crossed the Drava river with a battalion of Tito's partisans and tried to contact local resistance movements in the *Saualpe* area. They met heavy opposition, according to reports from the partisans, and sometime in early December Hesketh-Prichard disappeared during a battle. He was never seen again and was presumed killed by German troops.

British investigators in 1945 and 1946 suspected that this was not the real story, but they got no further. Only much later did it become clear that Alfgar had fallen victim to one or both political strands: the territorial ambitions of Slovene separatists and the geopolitical and ideological roots of what we now know as the Cold War. The partisans were happy to accept the parachuted arms and supplies that the British promised, and delivered. After all, the Russians were not in a position to provide such support.

The partisans, backed by Soviet officers, were determined to hinder SOE's progress in finding, training and supporting Austrian resisters. The Communist Party of Slovenia would not, as Frank Pickering put it in 1945, 'allow the British or Americans to use their lines for the purpose of infiltrating Austrians over whom they, the Slovene Communists, have no control'.[37] To prevent Alfgar Hesketh-Prichard from contacting and organising local non-Communist resistance groups, his partisan comrades 'almost certainly' murdered him soon after he sent his final report to SOE.[38] In it he had written, 'this is no place for a gentleman'.[39]

---

[1] For more on No 1 Special Force and the successful Italian operations, see David Stafford, *Mission Accomplished*, 2011, pp.27-86.

[2] Parties of NKVD agents, the *Pickaxe* missions were deployed to Western Europe by SOE, with limited success and considerable inter-Allied ill will. One party of four agents destined for Austria 'mutinied' and 'attempted to escape from NKVD with SOE's connivance'. See W J M Mackenzie, 2000, pp.395-399 and Donal O'Sullivan, *Dealing with the Devil: Anglo-Soviet intelligence cooperation during the Second World War* (New York: Peter Lang, 2010).

[3] TNA HS 6/13, AD/E to V/CD, 8th May 1944, HS 7/146, History of Clowder Mission, and James Darton, interviewed by Professor David Dilks, IWM Private Papers 14089 Maj James Garwood Darton, 23rd January 2002.

[4] TNA HS 6/13, 8th May 1944.

[5] They were Gerhard Heinrich Sykora (alias Gerhard Sanders, code symbol D/E168, referred to as Gerhard), Peter Johann Ulanowsky (alias Peter Brand, D/E166, Peter) and Israel Gold (alias Charles Gardner, D/E167, Charles). TNA HS 6/10-11.

[6] TNA HS 6/10, D/H98 (Gedye) to X (Thornley), 30th December 1943.

[7] Peter Dixon, *Setting the Med Ablaze*, 2020, pp.189-212, David Stafford, *Mission Accomplished*, 2011.

[8] The main SOE forward base, No 1 Special Force, known as *Maryland*, was at Monopoli. See David Stafford, *Mission Accomplished*, 2011 and Peter Dixon, *Setting the Med Ablaze*, 2020, pp.191-212.

9 TNA HS 6/10-11, various dates.
10 TNA HS 9/1245/3, D/H350 (Keir) to X (Thornley) 5th May 1944.
11 TNA HS 9/1245/3, 25th May-1st June 1944.
12 The purpose of this operation is unknown.
13 TNA HS 9/1245/3, 30th November 1944-15th January 1945. HS 6/19, X/A2 to AD/X1, 5th December 1944.
14 Hesketh-Prichard was known to the partisans under his 'war name' of 'Squadron Leader Cahusac'. Wilkinson and his team travelled from the airfield at Lecce in Brigadier Fitzroy Maclean's Dakota aircraft. Churchill had appointed Maclean as liaison officer to Tito in September 1943, after British support shifted from Mihailovich to Tito. On the political issues, see: Harold Macmillan, 1967, pp.526-530; *Slovene Claims to Carinthia 1919-1945*, 28th April 1945, by William Deakin, TNA FO 371/48826, reproduced in Thomas M Barker, 1990, pp.164-173; Peter Pirker, *British Subversive Politics towards Austria and Partisan Resistance in the Austrian-Slovene Borderland, 1938–45*, 2017; and Wilkinson's *Memorandum on the Revolt in Slovenia*, TNA FO 371/44255, also reproduced in Thomas M Barker, 1990, pp.83-116.
15 On this alternative to Operation *Anvil*, the landings in southern France, see for example Thomas M Barker, "The Ljubljana Gap Strategy: Alternative to *Anvil/Dragoon* or Fantasy?", *The Journal of Military History* 56, no. 1 (1992).
16 TNA HS 6/13, X to D/H98, 24th February 1944.
17 HS 6/13, X to AD/E 20th April 1944, covering Memorandum on the *Clowder* Plan.
18 TNA HS 7/146, History of 'Clowder' Mission, Summer 1943-Autumn 1945. IWM Personal Papers 12751 Peter Allix Wilkinson, *Notes on the Clowder Mission. Report on Clowder Mission*, 13th May 1944. *Clowder Mission Records*, November—December 1944, (TNA WO 204/1953), reproduced in Thomas M Barker, *Social Revolutionaries*, 1990, pp.141-145. The depleted *Greenleaves* party, the two men going under the names of Peter Brand and Charles Gardner, were brought under the *Clowder* umbrella (TNA HS 6/13, 10th February 1944).
19 M R D Foot, *SOE 1940-1946*, 2014, p.11, Peter Wilkinson and Joan Bright Astley, 1993.
20 Patrick Howarth, *Undercover: the men and women of the Special Operations Executive* (London: Routledge and Kegan Paul, 1980), pp.15, 38-39.
21 TNA HS 6/17, *Report on a Mission to Carinthia (Korosko), May to September 1944*, by Major C H Villiers. See Peter Pirker, *Subversion deutscher Herrschaft*, 2012, pp.284-285 for more on ÖFF).
22 Morton to Sporborg, 3rd May 1945, IWM 12751. Harold Macmillan, 1967, pp.344, 430. Although Wilkinson experienced warmth and hospitality among the Slovenian partisans, he had a different view of their attitude to the Allies: '[The Slovenians] have a blind (and almost pathological) admiration for the USSR (especially for the Soviet Army), a somewhat chilly respect for Great Britain (in particular for her democratic parliamentary institutions), and an

indifference almost amounting to contempt for the Americans.' (Memorandum on the Revolt in Slovenia, TNA FO 371/44255, p.84).

[23] The Austrian provinces of (southern) Carinthia (Kärnten) and Styria (Steiermark) are known to Slovenes as Korosko and Stajersko.

[24] TNA 6/3, Opinion and Morale in Austria, 25th January 1943, p.2.

[25] TNA HS 7/146, *History of 'Clowder' Mission, Summer 1943-Autumn 1945*. IWM Personal Papers 12751 Peter Allix Wilkinson, *Notes on the Clowder Mission. Report on Clowder Mission*, 13th May 1944. *Clowder Mission Records, November-December 1944*, (TNA WO 204/1953), reproduced in Thomas M Barker, *Social Revolutionaries*, 1990, pp.141-145.

[26] TNA HS 7/146, History of 'Clowder' Mission, Summer 1943-Autumn 1945.

[27] Franklin Lindsay, *Beacons in the Night: with the OSS and Tito's partisans in wartime Yugoslavia* (Stanford, CA: Stanford University Press, 1993), p.155.

[28] In addition to the Slovenes' secret arrangements with Moscow, knowledge of the British liaison with the Slovenian partisans sparked a competitive ambition within OSS to strengthen American presence in the area, which at this stage was limited to a few officers working alongside SOE (Dušan Biber, *Allied Missions in the Slovenian Littoral 1943-1945,* at IWM Personal Papers 12751 Peter Allix Wilkinson; Franklin Lindsay, 1993, pp.151-157, 173-174). On OSS/SOE cooperation in operations in and from Italy, see Tommaso Piffer, 'Office of Strategic Services versus Special Operations Executive: Competition for the Italian Resistance, 1943–1945.', *Journal of Cold War Studies* 17, no. 4 (2015).

[29] Both Dušan Biber and Peter Pirker have researched Yugoslav archives that show this to be the case. Dušan Biber at IWM 12571; Peter Pirker, *British Subversive Politics towards Austria and Partisan Resistance in the Austrian-Slovene Borderland, 1938–45,* 2017.

[30] They were Peter Ulanowsky (alias Peter Brand) and Israel Gold (alias Charles Gardner).

[31] Pyx consisted of Hans Zeilinger (aka 'Linger'), Hans Neufeld, (a Czech going by the name of Harry Newman) and Oskar Scheinmann (alias Oscar Stephens). TNA HS 7/146, *Activities of X Section in Italy*; and *'Clowder' Report*; HS 9/1638/6, Personal file Hans Zeilinger.

[32] TNA HS 6/17, *Report on a Mission to Carinthia*, pp.4-14.

[33] On Pickering, see Peter Dixon, *Guardians*, 2018, pp.100, 166.

[34] *Ibid*, p.171.

[35] When the *Clowder* mission withdrew from Slovenia, Pickering made an 'adventurous journey' out of the snow-covered Slovenian mountains, arriving in Italy on 5th January 1945 (TNA HS 7/146, *History of Clowder Mission*, Para 58).

[36] Thomas M Barker, *Social Revolutionaries*, 1990, p.36.

[37] TNA, WO 204/1954, *A Mission to the Untersteiermark (Stajersko) August 1944-January 1945* by Major Frank Pickering.

[38] Robert Knight, 'Life after SOE: Peter Wilkinson's journey from the Clowder Mission to Waldheim', *Journal for Intelligence, Propaganda and Security Studies* 2009, no. 1 (2009). More detail is in Thomas M Barker, *Social Revolutionaries*, 1990, pp.48-49 and Peter Pirker examines the different ways history has treated Hesketh-Prichard's death, in the context of Austrian post-war politics and the nascent Cold War (Peter Pirker, *'Partisanen und Agenten: Geschichtsmythen um die SOE-Mission Clowder'*, Zeitgeschichte 38, no. 1 (2011).

[39] TNA HS 6/17, 3rd December 1944.

CHAPTER 8

Out of Italy

Fighter ace in the mountains

PARTNERSHIP WITH THE SLOVENIAN PARTISANS was proving unfruitful. Meanwhile, a lesser-known wing of the *Clowder* mission was attempting to get through to Austria from northern Italy. SOE needed an alternative route into Austria, both for 'agents who in political colour would have been repugnant to Tito' and 'to keep the door open should the Jugoslavs at any time become completely uncooperative'.[1]

To establish it, Squadron Leader Manfred Czernin had parachuted on the night of 13th/14th June 1944 into the southern foothills of the Carnic Alps, accompanied by his Bolognese radio operator Piero Bruzzoni.[2] They linked up with anti-Fascist Italian partisan units, to set up despatch stations and courier routes into Austria, over the mountains between the Plöcken and Brenner Passes from a base some twenty miles south of the Austrian border.

Manfred Czernin was born in January 1913 in snowy Berlin, the fourth son of an Austro-Hungarian diplomat, Count Otto Czernin von und zu Chudenitz and his just as aristocratic English wife, Lucy.[3] The pair had met in Rome and married in London in July 1903. She was nineteen years old.

An adventurous child, Manfred grew up in Rome with his mother, by then separated from the Count. When he reached school age, he attended Oundle School, but instead of progressing to university he left to work on a plantation in Rhodesia, where his time was cut short by a bout of malaria. In 1936, aged twenty-three, Manfred joined the Royal Air Force Volunteer Reserve and saw action as a Hurricane pilot, gaining the Distinguished Flying Cross. In September 1943, health again curtailed his career, but it was SOE that benefited. The secret organisation recruited Squadron Leader Czernin through a tip from an air-marshal who knew of the work it was doing.

Manfred's experience of life in Italy and his command of the language made him a good fit for SOE's work alongside Italian partisans. He joined No 1 Special Force near Bari in November 1943 for paramilitary and parachute training. Impatient to get into action and accustomed to operating independently in a Hurricane fighter, he chafed at the discipline in the SOE training units. Only in June did his opportunity come.

Once Manfred Czernin had established himself with Italian partisans at Tramonti as the *Aunsby* party, he formed reception parties for drops of supplies for the partisans and of Austrian agents to head across the border. He was joined in July and August by the *Aunsby II* and *Bakersfield* parties, led by Captain Patrick Martin-Smith and Major Fielding respectively. They started to build capacity both to support the Italian partisans and to operate in Austria. The Italians knew Czernin as Manfredi.[4]

Later reinforcements came in the form of the *Seathrift* party, made up of Austrian volunteers trained by SOE. Manfred was surprised, though, to find that most of the new arrivals were in British uniform, expecting to carry out sabotage and paramilitary operations. They were unwilling to operate in Austria as undercover civilians, but this was the only way Manfred could send them to safe houses in Austria. So he kept most of them in Italy to give sabotage and weapons training to the Italian partisans.[5] The exception was Hubert Mayr, a Tyrolean who had parachuted to join Manfred's group in August 1944.[6]

Tyrolean patriot

Hubert Mayr was born in Innsbruck in November 1913 and worked in agriculture and forestry until 1936. Five feet nine inches tall, he had dark hair and eyes and a full moustache. His sturdy build betrayed the outdoor life of his youth in forest and mountain. His father, who had refused to allow the Hitlerjugend (Hitler Youth) to recruit Hubert's younger half-brothers, died in Sachsenhausen concentration camp in 1940. As Nazi power grew in Germany and Austria, Hubert left to fight for the left-wing Republicans in the Spanish Civil War. There he contracted tuberculosis, was wounded in battle and entered into a marriage that did not last. A committed socialist from his teenage years, he was also a vehement Austrian patriot and disagreed with the aim of the Revolutionary Socialists to build a pan-German socialist state. He would go on to fight for an independent Austria.

Hubert Mayr

After General Franco's victory in 1939, Hubert crossed into France, suffered horrific conditions in an internment camp and subsequently joined a French labour battalion. When French forces were defeated in 1940, Hubert ended up in North Africa and found employment with a French family as their gardener. When, in November 1942, the Allies launched Operation *Torch*, the invasion of French North Africa, Hubert saw his chance to join the anti-Nazi fight. Now bearing the name Jean Georgeau, he fought alongside French volunteers of the 'Special Detachments', part of SOE's *Brandon* Mission attached to the 1st British Army.[7] But Hubert was captured at Hammamet on 28th January 1943, a member of a party landed by submarine to demolish a bridge.[8] Freed from a PoW camp in Italy after the Italians changed sides in September 1943, he crossed the German lines to southern Italy and returned to SOE. This was initially for service in the Security Section at the *Massingham* base, but his potential as an undercover agent in Austria was quickly recognised.[9]

By April 1944, Hubert was under training at *Maryland* in Italy. After parachuting into northern Italy in Operation *Bakersfield*, he made several clandestine trips in civilian clothes to his homeland, building up a network of contacts but returning from the first to report that the Austrian people were 'apathetic, lacking in patriotic spirit and terrified of Nazi reprisals'.[10] He was supported by a forward base set up by Major George Fielding and Captain Patrick Martin-Smith in the Albergo Sotto Corona at Forni Avoltri, three miles from the Austrian border.[11]

Albergo Sotto Corona, exterior

Martin-Smith's wireless operator was Sergeant Charles Barker, whom Fielding sent on a dangerous 150-mile trip to collect some Allied PoWs. He completed his task, but weeks later he and Major Bill Smallwood were captured by the SS. Barker could have escaped, but stayed with the injured and vulnerable major. In captivity, he was frequently tortured, but survived in a prison camp long until the war came to an end.[12]

Albergo Sotto Corona, interior

Fielding and his comrades worked with the partisans of the Osoppo region, a non-political group founded by an artist with the *nom de guerre* 'Verdi' and Don Aurelio, a priest who was 'outstandingly brave physically' and had 'tremendous powers of physical endurance'. Operating out of uniform in an area patrolled by Germans, the soldiers faced danger every day. The nearest enemy garrisons were less than a dozen miles away, the Allies over 300 miles distant. The Italian partisans, whose support they needed, were divided among themselves, and often frustrated by the Allies' failure to drop supplies. Fielding's team were the nearest target for the partisans' anger.

Partisans of the Osoppo Vittoria battalion

Although the partisans at first more or less controlled this area, the Germans had garrisons in the area and were not unaware of the SOE and partisan presence. They launched a major offensive on 10th October and, despite spirited resistance by the Italian partisans, eventually drove them out. They offered a reward of 800,000 Lire for information leading to the capture of George Fielding. As winter approached, the combination of enemy pressure and lack of RAF supply drops in worsening weather made the group's situation impossible. They withdrew.

Their frustrated tension, as they promised the partisans supplies that never arrived, often surfaced in communications. George Fielding was later reprimanded for his message asking the Balkan Air Force to 'display more of the spirit of the Battle of Britain and less of the Bottle of Bari'.[13]

Meanwhile, back in the relative comfort of Monopoli, Jimmy Darton had felt that the most promising way into Austria was the network Hubert Mayr was building, and sent him a wireless operator to set up independent radio contact from the Tyrol. This man, 'Peter

Priestley', parachuted into the Friuli region and into a deteriorating situation with three others, not realising the disaster that awaited them.[14]

Michael Peter Priestley's real name was Egon Lindenbaum. Of Jewish origins, he had been born in Moscow to a Russian father and a Hungarian mother but became a naturalised Austrian citizen before his first birthday. In his teenage years, he had joined the Communist Youth League in Vienna. When the Gestapo surrounded a cafe where League members were meeting, Egon was one of those arrested. Found with a Walther pistol and twenty-five rounds of ammunition in his possession, he was sentenced to nine months in Dachau. His anti-Nazi rage increased, not least because the SS shot his brother during his imprisonment. Under his new name of Peter Priestley, he joined SOE in late 1942 and trained as a wireless operator.

Priestley's mission orders instructed him to report after landing to the senior British officer, who would provide Italian couriers to escort him over the mountains into Austria. There he was to act as Hubert Mayr's wireless operator. He was to consider himself under Mayr's command, as they attempted to reach the Innsbruck area in order to contact local anti-Nazi groups. Spreading black and white propaganda was also part of the task, as was reporting back the names of any escaped Allied prisoners.[15]

Priestley's three companions for the parachute jump on the night of 12th/13th October 1944 were Second Lieutenants William Taggart (real name Wolfgang Treichl), Richard Hauber (Nikolaus Huetz) and Stephen Dale (Heinz Günther Spanglet).[16] Their task, as the *Seafront* party, was 'to lay on a safe route to Salzburg, contact local resistance movements and carry out minor sabotage'.[17] Neither Priestley's nor *Seafront*'s mission was ever completed, but the true stories emerged only later.

A reception party for the parachutists was prepared and recognition signals arranged. But the pilot mistook lights shining from the windows of a German barracks at Tolmezzo for the drop zone. He did not wait for the recognition signal, and the four men dropped straight into German hands.

Peter Priestley landed in the middle of four German machine-gun posts and was captured. He immediately pulled out the self-destroying container in which his false German documents were stored, pulled out the pin and threw it away. The Germans took the container to be a bomb and kept away from it long enough for the incriminating documents to be burned. Stephen Dale escaped and hid in a hut in the mountains, burying his incriminating documents *en route*. He was subsequently discovered by some Cossacks fighting for the Nazis and surrendered. Both these men were able to convince their captors that they were British officers. They were treated well as PoWs.

Richard Hauber was luckier; he successfully evaded capture and eventually found his way to an Italian partisan group, who linked him up with the *Seathrift* party. William Taggart did not take his chances; tragically, he shot himself on landing to avoid falling into the hands of the Gestapo.[18]

Meanwhile, Hubert Mayr made several journeys into Austria, from the last of which he did not return. In January 1945, SOE posted him missing, last heard of at Dellach in the Drau valley. Search parties after the war found no positive trace of him. According to later research by Peter Pirker and Ivo Jevnikar, he made his way to Slovenia, hoping to continue the anti-Nazi fight alongside Slovenian partisans. But—like Alfgar Hesketh-Prichard—he and his courier fell foul of the partisans' suspicion of British influence. They were arrested and later executed by the Communist secret police.[19]

When in Rome

Soon after dawn on 6th June 1944, thousands of Allied soldiers landed in France, launching the Northwest Europe campaign and stealing Lieutenant-General Mark Clark's thunder. Famously, Clark had sped on 4th June into Rome, recently abandoned by *Generalfeldmarschall* Albert Kesselring, to liberate the Eternal City. But the war correspondents summoned by Clark to a carefully staged press briefing on the Capitoline Hill were talking excitedly about the news from Normandy.[20]

As the people of Rome emerged in relief that their city would not be the site of a battle, Austrians in Rome made their presence known. Former Austrian Foreign Minister, Egon Baron von Berger Waldenegg, joined with about a dozen others to raise the red-white-red flag over the former Austrian legation building. The group claimed that the 'Austrian Committee of Liberation' had been working undercover in Rome for several months, but Allied intelligence reports cast doubt on the claim.[21] Unfounded rumours that Waldenegg had been anointed by the Allies as head of a new independent Austrian government were quickly scotched. In pre-*Anschluss* Austria, he had been unpopular and closely connected with the repressive Dollfuss regime. His ambitions soon aroused censure from Austrian socialists in exile, and British officers in Italy received firm instructions not to encourage the Committee. Right or left wing, even the entire spectrum of Austrians in exile could not claim to represent Austrian opinion 'inside'. Also, connection with Waldenegg might damage the *Clowder* Mission's sensitive relations with the Slovenian Communists.

SOE Italy's Jimmy Darton treated Waldenegg with caution. Back in London, though, Evelyn Stamper and Clara 'Midge' Holmes were always on the lookout for new opportunities and saw one in Rome. The Austrians there might provide a way to contact Roman Catholic groups in their home country, particularly in the Tyrol. 'We could send an Austrian SOE officer to Rome', they proposed a few weeks after its liberation, 'to exploit those contacts'; the 'Catholic agrarian population, which comprises 40% of the population', had 'not been properly harnessed to the resistance movement'. Their suggested candidate was Ernst Weiss, a fervent 47-year-old Christian Social living in Hertfordshire, with whom the pair had been in close contact for over a year. Although Catholic, Weiss was of Jewish descent and had been 'a staunch Schuschnigg man'; for good reasons, he had left Austria in 1938. A sincere and hard-working man, he had been working on propaganda to Austrian Catholics. His British wife Enid could accompany him to Rome as his secretary. She too was thoroughly competent; she had served as a secretary in the Versailles

Treaty negotiations. The idea gained approval and the couple quickly became 'Captain and Mrs Wise'. He was instructed to 'get on with everyone', to allow nothing to interfere with his new subversive task and to 'let his wife manage the British'.[22] On learning that a wife was not permitted to serve as secretary to her husband, Midge Holmes leapt that hurdle by having Enid recruited into the First Aid Nursing Yeomanry: the FANY. Nevertheless, the process of installing the couple who became known as 'the Wise guys' was not simple. The arrival in Italy of a married couple brought a horrified response from men who had not seen their wives for months or years. Betty Hodgson quickly removed Enid from Monopoli and installed her in an apartment in Rome, instructing her to wear civilian clothes; her FANY uniform would instantly connect her with No 1 Special Force. Ernst quietly joined his wife in October 1944 and they started to find their way around. If anything, thought Jimmy Darton, Weiss was stirring up too much trouble, being 'rather too dynamic' instead of 'being a passive observer'. A visit by Enid to the formal and normally unflappable Sir D'Arcy Osborne, the British Minister to the Holy See, ruffled Foreign Office feathers. The sprightly sixty-year-old diplomat was suspicious of Enid's request for assistance in providing contacts in the Vatican and her refusal to disclose for whom she was working.[23] Ernst Weiss sent insightful reports from Rome on Catholic affairs and went on to work for SOE's post-war unit in Austria, No 6 SFSS, where his encyclopaedic knowledge of Austrian affairs proved invaluable.

Meanwhile, Darton thought that Baron Berger Waldenegg's conservative Austrian connections might be useful to SOE. And there was a way in. His son, Heinrich, was under SOE training in Southern Italy, with the code name *Baum*.[24]

The youthful Heinrich Berger Waldenegg had left Austria, carrying forged papers, to join his father in Rome in 1939 and had been called up for service in the Italian Army in 1941. He was commissioned in March 1942 and served in Yugoslavia until August 1943, fighting Tito's partisans. He was on a strategically arranged leave in Rome when Badoglio's government signed an armistice with the Allies. After the Allied landings in mainland Italy, he crossed the

German lines to southern Italy on the night of 23rd/24th September and contacted American forces. He 'rejoined' the Italian Army, now fighting on the Allied side.

A straightforward and intelligent young aristocrat, Heinrich's noble ambition was to return to Austria and build up resistance to the Nazis. He was confident that friends in Carinthia would give him shelter. British Military Intelligence passed him on to SOE, who started his training and gave him the cover name of Lieutenant Henry Burleigh. The deployment for which he was recruited never took place—overtaken by events—but he worked for SOE and subsequently MI6 in post-war Austria.[25]

The Baron's attempts to trade information on contacts in Austria for political recognition were unsuccessful. Recognising that the Baron's claims 'may be fairy tales', Darton got London's permission to 'share' him with MI6, OSS and A Force, who were all keen to exploit his information. But the *quid pro quo* for the Baron's contacts was to be provided in cash rather than political recognition.[26] Ultimately, Darton learned the name of the Baron's primary contact from a friend of the Waldenegg family and his information lost its value.[27]

Another Austrian who surfaced in Rome was Count Norbert von Trautmannsdorff, who knew the Baron and was from the same aristocratic background. An officer in the *Wehrmacht*, he had hidden in Rome for several months until the Allies arrived. SOE took him on board, giving him the cover name of Richardson and the unimaginative code name *Trout*. After training, he was to take charge of the *Bellington* party, consisting of himself, Waldenegg junior and a wireless operator code-named *Brenner* (Alois Bilisic). Their mission, after parachuting into a friend's estate near Graz, would be to contact conservative opponents of the Nazi regime.

As the summer of 1944 wore on, prospects for the mission became ever slimmer. Obtaining documents and Wehrmacht uniforms for the men took time. Aerial reconnaissance, pinpointing a suitable drop zone acceptable to the RAF, poor weather and lack of aircraft cost two 'moons'. By the third moon, two of the party had become ill and the

RAF were saying that drops into Austria would be impossible for three or four months.[28] The mission never took place.

The case of Baron Berger Waldenegg—the 'impulsive Austrian' as the Telegraph called him—caused a political and diplomatic furore in London, in Washington and in Italy itself. Ultimately, though, SOE's efforts with Waldenegg were of limited worth. Ronald Thornley advised Darton not to 'take these matters too seriously'. He inclined to the view that 'the émigrés have served their purpose and that the people who really matter are all 'inside'[29]'. Getting 'inside' was now the Austrian Section's principal aim.

By the Left

Theo Neumann arrived in Monopoli in September 1944 and quickly got to work with Jimmy Dalton planning the undercover assignments of socialist Austrian SOE agents. It was Theo's local knowledge from family vacations, for instance, that provided the site for Leo Hillman's night parachute jump near Krems an der Donau.

Theo was a charming and reliable native of Vienna, thirty-five years old, with a strong character and an attractive sense of humour. His appearance, though, was unimpressive. From his bald pate sprouted fringes of curly red hair to match the colour of his bushy eyebrows. And he suffered from a mild form of what we now know as bipolar disorder. He had been considered for SOE training in 1941 but had not been brought on board. The selectors had thought him unsuitable. True, he was older and less physically agile than other recruits. But the leaders of the social democrat émigrés in London were willing to work with SOE, primarily through the prominent Oscar Pollak.[30] Their pan-German policy had been dropped after the Moscow Declaration and they wanted to get socialists back into Austria. Theo was a significant member of the expatriate socialist community. Evelyn Stamper and Midge Holmes, particularly following the frustrating contact with right-wing groups in Rome, saw the socialist exiles as their best option for contacting opposition groups 'inside'.[31] As urgency grew, the political demands of the socialists and Ronald Thornley's operational priorities now seemed less incompatible.

When Theo started SOE agent training in January 1943, he was seen as a serious and conscientious student, exceptionally intelligent and a cautious thinker. Once he had made up his mind on an issue, he was not easily persuaded otherwise. He smoked incessantly, especially when deep in thought.[32] The smoking, and Theo's unconcern about where ash might fall, was a source of irritation to Neumann's room-mate during training, Eric Sanders (former name Ignaz Schwarz). According to the SOE plan, Eric was to serve as Theo's radio operator when they dropped into Austria.

Making up the trio travelling to Italy from Britain was Hans Hladnik. In his mid-forties, 'Hansl' was a farmer from Styria who had not joined SOE from the Pioneer Corps but had been recruited by the Austrian social democrats in London. He had fled Austria as a political refugee, having for many years smuggled banned left-wing publications into the country. Just before leaving England, he married his partner and thus 'legitimised' their English-born daughter. Whatever might happen to him, he needed to be sure that their financial future would be secure.

When Hansl arrived at Hatherop Castle in Gloucestershire, he was quiet and solitary, earning the nickname 'The Ghost'.[33] Despite his height and powerful build, he spoke softly and had kindly blue eyes. Although the three seemed an unusual group to their comrades, they got on well together.

In early August 1944, the trio left their final training school at Hatherop Castle to spend a few weeks in London. There they received falsified documents showing their fake identities, authentic 'Austrian-tailored' clothing and extensive briefings. Many of the discussions took place at Midge Holmes' house in De Vere Gardens, Kensington, where either Midge or fifteen-year-old Prudence answered the door and ushered them in. While the politically engaged Theo and Hansl went upstairs to make their plans, the apolitical Eric was offered coffee downstairs in the living room. On one occasion, he noticed a drably dressed man stepping down from an Army truck under armed guard. The cooperative Austrian PoW, for that is what he was, was taken upstairs to Theo and Hans to brief them on current conditions in Austria.

In London, Theo Neumann revealed to Eric Sanders what was in store for what was known as the *Dilston* party, although Eric was not much the wiser. Theo had frequently and mysteriously disappeared from the training schools. In fact, he had been helping to plan the socialist group's operation, because this was a joint venture between SOE and Austrian social democrats in London. Some contact with socialist colleagues in Austria had been maintained, and the group would be parachuted 'blind' into rural Austria to find like-minded local people. A month after their arrival in Italy after an overnight stop in Algiers, the trio were joined by Stefan Wirlandner (calling himself John Miller but known to his comrades as 'Wirl') and Walter Hacker (Walter Harris). Wirlandner had travelled from Istanbul to take charge of the party (see Chapter 6 above).[34]

By then, after a few weeks accommodated at Bari, the *Dilston* party had moved to 'Seaview', the remote house overlooking the Adriatic at Fasano near the SOE base at Monopoli and twenty miles southeast of Bari.

Again, Theo would disappear for days at a time, this time with Hansl, reappearing with Austrian newspapers and accounts of what they had learnt about the realities of life in the Nazi state. Eric later learned that the material came from the pair's infiltration into PoW camps in *Wehrmacht* uniform. There they gleaned useful information and sought out genuine anti-Nazis who might be recruited by SOE.[35]

Formed by agreement with the Austrian exiles, the *Dilston* party had more autonomy than many SOE groups or individual agents. Although they continued their training at the *Maryland* schools, with Jimmie Dalton's agreement they also met Italian social democrats in Rome, both to find potential contacts in Austria and to seek agreement on post-war political relations.[36] The discussions brought little agreement, and they continued to wait for the right conditions for *Dilston*'s deployment. That day never came. Even after they moved to the Villa Poderina near Siena in mid-March 1945, their goal did not seem any nearer. They sensed, but could not be certain, that the war was approaching a climactic end.

Long-awaited reports from Michael O'Hara, which would confirm the viability of the *Dilston* mission, indicated the opposite. The appetite among Austrians for opposing the Nazis was very limited. And by this stage the Allies were 'not anxious to encourage large-scale resistance in Austria'.[37] *Dilston* was not activated.

A very fine type

Reports by radio from Michael O'Hara were crucial to establishing the viability of the social democrat mission to Graz and Vienna. For the risk of parachuting into danger to be worth taking, insisted Jimmy Darton, a seedbed of potential resistance had to be already in place.

Theo, Eric and Hansl had got to know Michael O'Hara well, both during training in Britain and in their time together at 'Seaview', the house overlooking the Adriatic. Leo Hillman and Fred Warner had been living at the villa too. None of them discussed operational matters with each other: just their personal lives. Danger did not put O'Hara off; he already had one mission under his belt when he embarked on Operation *Evansville*, the reconnaissance mission for the socialist agents.[38]

Michael's real name was Egon Friedrich Berliner, and he was a native of Vienna. His banker father had died when Michael was seven years old and his widowed mother had returned to dressmaking, owning a fashionable dress shop in central Vienna. The family had left Austria in May 1939 as the Nazi grip tightened. His mother had settled in Switzerland, but Michael was by now relatively independent and escaped to Britain. He worked for a market gardener and a tractor firm in Cornwall for a year, but in May 1940 he was interned and sent to Canada.

Volunteering for the Pioneer Corps in April 1941, Michael served in the Royal Engineers, the Royal Army Service Corps and the Royal Electrical and Mechanical Engineers before being talent-spotted by SOE in September 1942. Tough and determined, but with no particular ideals or loyalties, he worked hard in training and was well liked by his comrades. He was fit and powerfully built. At over six feet in height, with brown eyes, a firm chin and with his dark brown hair brushed back, he made a strong impression. He was an individualist, a skilled mechanic and, according to his SOE interviewer, 'a very fine type'.[39]

Michael O'Hara (Egon Berliner)

By the spring of 1944, Michael was fully trained but with only a vague idea of a mission to the Tyrol in prospect. Meanwhile, an 'excellent opportunity' had 'suddenly arisen'. MI6, who were on good terms with the Italian Communist Party, had been put in touch with an Austrian Communist just arrived from Innsbruck via Bolzano. This man, calling himself 'Mario', wished to provide the well-organised Communists in Innsbruck with a wireless operator who could establish radio contact with MI6 in Italy. MI6 had therefore asked Jimmy Darton if they could 'borrow' a trained wireless operator to parachute into northern Italy near Mantua and travel onward to the Austrian Tyrol. Darton thought of O'Hara, and asked Ronald Thornley to send him to Italy 'fully documented and clothed' for the mission. Despite his reluctance to put O'Hara 'entirely in the hands of a Communist organisation, which we must automatically suspect of being penetrated', Thornley realised that O'Hara was 'anxious for a lone-wolf job'. He agreed, and instructed Evelyn Stamper and Midge Holmes to recall Michael from leave and respond positively to Jimmy Darton. One telling comment shows the contrast between the cooperative relationship between SOE and MI6 in the field and the mutual suspicion at headquarters level. We 'assume you are convinced' wrote X Section in London, that this is not a trick by MI6 'to obtain one of our W/T operators under false pretences'.[40]

Details had to be quickly worked out: authentic clothing and documents, a plausible cover story. Would the MI6 man from Innsbruck, asked Evelyn, give the address of a suitable engineering firm in Innsbruck to which 'Friedrich Knoll', O'Hara's fictitious identity, could have been instructed to report for work following the bombing of his factory in Wienerneustadt? What films had been shown in Vienna cinemas recently? When did Hitler last visit the Austrian capital? The preparations had not been completed on 7th June when Michael was due to fly to Italy. He had asked for some love letters from the fictitious Knoll's imaginary girlfriends to go with the photographs that he would carry with him; could Betty Hodgson (aka Harvey) in Italy oblige? His real girlfriend, a certain Senior Aircraftwoman Lovell in Taunton, was trying to divorce her husband in order to marry Michael.

The mission was known as Operation *Icecream*. O'Hara parachuted into northern Italy, near Bolzano, on the night of 28th/29th July 1944. Three days earlier, as was normal on embarking on a mission, his commission as a second lieutenant was confirmed. The plan was for his Tyrolean companion 'Mario' to escort him over the border to Innsbruck and hand him over to the Communist group there. Jimmy Darton had instructed Michael not to proceed beyond Bolzano until satisfied that all the onward arrangements were in place. He did not even get to make that judgement.

During the parachute landing, Michael lost contact with Mario and with the reception party, who had been forced by an air raid warning and the presence of Germans nearby to douse their lights. He heard shooting and went to ground. Although he tried for several days to find the others, he eventually decided to head south. From Mario via

MI6, SOE heard what had happened by radio, but had no other news of Michael for seven weeks. Jimmy Darton was bitterly disappointed. 'Highly trained and resourceful men like him as as rare as rubies', he said of Michael,.[41] But then an OSS party behind the German lines north of Rome reported that O'Hara had evaded capture and made contact. He was alive. He made his way through to Allied lines and arrived in Rome, exhausted but not discouraged.

Michael O'Hara was as keen as ever to get into action, so Darton assigned him the task of making a blind drop near Graz as a reconnaissance for the *Dilston* party. Theo Neumann and Eric Sanders were to follow him in, once he had made contact with socialist opposition groups. The mission was planned for November 1944, but winter weather caused its postponement. It was not until February 1945 that O'Hara could start Operation *Evansville*. On 7th February, he dropped 'blind' in the Koralpe mountains and made his way twenty miles northwest to Graz. Here he found that most of the socialists he had been sent to contact had been conscripted into the *Wehrmacht* or arrested. Conditions were too hot in Graz, so Michael was again on the run. He headed south and, although Jimmy Darton would have advised against it if he had been in contact in time, Michael joined up with a group of Slovenian partisans. He arranged a supply drop for this group, but SOE recognised the political sensitivity. Ronald Thornley already suspected that the Slovene Communists may have killed Alfgar Hesketh-Prichard, so considered it unwise to identify O'Hara with Hesketh-Prichard's mission.

Soon afterwards, Michael O'Hara went missing. X Section in Italy heard no further word from him, but the next news came from Moscow. The Slovene partisans had reported to their Soviet friends that they had captured someone they suspected to be German, but calling himself Flying Officer Chirgwin, Michael O'Hara's British alias.[42] At first, SOE dealt with this message suspiciously and passed the NKVD some personal test questions for the partisans to ask, such as 'what is the name of the town where your fiancee lives?'. Later, though, Jimmy Darton—who had been under intense pressure, with his people and files divided between Monopoli, Siena and Rome—

realised that Michael had passed some verification details via Moscow. He was genuinely in the hands of the Slovenes. The head of the German Directorate, as it now was, called the whole affair a 'blunder'.

None of this helped Michael O'Hara. Moscow reported on 20th April 1945 that the partisans had been involved in a skirmish with Germans. 'Chirgwin', i.e. O'Hara, was believed to be in German hands. Ominously, he had been captured in civilian clothes. Investigation immediately after the war ended provided corroboration. A downed US Air Force pilot, Melvin H Milbrath, had baled out into the middle of the partisan group in February 1945 and had met Michael there. Together with a small group of partisans, they had tried to cross the Drava river and escape. They had been captured by German troops near Maribor on 21st March 1945, and papers found on O'Hara revealed that he was a British agent. Also, the Slovene partisans captured with him denied his claim to have been shot down. Milbrath was sent to a PoW camp, but O'Hara was taken away by the SS. He asked the pilot to pass the information to No 1 Special Force, as he expected to be executed. He was right. With ten other men, Michael O'Hara—the courageous native of Vienna whose real name was Egon Friedrich Berliner—was shot by the SS on 3rd April 1945 at the Wetzelsdorfer Barracks in Graz.[43]

---

[1] TNA HS 7/146, *History of Clowder Mission*.
[2] TNA HS 7/146, *History of Clowder Mission*, Paras 31-46 and 65. *Notes on the Clowder Mission*, IWM Personal Papers 12751 Peter Wilkinson. Norman L R Franks, *Double Mission: RAF fighter ace and SOE agent, Manfred Czernin DSO MC DFC* (London: Kimber, 1976), pp.112-122.
[3] *Ibid*, pp.19-23, David Stafford, *Mission Accomplished*, 2011, pp.191-3.
[4] TNA HS 7/146, *Activities of X Section in Italy*. IWM Stephen Dale papers, '12 Force' document, letter from Christopher Wood to Stephen Dale dated 13th March 1994.
[5] TNA HS 7/146, *History of Clowder Mission*, Appendix D. The mission planned for the *Seathrift* party was named *Danbury*, with the aim of sabotaging railway lines in the Drautal. TNA HS 6/22, *X/AUS Section Operations into Austria from Italy*. Enrico Barbina and Jurij Cozianin, 'Autunno 1944, Danbury sul Monte Pala,' *La Panarie* 2018 (in Italian).

[6] Also known as Jean Georgeau and Lieutenant George Banks. TNA HS 9/1012/5.

[7] Peter Dixon, *Setting the Med Ablaze*, 2020, pp.58-60. The statement in Mayr's 'Short History' in TNA HS 6/22, written in 1945, that he was recruited by MO1(SP)—as SOE was known to the military—in May 1942, is probably inaccurate, as the Special Detachments were not formed until November 1942. Although some were recruited earlier, eventually French volunteers selected by SOE were enrolled in the *Corps Franc d'Afrique* and transferred to SOE on the same day (TNA HS 3/62, *Report on Brandon*, p.7); 'Jean Georgeau' would have been among them.

[8] Hubert Mayr, as 'Jean Georgeau' was one of the 'French' volunteers in the party led by Captain Eyre, which landed from HM Submarine *Unbroken* on the night of 28th/29th January 1943 to demolish a bridge near Hammamet under Operation *Felice I*. The party was captured during the operation (Brooks Richards, *Secret Flotillas Vol 2: clandestine sea operations in the Mediterranean, North Africa and the Adriatic*, 2nd ed. (London: Whitehall History Publishing in association with Frank Cass, 2004), p.217).

[9] On SOE's Field Security Sections and Massingham, see Peter Dixon, *Guardians*, 2018 and Peter Dixon, *Setting the Med Ablaze*, 2020 respectively.

[10] TNA HS 7/146, 'History of Clowder Mission', Para 36.

[11] Ernest Barker, *Behind Enemy Lines with the SOE* (Frontline Books, 2021).

[12] *Ibid*. Also Alan Ogden and Martin Fielding, *The Clowder Mission in and around Forni Avoltri, June-November 1944*, unpublished paper. This unpublished work is a detailed account of the *Clowder* Mission in this area, co-authored by George Fielding's son.

[13] Alan Ogden and Martin Fielding, 2020. The Balkan Air Force was the Allied formation tasked with air support of SOE and other special forces.

[14] TNA HS 7/146, *History of Clowder Mission*, Paras 65-66.

[15] TNA HS 9/1212/6, Personnel File: Michael Peter Priestley, *Brief for Operation Carlyle*, 28th September 1944.

[16] *Leutnant* Wolfgang Treichl was a *Wehrmacht* officer, from a Vienna banking family, captured at El Alamein and recruited by SOE in the Middle East (TNA HS 9/1482/2). Nikolaus Huetz came from Tyrol (TNA HS 9/759/1). Heinz Spanglet hailed from Berlin (IWM Oral History 14582 Dale, Stephen).

[17] TNA HS 6/22, *X/AUS Section Operations into Austria from Italy*.

[18] TNA HS 7/146, *History of Clowder Mission*, Appendix A, p.3. HS 9/1482/2, letter XF/A/294-JHD to AG/MR dated 29th October 1945. HS 6/21, letter XA/2 to AD/X-1 dated 23rd April 1945, based on information from Ernest Barker, who also reports the incident in Ernest Barker, 2021.

[19] TNA HS 9/1012/5, *Investigation Report*, 25th February 1947. Later research by Peter Pirker and Ivo Jevnikar in Slovenian archives has shown that Mayr fled German troops with his courier Rudolf Moser and tried to join up with partisans in Slovenia. But the Communist secret police—the OZNA— arrested them in Mid-November 1944, interrogated them for five days and executed

them (Peter Pirker and Ivo Jevnikar, 'So geheim wie möglich,' Die Presse, 14th April 2018).
[20] Antony Beevor, 2012, p.573.
[21] New York Herald Tribune, 7th June 1944. Daily Telegraph, 22nd June 1944.
[22] TNA HS 9/1571, memorandum dated 20th June 1944 and subsequent correspondence.
[23] TNA HS 9/1571, Holy See to Foreign Office dated 6th November 1944. For more on Osborne's role in helping escaping Allied POWs, see Sam Derry, *The Rome Escape Line: the story of the British organization in Rome for assistingescaped prisoners-of-war, 1943-44* (London: Harrap, 1960). On Osborne and on the Vatican's role in helping Jews escape Nazi persecution, see Gordon Thomas, *The Pope's Jews: the Vatican's secret plan to save Jews from the Nazis*, First Edition. ed. (New York: Thomas Dunne Books, 2012).
[24] TNA HS 6/12.
[25] TNA HS 9/1547/3, letter dated 22nd January 1946.
[26] TNA HS 6/12, X/A2 to X dated 14th July 1944, comment by X/Aus and subsequent correspondence. A Force was the organisation tasked both with PoW recovery and deception operations in the Mediterranean theatre. After MI6 had decided after all not to participate, SOE continued sporadic contact with the Baron.
[27] TNA HS 6/12, from Maryland dated 3rd August 1944.
[28] TNA HS 7/14, Activities of X Section in Italy.
[29] TNA HS 6/12, X to X/A2 dated 7th October 1944.
[30] Pollak and his colleagues were also in contact with OSS, and to some extent playing one ally off against the other. TNA HS 6/20, 6th March 1945; Christof Mauch, *The Shadow War against Hitler: the covert operations of America's wartime secret intelligence service* (New York: Columbia University Press, 2003), pp.241-248.
[31] X Section noted in 1945 that 'During the past four or five years there has been a constant ebb and flow amongst the groups representing Austria. Some organisations have completely changed their policy; others their character. The Austrian Centre, for instance, which started as a non-political organisation, has long since been the rallying ground for Communist activities; the Revolutionary Socialists, who were anti-Nazi but pro-*Anschluss*, have now come out strongly in favour of an independent Austria, whilst "Austria House, which at one time was H.Q. for a group of Austrian Social Democrats and others, has ceased to house political groups and become a restaurant'. TNA HS 7/146, *Austrian Emigre Groups in Great Britain*.
[32] TNA HS 9/1094/1 Personal File Theodor Neumann; Eric Sanders, 2008, p.177. Neumann took on the name 'Michael Norman'.
[33] Hatherop Castle (STS 45) was one of SOE's 'Holding Schools', where agents were accommodated pending deployment. It was STS 45 that spearheaded a more dynamic system, beyond simply 'waiting'. Agents accommodated at Holding Schools would attend specialised courses elsewhere but return to the

Holding Schools and consolidate their training in the context of their planned missions. (TNA HS 8/435 *History of the Training Section of SOE* p. 51.)

[34] Here and previous paragraphs: TNA HS 7/146, *Activities of X Section in Italy*; TNA HS 9/1612, Personal File Stefan Wirlandner; IWM Oral History 29954, Eric Sanders, Reel 2; Eric Sanders, 2008, pp.198-201.

[35] *Ibid*, pp.206-7.

[36] TNA HS 7/146, *Activities of X Section in Italy*.

[37] TNA HS 6/20, 18th March 1945.

[38] TNA HS 7/146, *Activities of X Section in Italy*. Michael O'Hara by Eric Sanders, in IWM Personal Papers 14089, Major J H Darton.

[39] TNA HS 9/134/5, Personal File Frederick Berliner (aka Michael O'Hara).

[40] TNA HS 9/134/5, 27th May-1st June 1944. O'Hara was known as '12E15'.

[41] TNA HS 9/134/5, 8th August 1944.

[42] TNA HS 9/134/5, cipher telegram 22nd March 1945.

[43] TNA HS 9/134/5: statement by 1st Lt Melvin H Milbrath, 25th May 1945; No 6 SFSS cipher telegrams 7/10th November 1945; *I Knew O'Hara* by Captain Hillman, in IWM Personal Papers 13326, Major A W Freud; Interrogation report of Candidus Cortolezis; Wolfgang Neugebauer, *Austrian Resistance*, 2014, p.37; Hans Janeschitz, *Felieferhof: ein Bericht über die amtlichen Untersuchungen der Massenmorde in der Schießstätte Felieferhof* (Graz: 1946). Other corroborating Austrian sources are cited in Peter Pirker, *Subversion deutscher Herrschaft*, 2012, p.419.

CHAPTER 9

Final Push

The final campaign

MANY EXECUTIONS LIKE THAT OF MICHAEL O'HARA tragically occurred during the last weeks of the war in Europe. We now know that Adolf Hitler committed suicide on 30th April 1945 and the final surrender document was signed eight days later. Yet Allied commanders, including those responsible for irregular warfare, knew the end was in sight but could not predict when and how it would come.

There was no alternative to fighting on.

The determination of the Nazi regime to resist to the last man, faced with certain defeat, is perhaps difficult to understand. Many factors played their part: the personal authority of Hitler; the repressive and severe security system; the propaganda-fed belief in *Wunderwaffen* that would miraculously turn the war's tide; and, not least, the Allied demand at the January 1943 Casablanca conference for unconditional surrender.

Any thought by German commanders to overthrow Hitler and make peace made no sense in the context of Roosevelt's announcement. Soldiers 'were unable to imagine life beyond the war and the impending German defeat'.[1] With their backs to the wall, the Germans would continue to hold out.[2]

The Normandy landings in June 1944 had launched the Northwest Europe campaign, and the Allies had slogged across the continent against heavy opposition. Setbacks like the December 1944 German counter-attack in the Ardennes—the 'Battle of the Bulge'—had led to a measured and cautious advance. Similarly in Italy, progress had been slow and bloody. However, France and the Low Countries were in Allied hands and the need for active SOE country sections diminished. In a general reorganisation to meet the new situation, X Section—until now a low priority—became a Directorate under Major-General Gerald Templer; 'all our energy and resources must be concentrated on the Reich itself', said the reorganisation report.[3] And that included Austria.

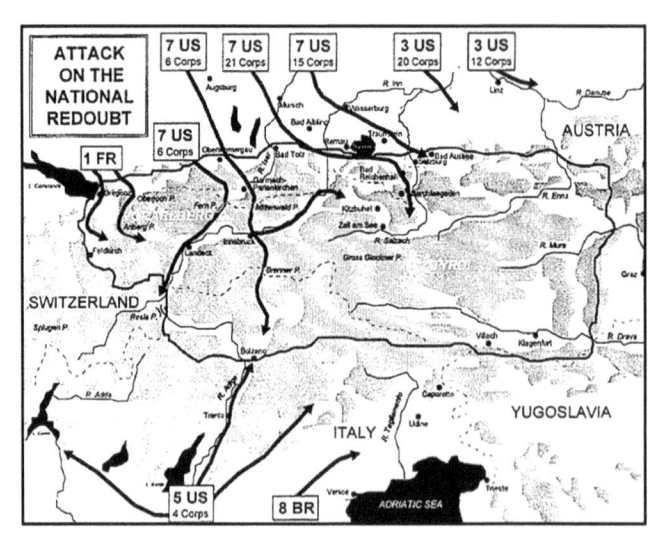

Map of planned attack on the rumoured National Redoubt

Under Operation *Rankin*, the Allies had prepared plans for restoring stability and securing victory under various scenarios of German collapse. Rumours abounded that the hard-core Nazis would retreat to an Alpine redoubt centred on Berchtesgaden. Rather late in the day, planners in London decided that 'operations into the German redoubt area ... should be considered of first class importance'.[4] Apart from their other tasks, Austrian agents sent into their homeland in the final months were ordered to find out all they could about the planned last stand, to 'establish whether a redoubt had been prepared or was already in existence in the Austrian mountains'.⁵ The problem, though, was that training agents and building resistance were slow processes, and there were not enough prepared agents or suitable ways to get them into Austria.

A man of mercurial temperament

Operation *Clowder* had not fulfilled its potential to get agents into Austria through Slovenia. In southern Italy, Jimmy Darton focused on direct parachute drops into Austria. But there was a third option. Even though the war was approaching its end, the Swiss connection was still in play.

Betty Hodgson had fled Switzerland in December 1943, leaving X Section without a representative. Only in August 1944 was she replaced by Squadron Leader Bill Matthey, whose journey to the neutral country had been almost as adventurous as Betty's escape from it. He had flown in an American aircraft with French politicians to Corsica and thence to an airfield in the newly liberated France. Travelling in a car powered by a wood-burner to a town near the Swiss border, he had been taken into Switzerland by mountain guides and a local farmer.

Describing himself as 'built more for comfort than for speed and not being an exactly perfect specimen of physical excellence', Matthey found the journey tough. Interrogation by the Swiss police, though, was polite and gentle. By this stage of the war, the neutral Swiss were much more willing to cooperate with the Allies than before.⁶

Once established in Bern in mid-September 1944, Bill Matthey focused on supporting potential Catholic resistance in the *Reich*. His contacts included priests, an anthropologist from Vienna, an unreliable Austrian sent into Austria by Swiss Intelligence seven or eight times, and a turncoat Nazi secret agent who subsequently found the Americans 'a more fertile field (more naïve, perhaps, and certainly freer with their money)'. But Matthey's 'only productive contact' was a 'man of mercurial temperament': Wilhelm Bruckner, code name *Black*.⁷

Born in Vienna in 1919, Bruckner was a medical student who had escaped to Hungary in 1938, was handed over to the Nazis and fled via Czechoslovakia and Switzerland to France in 1939. He was arrested by Swiss police in 1940 as he and his fiancée tried to return to Switzerland. They stayed in Geneva, but spent over two years under threat of deportation. That came to a sudden end in 1943, when Bruckner started to work with Swiss Intelligence. The robust Swiss neutrality was gradually shifting towards tacit support for resistance movements in the *Reich*. In return, the Swiss demanded intelligence that would help them defend their Alpine 'fortress', particularly if the Nazi collapse were to lead to chaos.[8]

Wilhelm Bruckner was a conservative Austrian nationalist who wanted to see his country liberated and founded an organisation dedicated to that aim: *Patria*. But their purpose was also to reunify the Tyrol as part of Austria. Today's South Tyrol is a partly German-speaking region of Italy (Trentino-Alto Adige), while the northern half, centred on Innsbruck, lies within western Austria. The divided nature of this Alpine region dates back to the dissolution of the Austro-Hungarian Empire in 1919 after the First World War. *Patria*'s ambitious aims were to foment resistance on both sides of the Brenner Pass that separates North from South Tyrol, to sabotage traffic over the Pass and to organise a general uprising when called for by the Allies.

Matthey felt that, if anyone could build up resistance among the Catholics in the Tyrol, this 'serious-minded young man' had the best chance. He promised to provide Bruckner with money, documents, weapons, ammunition, explosives and black propaganda. Matthey knew well that some of this material would go to the Swiss, who were themselves happy to keep quiet about the source of their supplies. Recruits came from the ranks of Austrian refugees who had arrived in Switzerland, and Matthey was willing to support up to ten agents. Further support would depend on demonstrated results.

With the strong support of London and Bruckner's close cooperation with the Swiss authorities—he carried a Military Intelligence identity card—*Patria* made impressive progress from

September 1944 until the accelerating Nazi defeat brought its efforts to a close. They sustained communication in one direction through messages in invisible ink in letters carried across the border, and in the other through coded messages transmitted by the BBC. At first, this did not work, as most radios had been confiscated, so Matthey asked London to send radio receivers too. Agents received little training, but they enjoyed full cooperation from the Swiss authorities until arriving across the border in Austria.

Messages from agents (*Little* and *Mills*) sent to Graz provided some military intelligence but confirmed other reports of the apathy among the population. The report by *Digger*, the agent sent to Innsbruck, was more hopeful, and Bruckner sent him back to the city to organise resistance.

In the South Tyrol, agents *Fortnum* and *Mason* had been able to contact Hans Egarter, who was known as *Barbarossa* and led a resistance group of 600 men in the Bolzano region. Support for this group became a priority. By April 1945, the activities of these and other agents—including *Matthew*, *Mark*, *Luke* and *John*—were building into something significant.[9] But on 8th May the war ended with the German surrender. As Squadron Leader Bill Matthey put it,

> It must always be a matter for regret that *Black* did not get into touch with us a year or more earlier, since there is no doubt that, given a little more time, we might easily have got Barbarossa's lot properly organised and from his group we might have slowly built up a network of smaller efficient groups in Austria. But ... we must content ourselves with the knowledge that there was at least one Austrian who got within measurable distance of effectively resisting the Nazis.[10]

Betrayed

At 1.30 am on 17th February 1945, a farm worker was awakened by knocking at a window and someone calling quietly 'Hallo, hallo!'. She cautiously opened the window, to find a young man in a parachutist's suit standing outside in the snow. 'I am a German soldier', he said. 'I was captured by the British and dropped by them by parachute. I need to report to the nearest police station or *Wehrmacht* unit'.[11]

She awakened the rest of the household and the farmer, Matthias Sattler, told her to let the man in. After they had given him coffee, he stripped off the suit to reveal a German uniform. 'I am Emil Fuchs from Graz', he explained. 'The British captured me and, when I was in the PoW camp, they asked for volunteers to drop into Austria. This was the quickest way for me to get home. I volunteered immediately, but I was determined not to do any spying work for the British. I have served in the SS'. He had dropped with two others, he explained, and gave a detailed description of their appearance and uniforms. They too had dropped near the farm, five miles from the town of Obdach, which was why he had knocked quietly. 'They are now harmless. Without me, they cannot do anything. I am the wireless operator'.

'The snow is too deep', said Herr Sattler, 'to get to the *Gendarmerie* in the town tonight. Sleep here until morning'. He was a Nazi, but not a fanatical one, and he knew the war was lost. He thought that Fuchs might change his mind overnight in order to save his comrades. Next morning, he offered Fuchs the opportunity to escape, by suggesting he go out and look for his parachute and rucksack. Fuchs refused: 'The police will have to come up later and find them for me'.

Thus it was that Farmer Sattler took the parachutist into Obdach and Fuchs told his story, first to the police and then again to the Nazi Party *Kreisleiter*, who had arrived within half an hour. Later the police apprehended two men dressed as German NCOs in the town and brought them to the station. When asked to identify them, Fuchs said nothing but just grinned. 'They still had revolvers', he explained later, 'They might have shot me'.

The two men were Josef Hemetsberger and Hans Prager, and both had been through SOE training in Italy with Emil Fuchs for their mission: Operation *Duval*. All three were 'Bonzos', agents recruited by SOE from amongst enemy PoWs.[12] Often, in Britain, captured *Wehrmacht* soldiers were identified as anti-Nazi during interrogation at Kempton Park and recruited before being registered with the Red Cross as PoWs, in violation of the Geneva Conventions.[13] In the PoW camps in Italy, though, prisoner processing was less formal and SOE had more flexibility. Austrian SOE agents like Theo Neumann would pose as prisoners and look for likely prospects.

Hemetsberger had been born in Graz but his family lived in Krems. Twenty-three years old, he was leader of the *Duval* party. Prager was much younger, still in his teens. Their mission was to travel to the Salzburg area, attempt to contact anti-Nazi elements, and prevent the destruction of important documents at the Gestapo headquarters in Salzburg.[14] Emil Fuchs' action brought it to a premature end. The three had been good friends in the PoW camp and had appeared inseparable during the months of SOE training in Italy.

The Austrian police questioned the three men separately but, to protect Fuchs from suspicion, placed them together in a cell and manacled all three for the journey to prison at Judenburg. The trick was transparent, though, and Hemetsberger quickly accused Fuchs of betrayal. After an all-night interrogation by the *Gestapo*, the three were returned to solitary confinement, but Fuchs was not handcuffed like the others. A few days later, all three were taken to *Gestapo* Headquarters in Vienna, where they were separated. Hemetsberger and Prager were taken to the infamous Mauthausen concentration camp and narrowly escaped execution. They survived the war.

Liberation of Mauthausen concentration camp, 1945

Because of SOE's policy of keeping agents from different countries isolated from each other, the pair probably did not know there were other SOE agents incarcerated with them. Mauthausen was the destination for prisoners from all over Europe; the *Gestapo* had shipped dozens of SOE agents to the camp after their capture.[15] Some had already been executed, but a few, like the two Austrians, were still alive. One was Edward 'Teddy' Zeff, a radio operator who operated in France for a year before being caught in early 1943. Known by his captors to be both a British agent and a Jew, he suffered cruel torture but survived until US forces liberated Mauthausen. A female SOE agent from the Dutch Section, Beatrice Terwind, was a KLM air hostess who was swept up as a result of *Unternehmen Nordpol* (Operation *North Pole*). Called the *Englandspiel* (England Game) by its mastermind, Hermann Giskes, it 'played back' false radio messages and captured dozens of MI6 and SOE agents parachuted into The Netherlands. Beatrix too survived Mauthausen, as did several more French Section agents—John Starr, Brian Stonehouse, Pierre Le Chêne and Bob Sheppard—and Brigadier E F 'Trotsky' Davies, captured in Albania.[16]

Others were less fortunate. Major John Sehmer and Viennese MI6 agent August Warndorfer were captured with Slovakian partisans on SOE/OSS operations and both executed in January 1945 at Mauthausen, where French Section agents Marcus Bloom, Gilbert Norman, Isidore Newman, Sidney Jones and George Clement had been killed the previous September. Arthur de Montalambert of the French Section died there in December. In October 1944 and February 1945 respectively, Belgian SOE agents André Schaepdryver and Valère Stiers were killed at Mauthausen. More shocking still, over forty Dutch agents of SOE's Dutch Section or MI6, mostly captured on landing as victims of the *Englandspiel*, were executed or died in captivity at Mauthausen.[17]

Emil Fuchs stayed in Vienna and later in Salzburg, helping *Gestapo* officer Johann Sanitzer deceive wireless operators at Monopoli. Sanitzer's role was to combat parachuted agents, and he had considerable success in *Funkspiele* (radio games) through violently 'persuading' captured Allied, especially Soviet, agents, to pass fake radio messages.[18] Fortunately, OSS had received an intelligence report in Bern, albeit 'of unknown reliability', that the *Sicherheitsdienst* was working at least three captured British wireless sets, one of which had been 'sent to Salzburg for Austrian resistance'. SOE London immediately instructed the base in Italy: 'If *Duval* makes contact with you, regard him as under enemy control'.[19]

Emil Fuchs was an unexpected gift to Sanitzer. He admitted to Captain Buckingham, who investigated the fate of the *Duval* party in June 1945, that he had operated his radio to Italy for the *Gestapo* but claimed he had only done so because of threats to his family. By the time he arrived in Salzburg, though, he could move about freely in civilian clothes. He fled the approaching Allies in company with *Gestapo* officers, supposedly 'because I wanted to find out where these people were going so that I could inform the Allies'.[20]

Buckingham did not believe a word of it. He was in no doubt that Fuchs had betrayed his comrades. A guilty verdict at trial would have earned the death penalty, but insufficient evidence was found to warrant taking the case forward. Josef Hemetsberger and Hans Prager were fortunate to be freed when US troops liberated Mauthausen, but Operation *Duval* had been doomed from the start.

Solo

Operation *Duval*, like Leo Hillman's *Electra* described in Chapters 1 and 2, was one of a series of direct parachute drops in the last months of the war. Any chance of patiently developing the Austrian will to oppose Nazi domination had passed. These operations would have more immediate priorities: harass the German retreat; incite *Wehrmacht* desertions; assist Allied PoWs if possible; report enemy troop movements; and report any German plans for post-surrender sabotage or guerrilla action.

The main political aim was to 'prepare the way for full implementation of the Moscow Declaration at a later date': in other words, to secure the independence of Austria.[21] As Spring brought improving weather and the collapse of Hitler's regime became more imminent, Jimmy Darton and Betty Hodgson pressed to get the remaining agents into Austria.

Like Michael O'Hara, ex-PoW Roman Haas (real name Roman Spreitzhofer) was a wireless operator on a lone mission: Operation *Eveleth*.[22] He parachuted alone on the night of 24th/25th March 1945, right on target in Styria, about forty miles southwest of Vienna. He found an uninhabited house in which to store his personal equipment, but he buried the container that held his radio. The area was familiar territory for him. Just an hour away in the Mürztal was the home of his sister Hilde, where to her surprise he appeared at 4.00 am. Later that day, she helped him discreetly collect his radio and batteries, hiding them in her home. They hoped that the two small children would not notice the unusual activity and excitedly tell their friends. Roman's brother-in-law brought him up to date on the local situation and put him in touch with opponents of the Nazis, including socialist Leo Geissrucker and a group of railway workers who did minor acts of sabotage.

Roman felt safe in the family environment, but the atmosphere soon heated up. As the Red Army advanced in the first days of April, the Mürztal was flooded with fleeing refugees and retreating German troops. The area was declared a military zone and Roman was in peril. He built a secluded bunker in which he could hide and contact SOE in Italy by radio. He had to rely on his sister for food, as his *Lebensmittelkarten,* the forged ration cards Betty Hodgson had given him, had expired two weeks earlier. With his Resistance contacts, Roman planned to remove demolition charges placed on bridges to slow the Allied advance and to place a bomb in the hotel requisitioned as a Nazi headquarters. But the weather proved too bad for the necessary equipment to be dropped, and the situation was changing daily.

Hilde's husband was called up for the *Volksturm* and ended up in Hungary. She could only visit Roman's hideout when out feeding the goats, as the district was swarming with soldiers. But on 8th May, the Russians finally broke through. Roman hid his wireless set in a disused mine and emerged from hiding. With Geissrucker, Roman formed a group of about twenty reliable people who acted as a local *Sicherheitsdienst*, wearing red/white armbands and attempting to keep the peace. This became more difficult once the Russians had received a vodka ration on 11th May to celebrate VE Day. The soldiers rampaged through the town, raping local women and looting private houses once they had emptied the shops. Women and girls who could get away fled.

When the vodka ran out, a semblance of discipline returned. Roman and his comrades had ousted the Nazi *Ortsgruppenleiter*—equivalent to Mayor—and reinstalled the pre-1934 *Bürgermeister*. The Russians used him as a point of contact and the armbanded Austrians were able to restore some kind of order.

Mountain Jump

In the early hours of 9th April 1945, a four-man team parachuted 'blind' into the moonlit Höllengebirge mountains of the Salzkammergut and landed in deep snow. This was Operation *Ebensburg*.[23] There was no reception party. The men quickly realised that they were some distance from their expected landing point near Bad Aussee.

More critically, they were separated from the four containers holding their equipment, which had been dropped minutes after they had jumped from Halifax 'Tango' of the RAF's 148 Squadron. The duty of the tail-gunner, Flight Sergeant Charlie Leslie, when not defending the aircraft and its twelve—later eight—'souls on board', was to report safe despatch of 'Joes' and packages to the pilot, Flying Officer Bill Leckie.[24] He had done so, and after landing Leckie gave the report familiar to all RAF aircrew: 'DCO', Duty Carried Out. There had been plenty of 'DNCOs'.

The containers were buried in snow, though, and the four men could only locate one of them. Relieved, they saw it was the container with the essential radio equipment with which they would be able to contact the SOE base in Italy. But on closer inspection they realised it was damaged beyond repair. The four men scrambled down the mountainside. Their names were Albrecht Gaiswinkler, Karl

Standhartinger, Karl Lzicar and Josef Grafl. They were all former PoWs: 'Bonzos'.

Hailing from Bad Aussee, Albrecht Gaiswinkler had a long history of fighting the Austrian and German Nazis, both before and after the *Anschluss*. A social democrat, he had been a political prisoner in 1934. In 1940 he helped to found the 'Aussee Group', which drew together a politically disparate range of opponents of Hitler in the heart of the Austrian Alps, the area the Allies expected to be the Nazis' final redoubt.[25]

However, he had been conscripted into the *Wehrmacht* and in August 1944 he was serving in a clerical job in Paris. The Allies had landed in Normandy in June and Gaiswinkler saw an opportunity. While in Brittany with a convoy of four trucks carrying munitions, he deliberately prepared engine trouble. With the help of the town mayor and local Frenchmen, the escort of fourteen German soldiers were driven off and Gaiswinkler went over to the Resistance with 'his' trucks. Six weeks later, he surrendered to American troops at Dinant.[26]

The Austrian Section had been struggling for over three years to find reliable information about and contact with active anti-Nazi groups in Austria. Despite the hopeful promises of the expatriate socialists and conservatives, they had had little success. The arrival on the scene of a man who had formed and led such a group was a welcome gift. And he had military training. Evelyn Stamper and Clara Holmes were on the lookout for just this kind of experienced 'Bonzo'.

Albrecht Gaiswinkler started SOE training. His wife and two children were still in Graz. Only a few months short of his fortieth birthday, Gaiswinkler did not have the physical fitness of younger soldiers. He had brown hair, 'thin on top', but was 'well built' and just short of six feet in height. His shooting improved once prescription glasses had been ordered and arrived. But he was 'probably well suited to be a leader as a result of his maturity and background', even if 'argumentative' and 'a little bossy with the other members of his group'. He became the leader of the 'willing and cheerful crew' whose task was Operation *Ebensburg*.[27]

Return to Vienna

Two of Gaiswinkler's comrades had also been extracted from the flow of *Wehrmacht* PoWs arriving in Britain. Karl Standhartinger, a 23-year-old machinist from Vienna, had been captured by Canadian forces twenty-five kilometres south of Rouen in Normandy. With blue eyes and light brown hair, he was of average height and slightly built. He had seen service in Russia, Belgium and France, including operating anti-aircraft guns, and 'disliked the Nazi regime intensely'. Like Albrecht Gaiswinkler, he was taken to SOE's Special Training School No 2 at Bellasis House near Dorking for assessment and interview, and was one of the few ex-PoWs selected for training at STS 5, Wanborough Manor. Karl Standhartinger joined Gaiswinkler at Wanborough and proved himself 'quite a smart fellow' who took things in quickly. He was a good shot, scoring highest of the group when firing pistol, sten and bren gun. As importantly, even though not brilliant he had 'all the Austrian virtues' and was 'pleasant and cheerful', never losing his temper.[28]

The third member of the *Ebensburg* group had also been born and raised in Vienna. Both of 27-year-old Karl Lzicar's parents had died. Short and stockily built with brown curly hair, he was 'fit, athletic and a keen triesr'. He had served in the pre-*Anschluss* Austrian Army and, between two periods in Hitler's army, he had spent four months in prison for distributing social democratic leaflets. During his *Wehrmacht* service, he had worked as a dispatch rider in Czechoslovakia, Russia and France. His fair knowledge of French and his solo travel through the countryside were advantages when he changed sides. He joined the French *Maquis* on 1st June 1944 and worked with them at Rouen until September, when he gave himself up to the Allies. In training, he was an accurate shot, but 'was inclined to be careless at first' with demolitions, a trait that was quickly addressed. He needed a strong leader, as he was 'inclined to be hot-tempered'.[29]

The wireless operator made up the four-man team. But the man being trained in Britain for the role, a miner from Graz named Sommer, had medical problems and was not deployed to Italy.[30] Betty Hodgson had just a few hours to find a local replacement. To make things worse, the request came as *Maryland* was moving forward to Siena. Jimmy Darton had already moved, but the RAF had decided not to move north from Brindisi, so Betty stayed behind at Monopoli. She would see off the operations for the current 'moon' and then follow. She was not looking forward to Siena—packed into one building with all the other special operators—but hoped that X Section would soon move into 'the promised land': Austria.

To replace the missing 'W/Op', Betty lighted on Josef Grafl, a trained Austrian wireless operator who appears to have been recruited by SOE from a PoW camp in Egypt in December 1944 and brought to Italy in January 1945.[31] She was able to equip him with a complete *Wehrmacht* uniform except for a belt, which she acquired by visiting a local PoW camp with a packet of cigarettes as payment. The *Ebensburg* group was ready for deployment and boarded Halifax 'Tango' just before midnight on 8th April 1945.

Operation Ebensburg

Landing by parachute at night in enemy territory is a daunting prospect, even on a prepared site where a reception party is waiting to whisk agents away. Landing on a desolate snow-covered mountainside, miles from where you expected to be, is an order of magnitude more challenging. Losing most of your equipment does not help.

Albrecht Gaiswinkler and his three companions took stock and struggled downhill through snow reaching up to their armpits, avoiding farm tracks where SS search parties might find them. They reached the railway station at Ebensee and quietly took a local train to Bad Aussee, their destination, jumping off the train just before reaching the town. There they established hiding places in the forest and cautiously contacted the disparate and disunited local resistance groups. Albrecht Gaiswinkler's family brought food to the hut where the group was hiding during the day. Gaiswinkler could visit his father's house in the hours of darkness and hold meetings with resistance leaders. Gradually, the groups started to work together, eventually forming a force of about three hundred guerrilla fighters to harass the retreating German troops. Operation *Ebensburg*'s mission was to carry out local sabotage and form the nucleus of an armed resistance force.[32]

In this, Albrecht Gaiswinkler and his comrades succeeded. According to a later report, not necessarily objective, on 'the part played by local resistance groups in hastening the end of Nazi rule in Austria', some twenty assorted resistance groups—Communist, socialist, Christian social, monarchist—had been working independently in the Bad Aussee area. Within three weeks, Gaiswinkler collected together 'a well-armed and well-organised band of 360 men'. Amid the confusion of early May 1945, as the Nazi regime was collapsing but before Allied troops had moved in, this group 'seized and imprisoned all the leading Gestapo, SD and Party officials in the district and took over control of the local *Gendarmerie*'.

The Bad Aussee guerrillas were also able to 'hasten the end of that part of the German 6th Army in the Bad Aussee area'. Apart from 'the usual tactics of attacking convoys and railways', they did this mostly by infiltrating Army and SS formations disguised as officers and spreading alarm and confusion by 'issuing as many conflicting orders as they could think of'. Even though a small area, the Ausseerland was at the heart of the 'Nazi Redoubt' and was the hideout of one of the most influential and brutal Nazis, Ernst Kaltenbrunner. Later, Albrecht Gaiswinkler's local intelligence laid the groundwork for the capture of Kaltenbrunner and other senior Nazis by the Americans.[33]

The partisans also secured two armoured personnel carriers 'by every conceivable ruse' from the German 6th Army and festooned them with red and white Austrian colours. They were 'the only Austrian Resistance Group to possess any armour'.

Not as spectacular but just as valuable was the partisans' seizure of 'prominent Nazis and other arrestable persons (who might have escaped in the confusion of the general collapse)'. They replaced all undesirable local civil servants and police officials, so that the Allies arrived to find a 'more or less ordered community'. When the Americans marched in, 'not a single house, bridge or street in Ausseerland was blown up and not a single shot was fired'. As to denazification, according to the Bad Aussee report 'there was not a single *Bürgermeister* or police official left who was not, and who had not always been, a true Austrian.[34] 'Nowhere in Austria can Military Government have been presented with an easier task': arriving American commanders appreciated the ease with which they could take over, and appointed Albrecht Gaiswinkler *Bezirkshauptmann*.

The seeds of debate and controversy over the extent of Austrian resistance to Nazi rule, which have endured during subsequent decades, emerge here. However, the *Ebensburg* story is thus far relatively clear and uncontroversial. Where it becomes difficult to disentangle fact from contested myth is in the history of the rescued art treasures.[35]

Four kilometres above the spa town of Bad Aussee, up a winding road bordered by fields of mountain flowers, the village of Alt Aussee lies on the western shore of a deep and cold lake. In 1942, the nearby salt mines provided the perfect temperature and humidity to store precious works of art from Viennese museums and protect them from Allied bombing. Progressively, the range of artworks stored in the mines expanded to include masterpieces looted from all over Europe, or 'purchased' from their Jewish owners.[36]

Adolf Hitler inspecting works of art

The number of items and the total value were huge, representing plunder amassed over the years of conquest. Adolf Hitler's dream was to build a monumental *Führermuseum* in his hometown Linz, according to his personal taste.

Back in the summer of 1939, Martin Bormann reported to Vienna the *Führer*'s instruction that both safeguarded and confiscated works of art would be 'available for his disposition'. This order referred to plunder in Austria following the *Anschluss*, but was extended in 1940 to 'territories occupied by German troops', in other words throughout Europe. Castles in Hungary, chateaus in France were stripped bare. In the twelve months to 31st March 1944, for instance, 881 paintings were 'purchased' for the proposed Linz museum, more than half of them representing the Netherlandish School.[37] Much of the booty taken from European museums, galleries and private collections arrived in crates at the Alt Aussee salt mines. Captured German records revealed that Alt Aussee housed '6,577 paintings; 230 drawings and watercolors; 954 prints; 137 pieces of sculpture; 128 pieces of arms and armor; 79 baskets of objects; 484 cases of unknown objects presumed to be archives; 78 pieces of furniture; 122 tapestries; 181 cases of books; 1,200 to 1,700 cases apparently containing books or similar matter; and 283 cases, the contents of which were entirely unknown'.[38]

*Ghent Altarpiece, **The Adoration of the Mystic Lamb**, 1432*

The claim, later mythologised, that the Paris Louvre's *Mona Lisa* had been in the mine was groundless. But works of inestimable value were there. Among them was the giant altarpiece removed from the Cathedral of St. Bavo in the Belgian city of Ghent: *The Adoration of the Mystic Lamb*. The altarpiece, a 'polyptych', had been completed by Flemish artists Jan and Hubert Van Eyck in 1432. Parts of it had suffered damage in a roundabout journey from Ghent via a chateau in Pau in southern France and the Neuschwanstein castle in Bavaria, before being brought to Alt Aussee in late 1944 to keep it out of Allied hands. Equally significant was the sculpture of the *Madonna and Child* created by Michelangelo in 1501 and taken from Bruges, but these two works of art are merely the highlights of a massive hoard. All of these were destined for destruction.

Adolf Hitler's 'Nero Decree' of 19th March 1945 ordered a 'scorched earth' policy: the entire infrastructure of the *Reich* was to be kept from the Allies through destruction, together with other 'objects of value'. This included the precious contents of the Alt Aussee salt mines.[39]

The Allies recognised the danger. SOE's American partner, the OSS, formed the 'Art Looting Investigation Unit', better known from the 2014 film starring George Clooney as *The Monuments Men*. At first a tiny unit, the ALIU was reinforced after the end of hostilities by fine art experts drawn from other Allied countries. They converged on Bad Aussee, where the ALIU established an interrogation centre and questioned Germans or Austrians who had been involved in the campaign of plunder.[40] The ALIU had searched out dozens of Nazi art repositories. But Lieutenant George Stout—the basis for Clooney's character in the film—said that Alt Aussee contained 'the very cream of the 'loot' from France, Belgium and the Netherlands'.[41]

The Nazis' intention to destroy the thousands of works of art was serious. August Eigruber, the Nazi *Gauleiter* of the Oberdonau district of Austria, mirrored the *Führer*'s wishes and ordered the destruction of the Alt Aussee hoard.[42] Under Eigruber's instructions, SS troops escorted a convoy carrying six large crates to the mine and guarded the entrance while men wheeled the crates along the narrow-gauge track deep into the mine. The miners discovered each crate contained an unexploded 500-pound bomb. Positioned at strategic locations, the bombs would damage the stored art and finish the job by destroying the pumps that prevented the mine's chambers from flooding.[43] Not least to protect their livelihood, the miners helped Professor Hermann Michel, a Communist art historian who had been working in the mine, to relocate the most important pieces. Subsequently, they appear to have removed the six bombs and sealed the mine entrances through controlled explosions.

How much of a role did the SOE team, and Albrecht Gaiswinkler in particular, play in saving thousands of works of art for posterity? Probably less than he later claimed, but more than his detractors asserted. Gaiswinkler's reputation became a major issue in post-war Austrian politics, particularly after he was elected to the Austrian parliament. Nevertheless, his small group of partisans were in full control of the region and were able to protect the mine from further Nazi attempts to destroy its contents. As importantly, when the Americans arrived, they recognised Albrecht Gaiswinkler as the key individual in preventing unnecessary destruction and bloodshed in the Aussee area. SOE later described the *Ebensburg* mission as 'an excellent example of an eleventh-hour rising and the only case of successful and highly organised resistance in Austria'.[44]

---

[1] Nicholas Stargardt, *The German War: a nation under arms, 1939-45* (London: The Bodley Head, 2015), p.540. On Nazi intransigence, see Antony Beevor, 2012, pp.716-756 and David Stafford, *Endgame 1945: victory, retribution, liberation* (London: Little, Brown, 2007).

[2] On opposition to Hitler, see Paddy Ashdown, 2018, on opportunities for peace Richard Lamb, 1987, on Casablanca Antony Beevor, 2012, p.404.

[3] W J M Mackenzie, 2000, p.709. Like other last-minute reorganisations, such as the formation of the *Etat-major des Forces Françaises de l'Interieur* on 1st July 1944 (see Peter Dixon, *Setting the Med Ablaze*, 2020, p.222), this one led to the assignment of officers who had not been involved in previous work. Misunderstandings and tense relationships resulted, e.g. when Italy did not inform London of Michael O'Hara's alias (TNA HS 6/22, 11th May 1945).

[4] TNA HS 6/20, 27th March 2022.

[5] Fred Warner, 1985.

[6] W J M Mackenzie, 2000, p.687; TNA HS 7/146, *Switzerland*.
[7] TNA HS 7/146, *General History from September 1944 to July 1945* and *History of Black's Activities*.
[8] TNA HS 9/225/2, Personal File Wilhelm Bruckner; Gerald Steinacher, 2001.
[9] They included Josef Ploder (Little), Franz Kummer (Mills), Karl Bitschnau (Digger), Johann Pircher (Mason), Albert Matt (Matthew), Eugen Cia (Mark), (TNA HS 6/21, 28th April 1945).
[10] TNA HS 7/146, *History of Black's Activities*.
[11] This narrative of Operation *Duval* is based on the subsequent investigation by Captain Buckingham, substantiated by interviews of those involved. Emil Fuchs himself told a different story (TNA HS 8/884, 22nd and 24th June 1945; HS 6/22, 6th June 1945). Dr Peter Pirker has added further detail, particularly on the post-war fates of members of the Duval party, in Peter Pirker, 'Tomorrow John Kitterer will play: the SOE Operation *Duval* and the Mauthausen Survivors Josef Hemetsberger and Hans Prager,' in *Who resisted? Biographies of Resistance Fighters from entire Europe in the Mauthausen Concentration Camp and Lectures from the International Conference 2008*, ed. Andreas Baumgartner et al. (Vienna: Edition Mauthausen, 2008).
[12] On Bonzos see Peter Dixon, *Guardians*, 2018, pp.168-169.
[13] TNA HS 8/883-4.
[14] TNA HS 6/19, 30th December 1944, List of Austrians in Italy.
[15] Alexander Prenninger et al., *Deportiert nach Mauthausen*, Europa in Mauthausen / Band 2 (Wien Köln Weimar: Böhlau Verlag, 2021).
[16] M R D Foot, *SOE 1940-1946*, 2014, pp.146, 195, 279; M R D Foot, *SOE in France: an account of the work of the British Special Operations Executive in France 1940-1944*, HMSO, 2006), p.193. Davies persuaded the Commandant of Mauthausen that he was a regular soldier and six months senior to him. He was sent to the Colditz PoW camp.
[17] The following list of the Dutch agents who died may be incomplete: Aart Alblas, Leonardus Andringa, Pieter Arendse, Arnoldus Baatsen, Karel Beukema toe Water, Mink Bloome, Pieter Boogaart, Cornelis Braggaar, Johannes Buizer, Jozef Bukkens, Johannes Cornelis, Johannes Dane, Oskar De Brey, Johannes De Haas, Arie De Kruyff, Cornelis Drooglever-Fortuijn, Jan Emmer, Cornelius Fortuyn, Jan Hofstede, George Jambroes, Roelof Jongelie, Hendrick Jordaan, Peter Kamphorst, Barend Kloos, Meindert Koolstra, Anton Mink, Willem Niermeijer, Herman Overes, Michiel Pals, Laurentius Punt, Evert Radema, Gozewin Ras, George Ruseler, Andre Schaepdrijvn, Hendrik Sebes, Horst Steeksma, Horst Straatsma, Thijs Taconis, Hermanus Ter Laak, Klaas Van De Bor, and cousins Pieter and Willem Van Der Wilden. In addition, Czech agents Jindrich Coupek, and Oldrich Pechel, Slovakian interpreter Margita Kockova, and Romanian paratrooper Aba Bardicev were executed at Mauthausen. At Mauthausen's satellite concentration camp Ebensee, French Section agent Marcel Clech was killed. I am grateful to Paul

McCue of the Secret World War 2 Learning Network, Dr Steven Kippax and Fred Judge for this information, but I take responsibility for any errors.

[18] Wolfgang Neugebauer, *Austrian Resistance*, 2014, p.39; TNA KV 2/2656, *Interrogation of Johann Sanitzer*. Sanitzer mentions Fuchs only briefly in his interrogation, giving more detail on the other British case, an MI6 agent parachuted into Styria. He focused mainly on 'playing back' Soviet wireless operators. The best-known and most successful *Funkspiel* was *Unternehmen Nordpol* (Operation North Pole) in the Netherlands, also known as the *Englandspiel* (England Game) which led to the arrest and execution of dozens of MI6 and SOE agents (Hans Schafranek, 'Unternehmen 'Nordpol': das 'Englandspiel' der deutschen militärischen Abwehr in den Jahren 1942-1944,' in *Krieg im Äther: Widerstand und Spionage im Zweiten Weltkrieg*, ed. Hans Schafranek and Johannes Tuchel (Vienna: Picus Verlag, 2004).

[19] TNA HS 6/20, 28th March 1945.

[20] TNA HS 8/884, 22nd June 1945.

[21] TNA HS 6/21, 16th April 1945, Operation Order Duncery.

[22] TNA HS 7/146, *History of 'Clowder' Mission*, Appendix H, *The Story of Operation EVELETH*; HS 6/22, 14th May 1945, *Agents in Field*.

[23] Details of the *Ebensburg* mission are primarily from TNA HS 7/146, German Section History, HS 9/553/3 Personal File Albrecht Gaiswinkler, HS 9/953/10 Personal File Karl Lzicar, and HS 9/1404/3 Personal File Karl Standhartinger. Also, Bernard O'Connor, *Operation Ebensburg: SOE's Austrian 'Bonzos' and the rescue of looted European art* (2018) is a comprehensive study of the operation and the team leader wrote a memoir, Albrecht Gaiswinkler, *Sprung in die Freiheit* (Salzburg: 1947), whose claims have been questioned.

[24] TNA AIR/27/996/32, Operations Record Book, No 148 Sqn, 8th-9th April 1945, Op *Edensburg* (sic).

[25] Peter Pirker, *Subversion deutscher Herrschaft*, 2012, pp.242-3.

[26] As recounted by Gaiswinkler to Sergeant Hartog at SOE's Special Training School No 5 (TNA HS 9/553/3).

[27] TNA HS 9/553/3, *Training Notes*.

[28] TNA HS 9/1404/3, *Training Notes*.

[29] TNA HS 9/953/10, *Training Notes*.

[30] TNA HS 8/883.

[31] TNA HS 6/20, 25th March 1945. In various post-war interviews, Grafl described a more adventurous anti-Nazi career starting in 1941, including partisan operations in the Far East and Greece, RAF pilot training and operational flying. None of this is supported by evidence. See Peter Pirker, *Subversion deutscher Herrschaft*, 2012, pp.239-240.

[32] TNA HS 6/22, 9th June 1945, *Bonzo Operations into Austria from Italy*.

[33] Kaltenbrunner, head of the Austrian SS, was appointed State Secretary for Security by Hitler in 1938 (Richard Evans, *The Third Reich in Power* (London: Penguin, 2012), pp.656, 660. His capture in a mountain chalet near Bad Aussee is described by Robert Matteson in an oral history interview at

https://collections.ushmm.org (Catalog 512456) and in *The Last Days of Ernst Kaltenbrunner*, released by the CIA on 22nd September 1993 (https://www.memoiresdeguerre.com). Kaltenbrunner was tried at Nuremberg trials and hanged in October 1946.

[34] TNA HS 7/146, *Extract from a Report by GSI, British Troops Austria*, citing a report submitted by the *Bürgermeister* of Bad Aussee to the *Landeshauptmann* of Upper Austria. The report was recognised as 'clearly that of an interested party, but from what we know of the general context of the facts given, there is no reason to suppose that the picture they present is over-drawn'. Other quotes are from HS 7/146, *History of 'Clowder' Mission*, Sheets 20-21.

[35] Gaiswinkler's autobiography (Albrecht Gaiswinkler, 1947) is described as 'pure fiction' in a short film about him that asks whether he was a hero or an impostor (Daniel Bernhardt et al, 'Albrecht Gaiswinkler: Held oder Hochstapler,' (Austria: 2009). A positive view of his role is taken in Charles de Jaeger, *The Linz File: Hitler's plunder of Europe's art* (Exeter: Webb & Bower, 1981) and Peter Harclerode and Brendan Pittaway, *The Lost Masters: the looting of Europe's treasurehouses* (London: Gollancz, 1999), while Dr Peter Pirker gives a balanced analysis in Peter Pirker, *Subversion deutscher Herrschaft*, 2012, pp.446-453, 487-490.

[36] Primary responsibility for locating and securing fine art rested with the Einsatzstab Reichsleiter Rosenberg. The mine was said to have been worked for 3,000 years and had a continuous history of operation from 1300 AD (TNA T 209/20/4, 12th Army Group Report, 10th July 1945). Charles de Jaeger, 1981 and Peter Harclerode and Brendan Pittaway, 1999 tell the story of plundered art and include material on Operation Ebensburg gained from interviews with some of the participants. They are used in this chapter selectively, especially as the latter makes some assertions that are not supported from primary sources.

[37] TNA T 209/29/16, Bormann letter 24th July 1939, Lammers letter 18th November 1940 (contemporary translations).

[38] TNA T 209/20/4, 12th Army Group Report, 10th July 1945.

[39] https://ghdi.ghi-dc.org. Also Volker Ullrich, *Hitler: Volume II, Downfall 1939-45* (London: The Bodley Head, 2020), p.558.

[40] Gregory Bradsher, 'The Monuments Men in August 1945: The Belgian Treasures', 2015, US National Archives. Also https://text-message.blogs.archives.gov/2015/10/15/monuments-men-august-1945/ (accessed 12 September 2022). The ALIU operated under the umbrella of the Monuments, Fine Arts and Archives (MFA&A) programme.

[41] T/209/20/4, HQ 12th Army Group report, 10th July 1945.

[42] ALIU, *Art Looting Investigation Unit Final Report* (Washington DC: Office of the Assistant Secretary of War, 1st May 1946).

[43] Johann Linortner, *Die Kunstgüter im Altausseer Salzberg 1943-1945* (Bad Aussee: Salinen, 1998), cited in Harclerode and Pittaway, 1999, p.108.

[44] TNA HS 7/146, *History of 'Clowder' Mission*, Sheet 20.

CHAPTER 10

Endgame

Coups de Main

WHEN X SECTION'S ITALY CONTINGENT WAS ORDERED in March 1945 to up sticks and move to Siena, Betty Hodgson remained behind in Monopoli to despatch Operations *Electra, Eveleth* and *Ebensburg*.[1] That done, she joined Jimmy Darton in Siena in early April to send in any remaining agents who had reached the necessary level of training. These para-military groups dropped in British uniform and had straightforward if rather vague objectives: to hasten the defeat of the *Wehrmacht* by disrupting communications on the line of retreat and to prevent destruction of infrastructure: 'counter-scorch'.[2]

The first group comprised just two men: 'Charles' Kaiser and 'Harry Williams'. Their mission, Operation *Hamster,* was to disrupt Bruck-Graz and Bruck-Leoben road and rail communications and 'to cause as much confusion as possible'.[3]

The Vienna-born Kaiser had kept his original identity, changing only 'Carl' to 'Charles'. He was a skilled linguist, speaking fluent French and Italian as well as his native German, and had served as an interpreter before enlisting in the Austrian Army. MI5 had screened him in late 1943 at its interrogation centres for 'enemy aliens', the Oratory School in Kensington and the Royal Victoria Patriotic School in Wandsworth, southwest London.[4] There his sincerity and the enormous bulk of documentary evidence in his possession convinced the interrogators that he was 'perfectly genuine in his desire to take up arms against the enemy'.

Charles Kaiser

Both his parents were Jewish, but he had been baptised Roman Catholic. He had taken part in the Vienna uprisings in 1934 and had served as an officer in the *Freiwillige Schutzkorps* until it was merged into the German *Wehrmacht*, where his Jewish parentage would have been disadvantageous. Hoping to emigrate to the USA, he had worked in Italy until receiving a US visa. En route in France, though, he was arrested and interned as an enemy alien. After five months, he obtained release by agreeing to serve in the French Army. He did so for a while, was discharged after France capitulated to Germany and worked as an agricultural labourer in southern France. On 11th November 1942, Germany occupied Vichy France. Although he described his politics as 'Imperialist Democrat', Carl's Jewish origins made him vulnerable if discovered. Carl made his escape into Spain with the help of Catholic priests. The Spanish police threatened to send him back but at the same time asked if he needed to change some money. He took the hint and handed over 2,000 Francs, accepted by the policeman in exchange for advice on the best route to take. After being again captured and having participated in a hunger strike with other internees, he was handed over to the British and reached Gibraltar.[5]

Carl's comrade Harry had changed his surname from 'Wunder' to Williams. Of average height and heavy, but physically fit and 'well-proportioned', he had brown hair and a dark complexion. Harry had been born in Vienna on 21st May 1924 to an Austrian mother and a Polish Jewish father, Isaak. The family escaped to Belgium in 1938, when Harry was fourteen years old, but the Nazis caught up with them there.

Isaak was deported to Poland. Harry believed that his mother Helene and his sister Cecilia had also later been deported. Harry had escaped from Belgium in August 1942, but did not arrive in Britain until October 1943, after spending time in French and Spanish prisons. In December, like many of his comrades, he was recruited by SOE from the Pioneer Corps. Younger than most of the other trainees and with a 'cunning quick-thinking brain', he was 'the most outspoken of the Austrian group' and had little time for 'the Berliners'. His casual attitude to security gave the trainers some doubts, but an interview in London cleared him for operations in the field. After training, Harry arrived in Italy from the Middle East in mid-1944.[6]

Charles Kaiser and Harry Williams parachuted 'blind' an hour after midnight on 21st April 1945, on target, in Styria about 30 miles northwest of Graz. One leg bag was too heavy and the rope broke, sending the bag hurtling into the darkness. A three-hour search, made cautiously near to the Rossbach barracks, yielded nothing. After hiding in woods during daylight, they made their way by night to a mountain hut, where they joined forces with an Austrian deserter named Hofer and made the hut their base. Although they were snowbound for several days, they were able to return to their drop zone and recover storage containers with some of their weapons, despite coming across a German platoon.

Progressively, they used local contacts to build up their small party from three to twenty, including *Luftwaffe* deserters. At midnight on 4th May in the town of Glein, Carl Kaiser secretly met representatives of 150 Hungarian Air Force personnel from the Zeltweg airfield. The Hungarian pilots had been forbidden to fly, because some had defected with their aircraft to Italy. Kaiser asked them to disarm the land mines on the airfield and try to contact Austrian officers who could take over the airfield and hand it over to the approaching Allies. These were the last days and even hours of the war in Europe, but the end was chaotic.

Hearing from the BBC on 7th May that the armistice would come in 'a matter of hours', Kaiser, Williams and their twenty men moved openly from their hideout into Glein. On the morning of 8th May, they marched into the town of Knittelfeld, where they were joined by a further 100 fighters from the suddenly emerging local underground. They obtained weapons from the police, who joined them, and a small troop of Germans agreed to withdraw. That afternoon, Williams worked on preventing demolitions and arrested the Nazi *Bürgermeister* and several suspected war criminals. Kaiser and his small force marched to Zeltweg airfield. The airfield was an important facility, not least because the Allies wanted to evacuate British and American PoWs from a nearby camp at Wolfsberg.

Joining forces

Meanwhile, another two paramilitary groups had dropped in the early hours of 25th April near the town of Judenburg. George Bryant (a Viennese lawyer whose real name was Georg Breuer), Frank Kelley (Franz König, a German wireless operator), Eric Rhodes (Erich Rohde, from Hamburg) and Fred Warner (Manfred Werner, another Hamburger) made up the Operation *Historian* team.[7] They too were to disrupt communications, but also to provide intelligence on military movements in the Judenburg area and on Slovenian activity. But in 'collapse or surrender conditions', they were to proceed to Zeltweg airfield and report on its condition.

Harry Stevens (Hans Schweiger, a middle-aged Austrian lawyer who had joined SOE from the Pioneer Corps) and Anton Walter Freud were the Operation *Duncery* team. They had more specific instructions regarding Zeltweg: to proceed there and 'make every effort to maintain Zeltweg airfield intact'.[8]

Their drop did not go as well as *Hamster*'s. The Liberator aircraft, flying at a height of 8,000 feet rather than the normal 1,000 feet because of nearby mountains, deposited them ten miles from the planned drop zone. They made a soft landing in a field in bright moonlight. Dismayed, they watched their explosives, food, clothing and wireless set descend into the middle of a village 300 yards away. Worse still, they lost touch with each other.

Stevens landed within a few yards of Bryant, and they spotted a parachute descending close to the village after the Liberator's second run. This turned out to be Kelley. Rhodes too appeared, reporting that he had landed in a back garden. The four moved off, but Warner and Freud were missing.

Heading for the prearranged emergency rendezvous in the mountains, the group met no activity on the way. The local German contingent did not stir from the town, but to cover their backs reported 'heavy fighting with parachutists'. The SOE party, lacking most of their equipment and their means of contacting their base, decided that the depleted *Historian* and *Duncery* should join forces. They agreed that their main priority should be the counter-scorch operations at Zeltweg. George Bryant took charge as the four set off by night for the airfield. One of their two missing comrades had beaten them to it.

Freud

That missing member of the *Historian/Duncery* party was Lieutenant Anton Walter Freud, who had refused the offer to anglicise his name and insisted on keeping his proud family identity. The grandson of pioneering psychoanalyst Sigmund Freud, he wanted Austria to know when the time came that a Freud was returning.[9] Walter had lived with his parents and sister in a spacious apartment. They had two servants and a nanny but could not afford to run a car. Walter moved entirely in Jewish circles, within a 'village' in central Vienna that could be crossed on foot in twenty minutes. Even his grandfather Sigmund's circle of friends and colleagues was Jewish, except for foreign professional contacts like Carl Jung. Walter was seventeen years old when the family fled the country.

Walter Freud's war had not started well. As a Jewish refugee from the Nazi *Reich*, he might have expected some sympathy in England. At first it was so. But when war came, Britain did not recognise Austria as separate from Germany. After all, the Austrians had welcomed the *Anschluss*, hadn't they? Walter was simply an enemy alien. As he put it, in the early stages of the war 'the English were quite extraordinarily blind in recognising their most ardent supporters'. Paranoia about German spies abounded.

Anton Walter Freud

Walter was sitting a mathematics exam at Loughborough College on 28th June 1940 when the police came for him. After a few nights in a dark, dirty police cell, he was taken to York Racecourse, where hundreds like him were living under canvas. A few days later, he was shipped to the Isle of Man and then to Liverpool, where he joined about 2,500 other internees in the cargo hold of the Hired Military Transport *Dunera*, guarded by hostile, suspicious and often cruel guards. For the nine-week journey to Sydney, it was hell on the ocean.[10]

Walter recognised, though, that Jews would have faced a worse fate if Hitler's plan to invade Britain or to install a puppet government had succeeded. In Australia, he was safe. To arrive by train at the internment camp at Hay, New South Wales, about 450 miles west of Sydney, was a relief. The hutted camp was reasonably comfortable, the Australian Army guards were rarely seen, and the food was good. Prisoners organised the camp. The predominantly well-educated Jews set up classes in every subject imaginable. Walter doubted whether 'there was another institution of such learning in all of Australia'.

In June 1941, Hitler turned his attention to the East and invaded Russia: Operation *Barbarossa*. At the same time, President Roosevelt was progressively preparing for war and easing American public opinion and Congress towards support for Britain and the Soviet Union. Effectively, he was waging undeclared hostilities against Germany, Italy and Japan. The Japanese attack on Pearl Harbor in December 1941, together with Hitler's declaration of war against the USA, gave him the trigger he needed to take the USA to war.[11] Britain's fear of invasion and of the threat from 'enemy aliens' subsided.

Winston Churchill, among others, recognised that the 'collar the lot' internment policy had been a major error. A Jewish British officer, Captain Julian Layton, came to Australia to 'sort the sheep from the goats' and seek volunteers for the Pioneer Corps. Walter was 'the most sheepy of the sheep and the very first person to be declared *persona grata*'. He signed up, returned to Britain in the SS *Glenifer* and joined the Pioneer Corps at Ilfracombe, learning military discipline, suffering what today would be called scams from crooked instructors and 'saluting everything in uniform, such as postmen and Land Army girls'. After Pioneer service, building Nissen huts for the expected American GIs and working in an ordnance depot, he was approached by an SOE recruiter. Without shedding many tears, he left behind the pick-and-shovel cap badge of the Pioneer Corps and entered SOE training in January 1943.

Walter's initial training and selection, at Special Training School No 3, Stodham Park near Liss in Hampshire and at STS 1, Brock Hall in Northamptonshire, followed the normal pattern of physical fitness training and familiarisation with weapons and explosives. The group of mainly Austrian trainees called themselves '12 Force'. According to Walter's training reports, he was inclined to be argumentative and to talk out of turn. After achieving satisfactory results in the preliminary training, Walter moved to the more demanding paramilitary training in the schools around Arisaig in the Scottish Highlands, to parachute training at Ringwood—today's Manchester Airport—and to operational training at Anderson Manor in Dorset and Hatherop Castle in Gloucestershire. Walter's training as a wireless operator was brief.[12]

After a year of training, he was more than ready to move to Italy. On 8th July 1944, he reported to a private apartment in Canning Place, London, to be kitted out by a woman who brought along her ten-year-old daughter. She was 'an obvious amateur', thought Walter, 'who sounded and acted like a rich, well-bred and connected society woman who wanted to do her bit for the war'. The lady called herself Mrs Moore, but he was probably underestimating Clara Holmes, who had many years of intelligence and operations work for MI6 and SOE behind her.

Walter took some embarkation leave with his father Martin and travelled by troop ship to Italy, where training continued. To refresher training in the paramilitary skills were added mountaineering and, for reasons he could not ascertain, mule-driving. His winter sports skills were used: having been at home on the snow since the age of three, he was asked to teach Peter Wilkinson and Charles Villiers to ski.

Walter was no fool. He recognised that Jimmy Darton was keeping the Austrian agents occupied and in peak condition until weather and operational conditions would allow them to parachute into Austria.

As the winter wore on, the agents became increasingly frustrated by the lack of deployment. And on the whole Walter thought little of his new comrades. Some of them were not Jewish refugees with a hatred of the Nazi regime, but ex-PoWs of Austrian descent who claimed to be anti-Nazi. He had observed the 'messianic reception' of Hitler when he arrived in Austria in 1938 and had difficulty imagining 'that any non-Jewish Austrian would be against him'. He did not trust them. Who could say how genuine their anti-Nazi claims were?

The Return

Walter Freud was dropped with the other five agents on 25th April 1945 at about 1.30 am. He was armed with a .30 American rifle, a .38 automatic pistol and a concealable .22 pistol. In a separate container were his radio and other heavy supplies. On his person were a large sum of money in different currencies and a rucksack with personal equipment. He drifted for several minutes and landed in a built-up area to the west of Judenburg, just off the main road leading down the Mur Valley. He did not know whether his comrades had jumped and, if so, where they might be. The container with his heavy equipment was also nowhere to be found. Thinking the Mur river was a small stream he had been expecting to be nearby, he attempted to cross, getting soaked to the waist and nearly being swept downstream. He went to ground, climbed into his sleeping bag and tried to recover.

Next morning, Walter set off across the mountains to the rendezvous agreed with Hans Schweiger. He bought food at isolated farms, where no questions were asked. Coming across a mountain hut, he settled in for a couple of days to dry out, warm up and take stock. He pressed on, but slowly realised that the chances of finding Schweiger at the RV were slim.

According to Walter Freud's account, he decided to head for Zeltweg airfield alone and claim it for the British. In the town of Schiefling, fifteen miles west of the airfield, he visited the *Bürgermeister*, the mayor. 'I am the vanguard of the British Army', he claimed, 'and I need to get to Zeltweg before the Russians'. Only the town fire engine had any fuel, so the *Bürgermeister* took the keys and drove Walter to Zeltweg. At checkpoints, he switched on the siren and they were waved through. They reached the Commandant's office without showing any documentation; 'a fire engine has free access to everywhere', wrote Walter later. 'I am Lieutenant Freud of the 8th British Army', he said to the German Commandant, 'I have come to take over your aerodrome'. The Commandant preferred this outcome to Russian occupation, but wanted to hear it from a more senior officer with proper documentation. He agreed that Freud could use the German radio to contact SOE in Italy and set this up. Walter sent the message, without encoding, but received no reply. He spent that night as the guest of the Commandant, dining well in the Officers' Mess and sleeping in a room in the barracks.

Next morning, he met with a group of officers and local Nazi officials and assured them that possession of the airfield would be on a 'first come, first served' basis. If they handed it over to him, it would become British. None of this had any basis in fact, but the Nazis were more concerned about potential war crimes trials and their personal fate.

One by one, half of those present drew Walter aside and explained that they had always been friends with the Jews. On the day after the meeting, a major accompanied Walter to General Rendulic's headquarters, where 'he was soon told he could have his airport'.[13] But on the way back to Zeltweg, after being bombed by Russian aircraft, they were stopped at a road block manned by a unit of Austrian deserters from the *Wehrmacht* and Walter's escorting major was arrested.

The Austrians would not let Walter continue to Zeltweg, instead escorting him westwards to the American front lines. After being questioned by a US Army intelligence officer, he spent a few days with the unit, flew to Paris, was handed over to the British Embassy and arrived in England on 8th May 1945, VE Day.

In Walter Freud's lone attempt to capture Zeltweg for Britain, he was successful in getting authority to take over the airfield. But putting that into practice was a longer and more complex action by the other members of the *Hamster*, *Historian* and *Duncery* teams. When they converged on the airfield, they were told of a 'very arrogant British officer' who had been there before them.

Zeltweg

As George Bryant, Frank Kelley, Eric Rhodes and Harry Stevens prepared to move to Zeltweg, they travelled cautiously. Bridges might be guarded, so they crossed rivers at shallow points. Hiding for the day in a deep gully, they were discovered by a local farmer, who was reassured to see British uniforms. He brought them food, reported that the alarm had been raised for the parachutists, and told them who could be trusted, and who not. As Bryant and his comrades met a series of local people over the coming days, each of them was able to tell the SOE men who was a Nazi to be avoided and who was 'a good Austrian'.

Hearing on 2nd May of the German surrender in Italy signed by General Heinrich von Vietinghoff, Bryant decided to come out into the open. The party moved into the village of Pusterwald and disarmed the local Nazis. The local population was in celebratory mood: an 'excellent meal, plenty of wine, general relief that the British had come'. They feared the Red Army alternative.

Bryant phoned the *Wehrmacht* garrison at Judenburg from the village Post Office. 'An armistice has been concluded', he said to the commander, Hauptmann Koch, 'and I wish to discuss details of your surrender. Please send a car for us'.

The car came, but the Germans in this area were not yet in a position to surrender. Instead, they took Bryant's party, under guard but keeping their weapons, to comfortable accommodation at their headquarters in Schloss Thalheim. Ironically, the castle had once belonged to Bryant's cousin.

In the discussions that followed, the sympathetic German officers walked a tightrope between their residual military duty and their wish to cooperate with the British. They helped find as much of the SOE party's hidden equipment as was still in place. The *Gestapo* had taken the wireless set to its headquarters in Murau, but a group of *Sicherheitsdienst* officers recovered it and explained that the two

Army Groups under Generals Rendulic and Löhr were keen to surrender, but not to the Red Army. Again able to contact base, Bryant reported this, but was instructed by the Allied Forces HQ to cut off any discussion of the *Wehrmacht* avoiding surrender to the Russians. Inter-Allied politics took priority. He was to concentrate on Zeltweg.

Here the stumbling block was the colonel in command of the airfield, an ardent Nazi. When Bryant phoned and demanded all details about the airfield, there was a danger that the colonel would send a squad to arrest Bryant's party and send them to a PoW camp. If so, promised their new *Wehrmacht* 'allies' at Schloss Thalheim, they would help to resist the arrest. Eventually, the colonel saw the writing on the wall and complied. The date was 7th May, Hitler had committed suicide and the war in Europe was within hours of ending.

At the Wolfsberg PoW camp, Bryant met a British major and captain of 'A Force' who were preparing to evacuate prisoners.[14] After offering them his help and agreeing that Zeltweg was crucial, Bryant joined the rest of his party at the airfield. By now, the Germans had left.

As requested by Charles Kaiser some days earlier, the Hungarians were in control and had disarmed land mines to prepare for Allied aircraft.[15]

On the following day, Kaiser himself arrived. Later in the day, Fred Warner, who had been missing since the 24th April parachute drop, also appeared. The European war was over, but the sensitive process of inter-Allied negotiations continued. The reunited *Hamster*, *Historian* and *Duncery* teams worked together, negotiating with arriving Russian forces the transfer of Soviet PoWs in exchange for British prisoners in Soviet-controlled territory. But Zeltweg lay to the north of the Mur River, in the area agreed at high level for Soviet occupation. Russian troops entered the airfield in force, putting an end to the question of which of the Allies would 'own' it. Only too happy to hand it over, the Hungarians went home.[16]

Ironically, the opening of the Zeltweg airfield had presented the last chance for the socialist *Dilston* party to deploy into Austria, but the opportunity collapsed. Stefan Wirlandner had already departed for Switzerland, but Jimmy Darton arranged for Theo and Eric to fly from Italy on 5th May 1945 to Zeltweg, to join their Austrian SOE comrades there. But the pilot who was due to fly them was too drunk and the flight never happened. Two days later, the war in Europe ended.

The mixed emotions of Eric Sanders in these final weeks of the war were no doubt shared by others. He knew he should be pleased to survive the war uninjured, but he shared his frustration with his diary: 'Deep inside me is an overwhelming desire to do something effective, to contribute something important to the defeat of Hitler'.[17]

Allies

The first days of May 1945 were a time of confusion. The Red Army consolidated its hold in the East and battled for Vienna. Hitler was dead. His successor, Admiral Dönitz, gave Field-Marshal Kesselring permission on 3rd May to surrender his Army Group G to the western Allies. Meanwhile, 'the war in Austria went on amid an aura of unreality: not really war, yet not quite peace'. In the West, 'there were three main drives, that of the French into the Vorarlberg, that of General Patch's 7th Army toward Landeck and Innsbruck, and that of General Patton's 3rd Army toward Linz'.[18]

As the Soviet and western Allies advanced into Germany and Austria in the last weeks of the war, the territory gained by each side differed from that agreed at the Yalta Conference. The confused situation on the ground did not match the neat lines drawn on maps by politicians and military top brass. *Wehrmacht* units were keen to surrender to American or British forces. Civilians too wished to head west if they could. A microcosm of this situation applied in the Judenburg/Zeltweg area, but in a north-south sense. By negotiation with Soviet officers, the SOE parties helped some fearful civilians cross to the south of the Mur river, fleeing the area controlled by the Red Army.

Similar tensions and parallel activities existed in the special operations field. This book has focused on SOE, but both the Soviet NKVD and the American OSS carried out undercover operations.

Following the liberation of France, the French secret organisation DGER (*Direction générale des études et recherches*) attempted to set up *Jedburgh* paramilitary operations in Austria.[19] Often, the Allies worked in ignorance of, or even in opposition to, each other.

The concealment from British undercover operators by Slovene partisans of their cooperation with Soviet officers was mentioned in Chapter 7. This led to the relatively successful formation of a Soviet-supported Slovenian partisan force, vigorously opposed by the Germans. Later, Communist-inspired Slovenian nationalist territorial claims threatened the territorial integrity of southeastern Austria. More directly, the NKVD parachuted dozens of agents to contact Austrian Communists. Many were arrested and 'played back' in 'radio games'.

On the American side, the OSS attempted several deployments in Austria, primarily to collect intelligence but also to encourage resistance. The most productive of these was Operation *Greenup*, which aimed to infiltrate the rumoured Nazi 'Redoubt' in the Tyrol. *Greenup* consisted of two skiers who had OSS Operational Group training, Friedrich Mayer and Hans Wihnberg, and an Austrian deserter, Franz Weber.[20] They parachuted into the Tyrolean mountains in February 1945 and reached the mountain resort village of Opferperfuss, where they were well received and installed their wireless link with Bari. Through courageous local contacts, they collected intelligence about traffic through the Brenner Pass. Captured as a result of a contact's betrayal, Mayer withstood torture but persuaded the local Nazi *Gauleiter* to surrender Innsbruck to US forces.

Post-war Austrian accounts played down Greenup's achievements, ascribing the bloodless handover of Innsbruck to native Austrian resistance, the so-called 'O5' movement and the associated multi-party political movement, the Provisional Austrian National Committee, or POEN (*Provisorisches Oesterreichische National-kommittee*).[21] At best, POEN was an attempt, rather late in the day, to persuade the Allies that a broad anti-Nazi movement existed in Austria to fill the post-war vacuum. Allegedly, POEN was 'fairly well organised, comprises all important Austrian political elements from right to left, including former Christian Socials, Social Democrats, Monarchists and Communists, as well as other Austrians without definite Party affiliations'. But much of it seems to have been 'smoke and mirrors'. It gained some French and American support, and Washington asked SOE to comment on some of the players, particularly Karl Hans Sailer, who had worked with Eric Gedye in Istanbul. On the basis of Gedye's assessment, SOE warned the Americans against him. Overall, SOE in London felt that 'reports on the existence of a big co-ordinated resistance movement known as POEN are in all probability grossly exaggerated and bear the stamp of tendentious émigré wishful thinking' and that OSS had 'swallowed the POEN story whole'.[22]

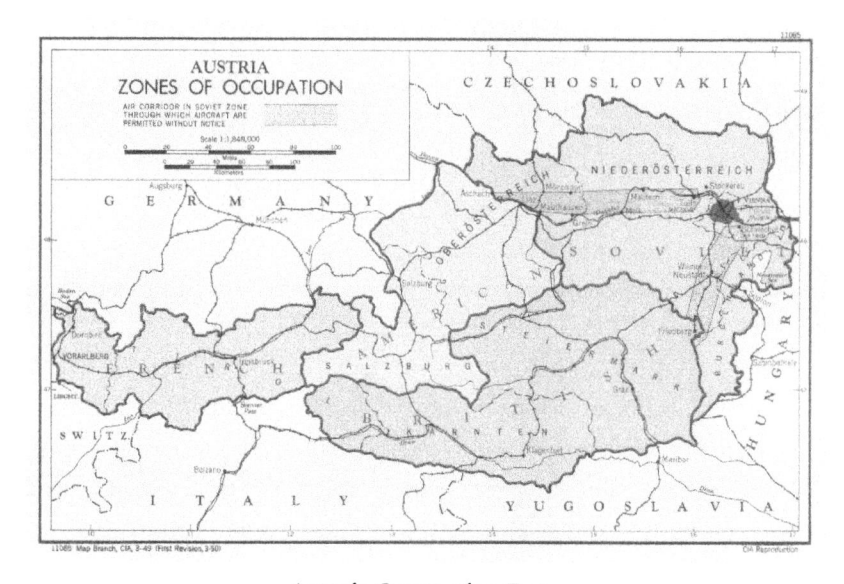

Austria Occupation Zones

Occupation

The immediate fate of Austria as the war in Europe ended was not much different from that of Germany. Austria was an occupied enemy country. Yet the Moscow Declaration had described Austria as Nazism's 'first victim' and Allied support for an independent Austria had grown as the war progressed. Thus the Allies dealt with occupied Austria separately from Germany and divided it into occupation zones agreed long before. Vienna was in the Soviet Zone, but under the combined four-power administration familiar to anyone who has watched Orson Welles' *The Third Man*.

After conquering Budapest in February 1945, the Red Army had advanced to Vienna, reassuring the inhabitants through leaflets that it would honour the Moscow Declaration to restore Austrian sovereignty; the target was not the people of Vienna but the German occupiers. The reality on the ground was different when the Red Army triumphed in mid-April: looting and rape were no less common than in the rest of Austria. But veteran politician Karl Renner set up a provisional government in Vienna, approved by the Soviets without consulting the western Allies, and declared Austria's independence from Germany.

The contribution of the Viennese to the defeat of the SS defenders of the city was limited. But when the Battle of Vienna was over, Radio Moscow broadcast the statement that 'the people of Vienna and elsewhere in Austria have helped the Red Army ... and rescued the honour of the Austrian nation'.[23]

Later in 1945, a prostrate and starving Austria started a process of reconstruction. Even then, though, the isolation of Vienna 100 miles inside the Soviet Zone brought with it the same potential for conflict and blockade that characterised the Berlin 'island'. Soviet hopes of dominating Austrian politics were dashed by the decisive election defeat of the Communists in November 1945.[24] Stalin was even more determined to maintain control of the Soviet Zone. The four occupying powers cooperated in the 'Allied Commission for Austria' and this was one of the few places in the world where East and West worked together as a matter of routine. Sometimes, though, it was through gritted teeth.

Suspicion and rivalry between the Soviet Union and the western Allies, which had continued throughout the war, became acute once they had defeated the common enemy. This was the Cold War.[25]

Cold War and Independence

While the term became common from 1945, the roots of the Cold War stretch back to the earliest days of the Second World War and beyond. Winston Churchill saw Stalin's Soviet Union as a threat comparable to that of the Nazis. Germany defeated, he watched with horror as the Red Army consolidated its hold over central and eastern Europe. Getting 'a square deal for Poland' was of particular concern. Churchill told his military chiefs of staff to develop contingency plans for *Operation Unthinkable*. 'Could we mount an offensive in July', he asked in mid-May 1945, 'to push the Red Army back'?

No support was on hand from the USA; although US troops were pressing forward towards Berlin, President Harry Truman intended to hand over to the Soviets the territory agreed in 1943-44. The planners concluded that the operation was indeed unthinkable, but meanwhile Soviet spies had reported on the plans. Stalin's paranoia was reinforced.[26] On the ground in Austria, the realities of the developing Cold War meant that denazification was not a great priority and the idea of Austria as a victim of Nazism was strengthened politically.

Another source of potential conflict in Austria, only loosely connected with East-West ideological or geopolitical rivalry, was nationalism. In the British occupation zone, Tito's Slovenian partisans had advanced into the southern Austrian province of Carinthia immediately after the German surrender. As warned by Lieutenant-Colonel Peter Wilkinson from his knowledge of the Slovenians, they had occupied the area around Klagenfurt, although Allied tanks beat them to the city itself by three hours.[27] A stand-off between them and British troops 'lasted for two weeks until Marshal Tito, under Western and Soviet pressure, ordered a withdrawal'. Eighteen months later, representatives of Tito's Yugoslavia argued their claim to a vast swathe of Austrian territory before the foreign ministers of the four occupying powers. It was rejected.[28]

After Stalin's death in March 1953, his eventual successor Nikita Khrushchev recognised the need to reduce military spending and therefore to reduce tension with the USA. One of his first steps was to authorise Foreign Minister Molotov to stop blocking Austrian statehood.

The May 1955 Austrian State Treaty, signed at the Belvedere Palace in Vienna, consolidated the existence of Austria's Second Republic. Austria 'recovered its full sovereignty within its January 1938 borders', with two provisos: 'no *Anschluss* with Germany and no alliance with either side in the Cold War'.[29] Occupying troops withdrew soon afterwards and the Austrian parliament declared the country's "perpetual neutrality". Ironically, western leaders mistrusted Soviet motives and greeted the Treaty and the associated neutrality with scepticism.

This is not the place to examine post-war Austrian history, how denazification was approached or the ways in which wartime resistance to Nazism have been reinterpreted. Others have done that more effectively than I could hope to achieve.[30] But it is interesting to note British historian Robert Knight's view that Austria's national consensus was 'too weak after the Second World War to allow a genuine confrontation with her recent past' and that 'it could only be successfully consolidated by avoiding one'. And the later 'Waldheim affair' highlighted the contradictions inherent in the mythologising of wartime resistance. Were Austrian nationhood and democracy 'born (or reborn) of the wartime suffering of Austrian victims of Nazism and heroes of the Austrian resistance movement'? Or was the role of Austrian resistance 'much inflated', hardly amounting to a 'movement'?[31]

Many former SOE agents kept quiet about having fought under a foreign flag: were they heroes or traitors?

Austrian and foreign historians have suggested various reasons for the delayed, but eventually successful, return to Austria's independence. Knight compares the different strands of opinion on the question and, instead of 'an unceasing Soviet attempt to absorb Austria into its sphere' or 'an Austrian struggle to be neutral', settles on 'the possibilities and difficulties of reaching agreement in a world moving into a state of polarisation'. Despite the geostrategic tightrope successive Austrian governments had to walk, he suggests, a 'successful Austrian variety of neutrality' was developed, accompanied by 'domestic prosperity and social stability'.[32]

What next for SOE?

The immediate priority of SOE in Austria after the German surrender was to find out what had happened to the agents who had disappeared into the chaos of the last months and weeks. Once they were located, the aim was to meet their aspirations as humanely as Army bureaucracy would permit. This 'liquidation' process was not as draconian as it sounds.

SOE's presence in occupied Austria was as 'No 6 Special Force Staff Section', under the command of Lieutenant-Colonel Charles Villiers. 6 SFSS employed some of those agents who had survived, as investigators or interpreters, and discharged others to their homes in Austria.

But many in SOE felt that their skill set was even more crucial in the face of the Soviet threat. For Austria, the key player in this was Lieutenant-Colonel Peter Wilkinson. He did his best to persuade London that members of the *Clowder* Mission should be attached to the military occupation forces in Austria (the Allied Military Government), and in due course to their civilian successors (the Allied Civilian Authority), for undercover operations in the new Cold War context. Wilkinson saw several threats to Austrian stability on the horizon: a lack of a common Austrian political programme; Communist efforts to control politics and the economy; Austrian opposition to separation from Germany; subversive action by Nazis; general dissatisfaction; and Tito's territorial claims. The *Clowder* team, he claimed, had the skills and knowledge to help deal with these problems.

For a time, the concept had a following wind: Allied Force Headquarters gave its support and extra agents were sent in. These were the *Bobby* operatives. In early May 1945, the first of these, 'John Miller', was sent in from Switzerland and made his way to the Vorarlberg. 'Miller' was actually Stefan Wirlandner, the Austrian socialist who had worked for SOE in Turkey and Italy. *Bobby Two* was

Theo Neumann and *Bobby Three* was Walter Hacker. The 'Bobbies' worked at first in Innsbruck, then in Salzburg and Vienna, whence they 'were able to send useful first-hand information' on Soviet activity.[33]

But resistance to a post-war role for SOE was evident at an early stage. The Foreign Office in London had at first responded positively, if in a lukewarm fashion, to the military request for a continued presence. The negative pressure built up and SOE's capacity in Austria was gradually reduced.[34] On 24th July 1945, the British Chiefs of Staff agreed that a small contingent of six SOE officers could stay in Austria, responsible to 8th Army. Only a few weeks later, the Chiefs of Staff accepted the recommendation of a 'Committee on the Future of SOE': the organisation would cease to exist and would become part of MI6.[35]

This was a triumph for those in the intelligence and diplomatic communities for whom SOE had been a thorn in the side since its formation in 1940. Since the July 1945 General Election, Winston Churchill was no longer Prime Minister; SOE had lost its 'top cover'. Nevertheless, disbandment would not take place until at least the end of the year and a small remnant would remain to carry out residual tasks into 1946.[36] The Foreign Office saw these tasks as being 'of a passive kind, being confined to the maintenance of certain contacts that have been built up during the war'.[37] Active subversion of the Soviet Union was out of the question for the new Labour government. Yet, although the organisation ceased to exist, individuals from SOE continued to work under the MI6 umbrella. As historian Richard Aldrich put it, 'many components of SOE marched out of the Second World War into the Cold War without breaking step'.[38]

---

[1] Captain Woodhouse, the Air Liaison Officer, remained with her (TNA HS 7/146, *Activities of X Section in Italy*).

[2] TNA HS 7/146, *Activities of X Section in Italy*. 'Counter-scorch' entails preventing a retreating enemy from carrying out a 'scorched-earth' strategy, destroying facilities and materiel that might be of use to the enemy (as ordered in Hitler's 'Nero Decree' of 19th March 1945).

[3] TNA HS 6/21, 16th April 1945, Operation Order *Hamster*.

[4] On the RVPS, see Peter Dixon, *Guardians*, 2018, pp.100-102.

[5] The documents showed Kaiser *inter alia* to have crossed from Spain into Gibraltar before disembarking in Liverpool on 24th July 1943 (TNA HS 9/818/2, Personal File Kaiser C).

[6] TNA HS 9/1596/3, Personal File Williams, Harry; Peter Leighton-Langer, *X steht für unbekannt: Deutsche und Österreicher in den britischen Streitkräften im Zweiten Weltkrieg* (Berlin: Berlin Verlag, 1999), p.203.

[7] TNA HS 7/146, *Activities of X Section in Italy*, Appendix E; Fred Warner, 1985; Eric Sanders, 2008, pp.243-248; Peter Leighton-Langer, 1999, p.201.

[8] TNA HS 6/21, 16th April 1945, Operation Orders *Historian* and *Duncery*.

[9] TNA HS 9/544/3, Personal File Anton Walter Freud. IWM 13326; Personal Papers Major A W Freud, unpublished manuscript *Before the Anticlimax*, from which Walter Freud's quotes in this section are taken. The story of the Freud family's experiences in the Second World War is recounted in Helen Fry, *Freuds' War* (Stroud: History Press, 2009).

[10] The court-martial of the officer in charge and several NCOs was reported in The Times, 25th June 1941.

[11] On the process of the USA's entry into the war, see Brendan Simms and Charlie Laderman, *Hitler's American Gamble: Pearl Harbor and the German march to global war* (London: Penguin Books, 2021).

[12] The SOE training system is described in more detail in Peter Dixon, *Guardians*, 2018, pp.14-17, 87-93.

[13] Daily Telegraph, 11th February 2004, Obituary, Walter Freud.

[14] The primary role of A Force was strategic deception in the Middle East and Mediterranean, under Lieutenant-Colonel Dudley Clarke. However, as cover for this it represented the escape and evasion organisation Military Intelligence 9 in the theatre, and a section of A Force organised the recovery of PoWs (Helen Fry, *MI9: A history of the secret service for escape and evasion in World War Two* (New Haven: Yale University Press, 2020); M. R. D. Foot and J. M. Langley, *MI9: escape and evasion 1939-1945* (London: Biteback, 2011), pp.88-93).

[15] TNA HS 9/1596/3, 9th May 1945.

[16] The airfield later became Royal Air Force Station Zeltweg and was handed back to the Austrian Air Force on Austrian independence in 1955 (Wolfgang Hainzl, *Die Luftstreitkräfte Österreichs 1955 bis heute*, 3rd ed. (Gnas, Austria: Weishaupt Verlag, 2000)).

[17] Eric Sanders, 2008, pp.206-7. In late April 1945, Sanders was offered a last-minute chance to parachute into his homeland. He turned it down. His allocated companion was an Austrian whom he had spent weeks training as a wireless operator, without any discernible progress. Eric had no confidence in his reliability (*ibid*, p.235).

[18] Charles B MacDonald, *The Last Offensive*, United States Army in World War II: The European theater of operations, vol. CMH Pub 7–9 (Washington, DC: US Army Center for Military History, 1973), p.440.

[19] TNA HS 6/1.
[20] Weber was a Tyrolian Catholic who had joined the Italian partisans near Viareggio. His companions, Mayer and Wijnberg, were Jewish refugees from Freiburg im Breisgau and Amsterdam respectively. The full story is in Peter Pirker, *Codename Brooklyn: jüdische Agenten im Feindesland, die Operation Greenup 1945*, 2nd ed. (Innsbruck: Tyrolia Verlag, 2019) and is the basis for the fictionalised Quentin Tarantino film *Inglorious Basterds*.
[21] Fritz Molden, *Fires in the Night: the sacrifices and significance of the Austrian Resistance, 1938-1945*, trans., Harry Zohn (Boulder: Westview Press, 1989).
[22] TNA HS 6/20, Letter No 632, 5th April 1945; HS 6/23, Jean Lambert and POEN.
[23] Erika Weinzierl, '*Vor- und frühgeschichte der Zweiten Republik*,' in *Österreich und die Sieger*, ed. Anton Pelinka and Rolf Steininger (Wien: W. Braumuer, 1986), pp.114-115.
[24] Peter Calvocoressi, *World Politics, 1945-2000*, 8th ed. (Harlow: Longman, 2001), p.16.
[25] A recent history of the Cold War, taking into account Russian and Chinese archive material is John Lewis Gaddis, *The Cold War: a new history* (New York: Penguin Press, 2005).
[26] Antony Beevor, 2012, pp.762-3.
[27] Peter Wilkinson, *Foreign Fields: the story of an SOE operative* (London: I B Tauris, 1997), pp.234-5; TNA WO 204/1613, 13th May 1945.
[28] TNA WO 204/1614, 8th May 1945; Robert Knight, 'Ethnicity and Identity in the Cold War: The Carinthian Border Dispute, 1945-1949', *The International History Review* 22, no. 2 (2000): p.277; Robert Knight, *Life after SOE: Peter Wilkinson's journey from the Clowder Mission to Waldheim*, 2009. Tito made similar territorial claims with respect to the port city of Trieste and the surrounding region of Venezia Giulia (TNA WO 204/1613, 204/1614, 204/6406). He 'considered that his country should be allowed to occupy this territory as a reward for all their efforts in the Allied cause and expenditure in blood and resources' (WO 204/1613, 8th May 1945).
[29] Peter Calvocoressi, 2001, p.26. A detailed look at the process towards the State Treaty is in Manfried Rauchensteiner, '*Österreich nach 1945: der Weg zum Staatsvertrag*,' in *Österreich und die Sieger*, ed. Anton Pelinka and Rolf Steininger (Wien: W. Braumuer, 1986)(in German).
[30] Anton Pelinka and Rolf Steininger, *Österreich und die Sieger* (Wien: W. Braumuer, 1986); Peter Pirker, *Subversion deutscher Herrschaft*, 2012, pp.535-9.
[31] Robert Knight, 'The Waldheim context: Austria and Nazism', *Times Literary Supplement* 4357 (1986).
[32] Robert Knight, 'British Policy towards Occupied Austria 1945-1950' (London School of Economics, 1986), pp.7, 15.

[33] TNA HS 7/146 and HS 6/22. Neumann had changed his name to Michael Norman and Hacker used the alias Walter Harris. A report by Wirlandner on the 'Situation in the Russian Zone' is on HS 9/1613, 5th July 1945.
[34] Peter Wilkinson and Joan Bright Astley, 1993; TNA 6/13, *Aide memoire from MXA to CD, Outline Plan (Trigger Two) for Future Special Operations in Austria* and covering Foreign Office response, 28th March 1945.
[35] David Stafford, *European Resistance*, 1980, pp.202-3.
[36] W J M Mackenzie, 2000, p.715; David Stafford, *European Resistance*, 1980, pp.258-9.
[37] TNA FO 371/46603, 28th July 1945.
[38] Richard Aldrich, 'Unquiet death: The post-war survival of the Special Operations Executive (1945-51),' in *Contemporary British History 1931-61: Politics and the limits of policy*, ed. Tony Gorst et al. (London: Institute of Contemporary British History, 1991), p.193.

Conclusion

Failures and Successes

THE CONTRIBUTION OF SOE to winning the war in Austria was not spectacular. More missions failed or were betrayed than succeeded. And most of the missions that went ahead were launched in the final months or even weeks of the war. Before that, the British Chiefs of Staff had other priorities for resources, especially aircraft. The faith of Air Chief-Marshal 'Bomber' Harris in the effectiveness of strategic bombing was a force of nature that overpowered other arguments.

In countering Nazi propaganda with their own, SOE and the Political Warfare Executive made a difference to the morale of enemy soldiers and population. But, even within SOE, operational priorities were focused elsewhere. British soldiers trained in unconventional warfare were more likely to be deployed to France, Greece, Yugoslavia and later northern Italy than to Austria.

Recruitment, planning and training all took time. Only in 1944 did a supply of trained Austrian agents come on stream. Many were recruited from the burgeoning numbers of PoWs who had not been available earlier. By the time they reached the hastily mounted SOE base in Italy, the strong British presence in Yugoslavia seemed to offer a route to smuggle agents into Austria overland. Yet Slovenian nationalist priorities and the clandestine Soviet relationship with Tito's distrustful partisans proved insurmountable political barriers. The Swiss route and direct parachute drops into Austria were the only options remaining. But aircraft were scarce and by then the Alpine winter had set in. Frustrated agents faced delay after delay as they waited for the next full moon, and then the next. By the time significant effort could be applied to sabotage and guerrilla warfare, the war was nearly over.

Within Austria itself, the seedbed in which to plant resistance to Nazi power was hard to find. In some parts of the country, a minority of inspiring Austrians were willing to organise resistance. They were divided and lacked strategy, but this was true in other countries, where resistance did grow. In Austria, the brutal efficiency of the Nazi state snuffed out most of the glimmering flames. Among others, Evelyn Stamper recognised that most of the courageous men and women who could resist were in concentration camps.[1] Many did not survive.

The men and women of X Section were realistic. Even in occupied countries like France, the proportion of the population who risked joining the Resistance was small, and their reasons were various: some political, some personal, others simply pragmatic. In a population under foreign occupation, the goal of the overwhelming majority is for their families to survive. Even the French people were 'divided between those who collaborated with the Germans, those who resisted them, and those in the middle who 'muddled through' and resigned themselves to the situation'.[2] Few actively collaborated, and even fewer heroically resisted. The same was true in Austria, but more so.

The *Gestapo* successfully suppressed most Austrian opposition to Nazi dominance. Many opponents of the regime fled abroad and were in principle available to SOE's small Austrian Section as potential agents.

Yet several factors made it difficult to get them into the field: the political divisions of exiled Austrians; the way Allied policymakers at first treated the *Reich* as one entity; the justified scepticism about local support; and the practical difficulty of access to Austria. Political change, increased priority and the chance to operate from Italy came too late to allow significant progress. The men of the *Clowder* Mission in Slovenia and northern Italy battled against immense odds to get agents into Austria. Mostly, though, the obstacles were insurmountable.

For operational teams that successfully reached Austria, the effectiveness of the *Gestapo*'s counter-intelligence apparatus was a formidable obstacle. Through informers, arrests, brutal interrogation and fake wireless messages, *Gestapo* officials like Johann Sanitzer neutralised many of SOE's efforts. Similar processes were in place in occupied countries like France and Belgium, but there a kernel of resistance was ready to be nurtured, organised, trained and equipped. Not so in Austria.

As William Mackenzie put it, 'on the whole the story is one of low priorities and hope deferred'.[3]

Yet a tiny group of men and women in SOE helped to keep the flame of Austrian independence alive, after Hitler's takeover in March 1938. SOE's X Section overestimated the number of Austrians who were willing to challenge the Nazi domination of Austria. Evelyn Stamper's and Clara Holmes' experience of the *Anschluss* had led them to conclude that it was German efficiency that had led to its success, rather than overwhelming Austrian popular support. However exaggerated their view of anti-German feeling in Austria, they spoke from their love of the country. But they also saw encouraging an Austrian spirit as a pragmatic way of undermining Hitler's war effort. In the early years of the war, few such weapons existed.

The Austrian Section was persistent in arguing against the Foreign Office policy of accepting Hitler's Greater Germany as fact. Why concede the moral advantage, they thought. Gradually, their view prevailed, culminating at the highest level in the Moscow Declaration. Even then, the Allies did not give political guarantees about the post-war future of Austria, called for by SOE and by anti-Nazi Austrians. An incentive to throw off the German yoke was not provided. As victory approached, though, the final SOE missions were grounded in a political framework that assumed rebuilding an independent Austria. When surrender came, Austria was occupied, but as a separate entity from defeated Germany. In the context of Cold War hostility between East and West, it would take another decade before Austria would regain her sovereignty. But the handful of seeds had been sown by a few men and women with a vision of what might be.

Like those who opposed Nazism in large or small ways, in their cities, towns and villages, the refugees who volunteered to return and fight deserve to be remembered with respect. Particularly in the last weeks, brave Austrian and British SOE agents played their part in reducing the loss of Austrian lives. The men and women of X Section helped to fan the uncertain flame of Austrian independence until geopolitics made it a reality.

Later life—for survivors

The characters in this story were diverse. They were Austrian and British, women and men, young and old. Some worked in offices—in Britain, Switzerland, Turkey or Italy—but were far from 9-to-5 bureaucrats. Those 'office-workers' may have thought themselves 'a small and second-rate lot [who] were mainly a channel of communication, rather than action lads'.[4] But they worked all God-given hours and lived constantly with the stress of knowing they were putting young men in harm's way.

Those young men might parachute into an Austrian forest clearing or they might train and train and do yet more training but never be deployed; the SOE leaders were often cautious about risk. Those who did go 'into the field' might succeed or fail in their mission, often through circumstances they could not control. Some were captured, imprisoned, interrogated under torture. Some were murdered.

The more fortunate ones lived on after the war, to take up new occupations or return to their old ones. The bitter memory of pre-war experiences made some of them retain their anglicised names and identities, and make new lives outside Austria. For those who returned, the danger of being seen as traitors to their country was always present.[5]

A few continued in work similar to that they had learnt since 1941, but in a new context: the Cold War. For these, little can be said about their post-war activity, and what there is often cannot be verified. But there are some who re-emerged into the open and we can trace the paths of their post-war lives.

The journalist and secret agent turned agent-handler **Eric Gedye** returned to Vienna as a correspondent, representing the British papers the *Daily Herald*, *Observer* and *Manchester Guardian*. His years of service were recognised in 1946 by the award of an MBE (Member of the British Empire). He and Litzi married in 1947 and he led the Vienna Bureau of Radio Free Europe, the American anti-Communist station broadcasting to Soviet satellite countries. On retirement in 1961, Gedye returned to England and started work on an autobiography. He died in Bath in 1970 before he could finish it.[6]

Walter Freud did not stay long in his native Austria. Three months after the end of the war, he was posted to the War Crimes Investigation Unit at Bad Oeynhausen in Germany, where he collected harrowing evidence of the Nazi death camps. After a serious car accident in July 1946, he was discharged from the Army in September. Just under a year later, he married his Danish fiancée Annette, and started a new civilian life as a chemical engineer. He died in February 2004.[7]

In 1945, **Albrecht Gaiswinkler** became a member of the Austrian Parliament for four years as a social democrat politician. He died in 1979 in his home town of Bad Aussee.

Leo Hillman continued his military career in the Intelligence Corps, serving as a Field Security Officer in Hamburg, the Suez Canal Zone and Cyprus. In 1959, he transferred to the Canadian military and subsequently retired in Canada.[8]

Clara 'Midge' Holmes lived after the war in southern England, and died in Chichester, Sussex in April 1992. Her daughter, **Prudence**, married and had four children; she passed away peacefully in June 2021 while staying with her son in Warwickshire.

Friedrich Reitlinger, who had tried so hard to return to the fight in the Tyrol, did eventually return to his homeland in peacetime.[9] He served as an interpreter for the Allied Commission in Austria and in the 1960s pursued a career as a translator and journalist. He had married Anna Berger Waldenegg in June 1945. They appear both to have died on the same day in December 1988.

Lieutenant-Colonel (later Sir) **Peter Wilkinson** joined the British Diplomatic Service after the war and served as Ambassador in Vienna in the 1970s. He wrote about his wartime and diplomatic experiences in his autobiography *Foreign Fields*.[10]

Harry Williams joined the Control Commission in Hamburg, Germany, in 1946 as an interpreter.[11]

Squadron Leader Count **Manfred Czernin** worked for the Fiat motor company as a sales manager. He died in 1962, a few months before his fiftieth birthday.

****

Thank you for reading *Return to Vienna*!

If you have found it an interesting read, perhaps you could spend a few minutes leaving a review at Amazon, Goodreads or wherever you bought it. Reviews show potential readers what to expect and are crucial for independent authors.

Thank you!
Peter Dixon

P.S. Why not check out my other SOE books?

Guardians of Churchill's Secret Army:
Men of the Intelligence Corps in the Special Operations Executive

Setting the Med Ablaze:
Churchill's Secret North African Base

Or join our email newsletter for occasional updates and download a free sample chapter of the ebook edition of *'Guardians'*. The self-contained chapter tells the moving story of SOE French Section agent Teddy Bisset. Find out more at https://cloudshillpress.com or scan the QR code.

[1] TNA HS 6/3, 21st January 1941.
[2] Robert Gildea, *Fighters in the Shadows: a new history of the French Resistance*, Main ed. (2015).
[3] W J M Mackenzie, 2000, p.687.
[4] Peter Jellinek to historian Neville Wylie, quoted in Neville Wylie, 2006, p.157.
[5] Peter Pirker covers this aspect of former SOE service in Peter Pirker, 'Die Remigration sozialistischer Exilanten nach Österreich: Exilpolitik-Netzwerke-Nachkriegsintegration,' in *Vision and Reality: Central Europe after Hitler*, ed. Richard Dove and Ian Wallace (New York: Brill, 2014) and Peter Pirker, *Subversion deutscher Herrschaft*, 2012, pp.474-490.
[6] Obituary Litzi Gedye, Daily Telegraph, 3rd September 2005.
[7] Helen Fry, *Freuds' War*, 2009.
[8] Hillman commanded 309 FSS in Hamburg and 147 FSS, transferring from the Canal Zone in early 1955 to Wolseley Barracks, Nicosia, during the EOKA campaign (information courtesy of Fred Judge at the Intelligence Corps Museum); also Supplement to the London Gazette, 7th July 1959.
[9] Source: http://www.hohenemsgenealogie.at, accessed 6th September 2021.
[10] Peter Wilkinson, 1997. See also: his obituary in The Independent, 5th July 2000; *ibid*; Robert Knight, *Life after SOE*, 2009.
[11] TNA HS 9/16596/3, 2nd February 1946.

Acknowledgements

'WE STAND ON THE SHOULDERS OF GIANTS': a cliché, but no less true for that.

Numerous individuals have helped with the preparation of this book. Thanks to the internet, a he vibrant 'community of interest' exists that focuses on the Special Operations Executive. It has members worldwide, linked by an online forum founded by Dr Steven Kippax. Steven has also spent innumerable days at the National Archives at Kew, near London, winnowing out contemporary documents on SOE and the other undercover agencies of the Second World War. A major contributor to the knowledge base of the community is Fred Judge of the Intelligence Corps Museum, who has worked tirelessly on a massive database of SOE personnel and on unravelling the often-contradictory lists of abbreviations.

Another network with a similar focus is the non-profit Secret World War 2 Learning Network (https://www.secret-ww2.net), with a particular heart for ensuring that those who gave their lives in the undercover fight against Nazism are properly remembered. Paul McCue of SWW2LN generously gave of his time to check a draft of this book for accuracy and to improve the narrative. Others who made a similar sacrifice of time, not least to save me from historical howlers, include my Royal Air Force comrade Ted Mustard, my PhD supervisor Dr Philip Towle, family member Steve McCormack and SOE researchers Alan Ogden and Martin Fielding (son of Major George Fielding). I thank them all.

I am also most grateful to Dr Michael Zimmerman, Austrian Ambassador to the United Kingdom for contributing the Foreword, with its focus on relations between Austria and Britain, and to his First Secretary (Political Affairs), Mario Gavenda, who also made helpful comments on the text.

Family members of some of my other 'characters' have also commented on drafts and have generously given access to family archives, photographs and private information: for Clara Holmes, Adrian Hopkinson, Katherine Laing and Richard Holmes; for Eric and Litzi Gedye, Robin Gedye. Similar generosity was shown by agents and staff officers of SOE whom I cannot thank. Most are long deceased, but donated their personal papers and their memories, in written and oral form, to the rich resource that resides in the Imperial War Museum. I acknowledge their contribution individually in the Notes to this book and more generally, and wholeheartedly, here.

Some of those written memories have been committed to published works, either by the individuals themselves or by other writers of history. Many distinguished researchers have gone before me. After I decided to build on my two earlier books on SOE and started researching its work in Austria, I realised that much of my research parallels that of Dr Peter Pirker. Dr Pirker, an expert on Austrian resistance, wrote his doctoral thesis on the role of SOE. He has of course gone into much more depth than I have, and the book developed from his doctorate is a masterpiece of detail. In the present book I have had a different purpose, namely to bring some stories to a wider audience that illustrate how Austrian agents and their British partners worked to undermine Nazi domination. In doing so, I have used many of the same primary and secondary sources as Dr Pirker, but would not claim to equal his diligence and comprehensiveness.

Along the way, I have been blessed to have patient and supportive family members, most important among them my wife Ingrid, who in every sense keeps me alive.

Dramatis Personae

This incomplete list of individuals named in this book shows the main contexts in which they appear and, where appropriate, a military rank representative of the period covered. I have made no attempt to describe any individual's full career.

Heinrich Allina	Austria Office London
Major-General Walter Bedell Smith	Chief of Staff, Eisenhower's Allied Forces Headquarters
Oskar Behron	SOE agent, Istanbul
Kenneth Benton	MI6 Vienna
Peter Brand	*Greenleaves* party, (Peter Ulanowsky)
General Josip Broz)	Yugoslav partisan commander
Piero Bruzzoni	Czernin's wireless operator, N Italy
Unteroffizier Heinrich Bruckner	SIG
Wilhelm Bruckner	*Patria* group, Tyrol ('*Black*')
2nd Lieutenant George Bryant	Operation *Historian* (Georg Breuer)
Captain Herbert Buck	SIG
Colonel Maurice Buckmaster	F Section head
Lieutenant-Colonel Euan Butler	SOE Stockholm
Brigadier-General Giuseppe Castellano	Italian armistice negotiator
Lieutenant-Colonel Brien Clark	First head of X Section
Squadron Leader Manfred Czernin	*Aunsby* party, N Italy
2nd Lieutenant Stephen Dale	*Seathrift* N Italy (Heinz Spanglet)
Hugh Dalton	Labour politician, first head of SOE

Claude Dansey	SIS/MI6 Deputy Director and controller of 'Z Organisation'
Major James Darton	X Section representative with No 1 Special Force in Italy
Captain David Dobell	X/AUS staff officer, Killed in Action 16th February 1945 in Germany
Josef Dobretsberger	SOE Agent, Istanbul
Major Douglas Dodds Parker	*Massingham*
Engelbert Dollfuss	Chancellor of Austria 1932-34
Major General 'Wild Bill' Donovan	OSS Director
Lieutenant General Dwight D. Eisenhower	Commander, Mediterranean operations
Feldwebel Walter Essner	SIG
Colonel Bonner Fellers	Military Attaché, US Embassy, Cairo
Herbert Feuerlöscher	SOE agent, Istanbul
Major George Fielding	*Bakersfield*, N Italy
Sir George Franckenstein	Austrian diplomat, Envoy in London 1920-1938.
2nd Lieutenant Anton Walter Freud	Operation *Duncery*
2nd Lieutenant Emil Fuchs	Operation *Duval*
2nd Lieutenant Abrecht Gaiswinkler	Operation *Ebensburg*
2nd Lieutenant Charles Gardner	*Greenleaves* party (Israel Gold)
G E R (Eric) Gedye	Journalist, MI6 agent, SOE Middle East
2nd Lieutenant Josef Grafl	Operation *Ebensburg*
Major Laurence Grand	MI6 Section D
Karl Gerold	Member of *Lex* group, Zurich
Karl Groehl	Member of *Lex* group, Paris
Major-General Colin Gubbins	SOE Director of Training and Operations, SOE Director (CD) from September 1943.
2nd Lieutenant Roman Haas	Operation *Eveleth* (Roman Spreitzhofer)
Sir Charles Hambro	Director of SOE (known as CD), April 1942-September 1943
Julius Hanau	Section D Yugoslavia (*Caesar*)
Archduke Otto von Hapsburg	Monarchist leader
2nd Lieutenant Walter Harris	*Dilston, Bobby*, (Walter Hacker)
Lieutenant-Colonel John Haselden	SAS North Africa
2nd Lieutenant Richard Hauber	*Seafront*, N Italy
2nd Lieutenant Josef Hemetsberger	Operation *Duval*
Elsa Herberger	Member of *Lex* group in Zurich

Major Alfgar Hesketh-Prichard	*Clowder* Mission, Slovenia
2nd Lieutenant Leo Hillman	AMPC, 51 (ME) Cdo, SIG, 1 SAS, SOE X/A (aka Charles Kennedy)
Elizabeth 'Betty' Hodgson	MI6 Vienna, MI6 Section D/JBC, SOE Austrian Sub-section, Switzerland Italy (aka Betty Harvey)
Clara Holmes	MI6 Vienna, MI6 Section D, SOE Austrian Sub-section
Lieutenant-Commander Gerald Holdsworth	Commander, *Massingham* para-naval section and *Maryland*
Major Jo Holland	MI(R)
Hans Hladnik	SOE socialist agent, *Dilston, Bobby*
Dr Hans Hollitscher	'No 8', SOE collaborator in Switzerland
Company Sergeant-Major 'Ginger' Hughes	*Clowder* Mission, Slovenia
Robert 'Peter' Jellinek	SOE Switzerland
Captain James Joll	X/AUS staff officer
Lieutenant Augustin Jourdain	Free French SAS, North Africa
2nd Lieutenant Charles (Carl) Kaiser	Op *Hamster*
Lieutenant Allan Keir	Conducting Officer, X Section
2nd Lieutenant Frank Kelley	Operation *Historian* (Franz König)
Captain Thomas Kendrick	MI6 Vienna
Sir Hughe Knatchbull-Hagessen	British Ambassador, Ankara
Eva Kolmer	Communist, Austrian Centre
Bruno Kreisky	Austrian socialist exile in Stockholm later Chancellor of Austria
Alice 'Litzi' Lepper	SOE Middle East, later wife) of Eric Gedye
2nd Lieutenant Karl Lzicar	Operation *Ebensburg*
Captain Patrick Martin-Smith	*Aunsby II*, N Italy
Squadron Leader Bill Matthey	SOE Bern, Switzerland
2nd Lieutenant Hubert Mayr	*Bakersfield,* N Italy (Jean Georgeau)
John McCaffery	SOE Bern, Switzerland (Italy Section)
Brigadier Eric Mockler Ferryman	Director, 'London Group'
Desmond Morton	10 Downing Street
Theo Neumann	SOE/socialist agent, *Dilston, Bobby*
2nd Lieutenant Harry Newman	*Pyx* (Hans Neufeld)
2nd Lieutenant Franz Novy	Austrian socialist exile in Stockholm
2nd Lieutenant Michael O'Hara	Viennese SOE agent (Egon Berliner), Operation *Icecream* (MI6) Operation *Evansville*

Karl Otten	Member of *Lex* group, London
Kim Philby	Soviet 'mole' in MI6
Captain Frank Pickering	FSS, *Clowder* Mission, Slovenia
Oscar Pollak	Revolutionary socialist
2nd Lieutenant Hans Prager	Operation *Duval*
Franz Preiss	SOE agent, drowned *en route* February 1941
[Michael] Peter Priestley	*Seathrift,* N Italy (Egon Lindenbaum)
Friedrich Reitlinger	Tyrolean SOE agent
Eric Rhodes	Operation *Historian* (Erich Rohde)
Lieutenant David Russell	Conducting Officer, X Section
Karl Hans Sailer	SOE Istanbul
2nd Lieutenant Eric Sanders	Austrian SOE agent (Ignaz Erich Schwarz), *Dilston Bobby*
Gerhard Sanders	*Greenleaves* party (Gerhard Sykora)
Johann Sanitzer	*Gestapo*
Theodor Schuhbauer	SOE agent, drowned *en route* February 1941
Kurt von Schuschnigg	Chancellor of Austria, 1934-38
Dr Gregor Sebba	SOE agent, New York, Founder member, Austrian Action.
Commander John Senter	SOE Head of Security
Arthur Seyss-Inquart	Chancellor of Austria 1938 pre- *Anschluss*
Admiral Sir Hugh Sinclair	Director MI6 ('C')
Evelyn Stamper	MI6 Vienna, Section D, SOE Austrian Sub-section (aka Evelyn Graham-Stamper)
2nd Lieutenant Karl Standhartinger	Operation *Ebensburg*
2nd Lieutenant Oscar Stephens	*Pyx* party, Slovenia (Oskar Scheinmann)
Sir William Stephenson	BSC New York
2nd Lieutenant Harry Stevens	Operation *Duncery* (Hans Schweiger)
Captain David Stirling	SAS, North Africa
Major Bickham Sweet-Escott	SOE staff officer
Second Lieutenant William Taggart	*Seafront,* N Italy (Wolfgang Treichl)
Lieutenant-Colonel Ronald Thornley	Head of X (Germany) Section
Major Henry Threlfall	SOE Stockholm
Count Norbert von Trautmannsdorff	*Bellington* party, not deployed
Major Charles Villiers	*Clowder* mission, Slovenia No 6 SFSS
Egon Baron von Berger Waldenegg	Rome
Heinrich Berger Waldenegg	SOE Agent, not deployed
2nd Lieutenant Fred Warner	Operation *Historian* (Manfred Werner)

2nd Lieutenant Harry Williams	Operation *Hamster* (Harry Wunder)
Ernest Wise	SOE Rome (Ernst Weiss, with wife Enid)
Lieutenant Colonel Peter Wilkinson	SOE staff officer, *Clowder* mission, Slovenia
Stefan Wirlandner	SOE Istanbul, Italy, *Bobby*
2nd Lieutenant Hans Zeilinger	*Pyx* party, Slovenia

Chronology

The following chronology was compiled from a range of public domain sources,

1919	
June	Treaty of Versailles ends WW1
1920	
1st October	Austrian Federal Constitution established
1933	
30th January	Adolf Hitler becomes Chancellor of Germany
7th March	Chancellor Dollfuss dissolves Austrian parliament
1934	
25th July	Chancellor Dollfuss assassinated
1938	
12th March	*Anschluss:* German troops enter Austria, pre-empting Chancellor Schuschnigg's planned referendum
1939	
1st September	Germany invades Poland
3rd September	Britain and France declare war on Germany
1940	
9th April	Germany invades Denmark and Norway
10th May	Winston Churchill becomes Prime Minister; Germany invades Low Countries and attacks France
10th June	Italy enters war as ally of Germany
26th May—4th June	British vessels evacuate Allied forces from Dunkirk
22nd July	Churchill forms Special Operations Executive under Hugh Dalton
13th September	Italians invade British-controlled Egypt from Libya.
1941	

22nd June	Germany invades the Soviet Union (Operation *Barbarossa*)
7th December	Japan attacks US ships at Pearl Harbor and declares war on the USA and Britain. Hitler signs *Nacht und Nebel* decree, ordering that guerrillas should 'disappear'.
16th December	Afrikakorps starts to withdraw
25th December	Allied forces retake Benghazi, Libya, but hold it only until 29th January 1942
1942	
21st June	Tobruk falls to Rommel
1st July	First Battle of El Alamein begins, lasting 25 days and developing into stalemate
13th July	Churchill appoints General Bernard Montgomery to command Eighth Army
19th July	Operation Jubilee, the Canadian/British raid on Dieppe, fails and impacts planning for Allied invasion of France
18th October	Hitler issues Commando Order, ordering execution of captured commandos
23rd October	Second Battle of El Alamein begins, leading to German retreat on 3rd November
8th November	Allies launch Operation Torch invasion of Vichy Algeria and Morocco accompanied by French resistance coup in Algiers
10th November	Germany occupies Vichy France Admiral François Darlan orders ceasefire in North Africa
13th November	Montgomery's 8th Army recaptures Tobruk and continues into Tunisia
1943	
14th 24th January	Allied Casablanca Conference
18th 20th March	Allies advance into Tunisia from east and west, linking up on 7th April and forcing surrender of *Afrikakorps* and Italians on 13th May
10th July	Allied invasion of Sicily (Operation *Husky*) begins, achieving full control on 17th August
25th July	King Victor Emmanuel III arrests Mussolini and appoints Marshal Pietro Badoglio as Prime Minister of Italy
6th August	German troops take over defence of Italy
17th 24th August	Quebec Conference
3rd September	Italians sign secret armistice
3rd 9th September	Allies land in mainland Italy
30th October	Moscow Declaration on future of Austria signed
28th November	Tehran Conference begins, ending on 1st December
1944	
22nd January	Allies land at Anzio, Italy but are held in the beachhead until May

14th February	General Eisenhower forms Supreme Headquarters Allied Expeditionary Force (SHAEF)
6th June	Allies invade Normandy (Operation *Overlord*)
20th July	Attempt to assassinate Hitler fails
15th August	Allies land in Southern France (Operation *Dragoon*)
1945	
30th March	Red Army invades Austria
15th April	Soviet occupation of Vienna
29th April	German forces in Italy surrender
30th April	Hitler commits suicide
7th May	Germany surrenders
9th July	Allies agree occupation zones
25th November	First post-war elections in Austria
1946	
15th January	SOE disbands
1955	
27th July	Austrian State Treaty signed

Glossary

The following list unpacks a selection of relevant SOE-related terms and abbreviations. Some are abbreviated or appear in this book. Others are included here as being useful for further research.

51 (Middle East) Commando	Raiding formation raised from 401 (Palestine Company AMPC.
Abwehr	German military intelligence
Operation *Agreement*	Allied attack on Tobruk, September 1942
AMPC	Auxiliary Military Pioneer Corps
Anschluss	Incorporation of Austria into the German Reich in March 1938
Aunsby	Party of agents deployed to northern Italy, intended for Austria (Czernin, Bruzzoni. Also *Aunsby II* (Martin-Smith, Barker)
Austria Office	Social centre in Eaton Place, London' with social democratic political connections
Austrian Centre	Organisation formed in 1939 to aid Austrian refugees that gradually became dominated by Communists
Bakersfield	Party of agents deployed to northern Italy, intended for Austria (Fielding, Buttle, Smallwood Georgeau)
BBC	British Broadcasting Corporation
Black propaganda	Propaganda whose source is hidden
Beaulieu	UK base of SOE 'Finishing Schools'
BLO	British Liaison Officer (e.g. with partisans in the Balkans and Northern Italy)
Bonzo	SOE agent recruited from among PoWs
Brandon	SOE Mission in support of Allied invasion of North Africa in late 1942
BSC	British Security Coordination (New York
C	Head of Secret Intelligence Service / MI6
CD	Executive Director of Special Operations Executive

Clowder	Operation to infiltrate agents into Austria via Slovenia, in 'cooperation' with Yugoslavian partisans
Combined	Multinational operation or organisation.
D/F	[Head of] SOE Section for clandestine escape
DGER	(*Direction générale des études et recherches*) French intelligence agency
Dilston	SOE/socialist mission (Neumann, Sanders, Hladnik)
Dragoon	Operation to invade Southern France August 1943 (formerly *Operation Anvil*)
Duncery	SOE operation to secure Zeltweg airfield (Stevens, Freud)
Duval	SOE paramilitary Bonzo mission (Hemetsberger Prager, Fuchs)
DZ	Dropping Zone
Ebensburg	Operation in Salzkammergut area around Bad Aussee (Gaiswinkler, Standhartinger, Lzicar, Grafl)
EH	Foreign Office propaganda unit at Electra House London
Electra	SOE operation in Vienna (Leo Hillman)
Eveleth	Solo SOE mission in Styria (O'Hara)
FANY	First Aid Nursing Yeomanry
FO	Foreign Office
Force 133	SOE operations into Balkans
Free Austrian Movement	UK-based group formed in 1941, aiming to secure Austrian self-determination, later apparently dominated by Communists
FTP	*Francs-Tireurs et partisans*
FSS, FSO	Field Security Section/Officer
Funkspiel	'Radio game', transmitting false wireless messages from captured agents' sets
Gestapo	German secret police (*Geheime Staatspolizei*)
Greenleaves	Party of Austrian agents planned for infiltration via Yugoslavia (Sanders, Brand, Gardner)
Greenup	OSS operation in Tyrol (Mayer, Wihnberg, Weber)
Hamster	SOE operation in Graz area (Kaiser, Williams
Heimwehr	Austrian nationalist paramilitary group
Historian	SOE operation near Judenburg (Bryant, Kelley, Rhodes, Warner)
ISLD	Inter-Services Liaison Department (cover for MI6)
ISRB	Inter-Services Research Bureau (cover for SOE)
J	[Head of] SOE Italian Section
Jedburgh	Three-man teams for post-invasion liaison with Resistance
JBC	Joint Broadcasting Committee (controlled by MI6 Section D)
Joint	Involving two or more armed services.
Lex	Anti-Nazi group based in France and later in Switzerland

LRDG	Long Range Desert Group
LZ	Landing zone
Maryland	Code name for No 1 Special Force, based at Monopoli and responsible for all SOE activity in and from Italy except Force 133
Massingham	Code name for SOE North Africa base near Algiers
Maquis	Guerrilla units, rural France From maquis, Corsican scrub vegetation (members were *maquisards*).
MBE	Member of the British Empire.
MEW	Ministry of Economic Warfare
MI5	Security Service
Ml6	Secret Intelligence Service
Ml9	War Office section assisting escaping airmen and POWs
MI(R)	Military Intelligence (Research formed 1938 in War Office to develop subversion tactics
MO1(SP)	SOE cover name, especially with military
MOI	Ministry of Information
Moscow Declaration	Statement by Allies in October 1943 regarding Austria's potential independence
NCO	Non-commissioned Officer
NKVD	Soviet intelligence agency
No I SF	No I Special Force, SOE formation in Italy
No 6 SFSS	No 6 Special Force Staff Section, the SOE unit in Austria immediately post-war
OKW	*Oberkommando der Wehrmacht*, German High Command
OSS	[United States] Office of Strategic Services
OSS/SI	Intelligence element of OSS
OSS/SO	Special operations element of OSS
Overlord	Allied invasion of northwest Europe, June 1944
Patria	Tyrolean anti-Nazi organisation
PCO	Passport Control Officer, cover for MI6 officer in British embassies
PE	Plastic explosive
PID	Political Intelligence Department, Foreign Office
Pioneer Corps	British military unit that accepted enemy aliens
POEN	*Provisorisches Österreichisches Nationalkomitee* (Provisional Austrian National Committee)
PoW	Prisoner-of-War
PWE	Political Warfare Executive
Pyx	SOE party intended for Austria via (Linger, Newman, Stephen)
RAF	Royal Air Force
RAF Ringway	Parachute school, Manchester.
Rankin	Allied contingency plans for various degrees of collapse of the Nazi regime

Republikanischer Schutzbund	(Banned) paramilitary arm of Austrian Social Democratic Workers' Party
Revolutionary Socialists	Austrian political group initially favouring union with Germany
RN	Royal Navy
SAARF	Special Allied Airborne Reconnaissance Force, formed March 1945 to protect PoWs
SAS	Special Air Service
SD	*Sicherheitsdienst* (Security Service)
Seafront	Party of agents deployed to northern Italy, intended for Austria (Taggart, Hauber)
Seathrift	Party of agents deployed to northern Italy intended for Austria (Dale, Priestley)
Section D	MI6 department formed June 1938 to develop subversion tactics (cover name 'Statistical Research Department')
SF	Special Forces
SFHQ	Special Forces Headquarters
SHAEF	Supreme Headquarters Allied Expeditionary Force
SIG	Special Interrogation Group
SIM	*Servizio Informazioni Militare* (Italian counter-espionage service)
SIS	Secret Intelligence Service (MI6)
SOE	Special Operations Executive
SOE/SO	British/American combined predecessor of SFHQ
SOM	Special Operations (Mediterranean)
Speedwell	(After advance into Italy) Command post of *Massingham* and *Maryland*, attached to Allied Forces HQ (wherever situated)
SS	*Schutzstaffel*, Nazi paramilitary and military organisation
Temple	SOE party intended for Austria via N Italy (Baum, Brenner)
STS	Special Training School
TNA	National Archives, Kew, UK
Torch	Allied operation to invade North Africa
Ultra	Intelligence product of Bletchley Park codebreaking
USAAF	United States Army Air Forces
Volkssturm	Last-ditch militia formed in October 1944
Wehrmacht	German armed forces
White propaganda	Propaganda whose source is acknowledged
W/T	Wireless telegraphy
X	[Head of] SOE German Section (Directorate post-1944)
X/Aus	[Head of] SOE Austrian sub-section (or X/A)

Sources and Further Reading

Sources and suggested further reading are noted below, divided into primary sources, memoirs, secondary sources and images. Primary sources include files at the British National Archives (TNA) in Kew, records at the Imperial War Museum (IWM) in London, (www.iwm.org.uk/collections) and files at the National Archives and Records Administration (NARA, https://www.archives.gov), College Park, Maryland, USA. Much of the information in this book derives from SOE's operational files (HS 6 series), contemporary SOE history files (HS 7 series), headquarters records (HS 8 series) and personal files of SOE members (HS 9 series) at TNA. Other files are in the Air Ministry (AIR), Cabinet (CAB), Foreign Office (FO), MI5 (KV), Treasury (T) and War Office (WO) series. All these files can easily be found via the TNA Discovery search engine.

Primary Sources

National Archives: Files Consulted
Air Ministry Files: AIR/27/996/32; 996/30.
Cabinet Files: CAB 65/34/40; 101/131.
Foreign Office Files: FO 371/46603; 371/30095; 371/44255; 898/1; 954/1A/88; FO 954/1A/91.
SOE Files:
HS 3/62; 3/222.
HS 6/2-4; 6/8; 6/10-11; 6/13; 6/17-23; 6/669; 6/775; 6/692;

HS 7/3; 7/5; 7/145-6; 7/199; 7/253; 7/263-4.
HS 8/435; 8/883-5.
HS 9/116/6; 9/134/5; 9/225/2; 9/436/8; 9/544/3; 9/553/3; 9/711/2; 9/759/1; 9/806/2; 9/818/2; 9/825/9; 9/915/2; 9/953/10; 9/1012/5; 9/1094/1; 9/1209/1; 9/1212/6; 9/1245/3; 9/1329/6; 9/1404/3; 9/1465/8; 9/1482/2; 9/1547/3; 9/1571; 9/1596/3; 9/1612-13; 9/1638/6; 9/1643.
MI5 Files: KV 2/2171-2; 2/2517-2523; 2/2656.
Treasury Files: T 209/20/4; 209/29/16.
War Office Files: WO 204/1613-14; 204/1953-4; 204/6406; 218/159; 373/46/64; 373/100/142.

Imperial War Museum
Personal Papers: 12751 Peter Allix Wilkinson; 14089 Major J H Darton; 13326 Major A W Freud.
Audio and Oral History: 18591-3/18605-11/18583-90 SOE Conference; 29954 Eric Sanders; 13289 Peter Wilkinson; 12069 Patrick Martin-Smith; 10505 Basil Davidson; 8775 Herbert Radley; 26813 James Darton; 8238 Henry Threlfall; ; 31577 Richard Barry; 31589 Peter Murray Lee; 27773 Robert Clark; 23142 Mildred Schutz; 11087 Gwendoline Rees.

Additional material from:
Documentation Centre of Austrian Resistance (*Dokumentationsarchiv des österreichischen Widerstandes*) (https://www.doew.at/)
National Archives and Records Administration (NARA) (https://www.archives.gov/)
Central Intelligence Agency (https://www.cia.gov/resources/)

Memoirs and Secondary Sources

Books

Popular general histories by Sir Antony Beevor and Sir Max Hastings, respectively, present a narrative of the overall course of the war and of undercover operations.[1] On the world of intelligence, the official histories of MI5 and MI6 by Christopher Andrew and Keith Jeffery are comprehensive.[2]

Histories more focused on SOE by William Mackenzie and M R D Foot describe its structure, equipment, agent selection and training, operations and political relationships. Other books about SOE that stand out include Bickham Sweet-Escott's memoir, the biography of Colin Gubbins by Joan Bright Astley and Sir Peter Wilkinson, the brief descriptions of many SOE agents by former SOE member Michael Howarth, and the often-entertaining view of coded wireless communications and SOE culture by cryptanalyst Leo Marks.[3]

On Austria itself, Wolfgang Neugebauer has written on Austrian resistance to Nazi rule, while Thomas Barker examined the Slovenian partisans and their relationship with SOE.[4] Memoirs that include at least some reference to SOE and Austria include Sir Peter Wilkinson's autobiography, Patrick Martin-Smith's and Ernest Barker's memories of operations in northern Italy and OSS agent Franklin Lindsay's memoir of operations with the Yugoslav partisans.[5] Alliances are not often harmonious; Matthew Jones covers political relations between the USA and the UK in the Mediterranean, while Jay Jakub focuses on rivalry between OSS and SOE, and Tommaso Piffer highlights their rivalry in Italy.[6] On the post-war period in Austria, both Rolf Steininger's history and Warren Williams' PhD thesis are valuable resources, if obtainable.[7] Many other books and articles are included in the Notes and Bibliography, but the *doyen* of researchers on SOE and Austria is Dr Peter Pirker, who has devoted much of his academic career to studying the subject. His published articles are available, but many of them are based on his doctoral research, which was published in German in 2012.[8]

Websites

A range of general resources on undercover operations in the Second World exists, many of them available online. They include the Secret World War 2 Learning Network (https://www.secret-ww2.net), WW2 Talk (ww2talk.com) and the Gerry Holdsworth Special Forces Charitable Trust (https://holdsworthtrust.org/soe/). Also, Nigel Perrin has collated a collection of books and DVDs on SOE at https://nigelperrin.com/soebooks.htm.

Other websites consulted include:
www.operationdarkofthemoon.org.uk;
www.commandoveterans.org/51MEComando1941;
www.jewishvirtuallibrary.org/mauthausen-trial;
https://aviation-safety.net/database/record.php?id=19430601-0;
https://avalon.law.yale.edu/wwii/moscow.asp;
https://collections.ushmm.org/search/catalog/irn512456;
https://www.memoiresdeguerre.com/article-the-last-days-of-ernst-kaltenbrunner-83009915.html; https://ghdi.ghi-dc.org.

Image Sources

Image	Page
Map of Austria, 1930s, Public Domain (PD), US National Archives and Records Administration (NARA)	6
Map of Europe between the wars, PD (courtesy of the United States Military Academy Department of History)	10
Map of Austria and neighbouring countries, by James Morgan	28
Map of districts of Vienna, 1938, PD	29
Memorial on the site of the former Hotel Metropole Morzinplatz, Vienna©2018, C.Stadler-Bwag, CC-BY-SA-4.0	31
Duke and Duchess of Windsor with Hitler, 22nd October 1937, Berchtesgaden, published *Le Nouvelliste d'Indochine*, 14 November 1937, PD	45
Referendum poster, 13th March 1938, PD, Mediathek	49
Jews forced to scrub pavement, Vienna 1938, PD, after Nazi annexation 1938, PD, National Holocaust Museum, courtesy of NARA	51
Post- Anschluss Austria: the *Ostmark* 1941 (CC BY-SA 4.0 2015, XrysD)	52
Eric Gedye, courtesy of Robin Gedye	56
Clara Holmes and Prudence, Vienna c. 1934, courtesy of Adrian Hopkinson	61
Lieutenant-Colonel Ronald Thornley PD*	83
Poster for Auxiliary Military Pioneer Corps, PD*	92
Friedrich Reitlinger, PD*	94
Greater Germany, 1942 (CC BY-SA 3.0 Mackay 86 at English Wikipedia)	103
Litzi Gedye, Vienna 1959 courtesy of Robin Gedye	111
Stefan Wirlandner, PD*	115
Map of southern approaches to Europe 1942-1945, PD (US Army Center of Military History)	129
Map of the Balkans as seen from Germany 1940, PD (*The War in Maps*, German Information Service in USA)	137
Major Alfgar Hesketh-Prichard, PD*	139
Hubert Mayr, PD*	147
Albergo Sotto Corona, exterior, PD (courtesy of Albergo Sotto Corona and Alan Oden)	148
Albergo Sotto Corona, interior, , PD (courtesy of Albergo Sotto Corona and Alan Oden)	149

Partisans of the Osoppo Vittoria battalion, PD (courtesy of Alan Ogden)	150
Michael O'Hara (Egon Berliner), PD*	160
Map of planned attack on the rumoured National Redoubt, PD (US Army Center of Military History)	168
Liberation of Mauthausen concentration camp, 1945, PD (US Army)	173
Adolf Hitler inspecting art, PD (NARA 242-HB-32016-3)	182
Ghent Altarpiece, 1432, PD	183
Charles Kaiser, PD*	192
Lieutenant Anton Walter Freud, PD (Imperial War Museum, personal papers)	196
Austria Occupation Zones, PD (CIA)	205
* Contains public sector information licensed under the Open Government Licence v2.0	

[1] Antony Beevor, 2012; Max Hastings, *The Secret War: Spies, codes and guerrillas, 1939-1945*, (2015).

[2] Christopher Andrew, *Defence of the Realm*, 2009; Keith Jeffery, 2010.

[3] W J M Mackenzie, 2000; M R D Foot, *SOE 1940-1946*, 2014; Bickham Sweet-Escott, 1965; Peter Wilkinson and Joan Bright Astley, 1993; Patrick Howarth, 1980; Leo Marks, *Between Silk and Cyanide: A codemaker's story 1941-1945* (Stroud: History Press, 2008).

[4] Wolfgang Neugebauer, *Austrian Resistance*, 2014; Thomas M Barker, *Social Revolutionaries*, 1990.

[5] Peter Wilkinson, 1997; Patrick Martin Smith and Peter Pirker, *Widerstand vom Himmel: Österreicheinsätze des britischen Geheimdienstes SOE 1944* (Wien: Czernin, 2004) Ernest Barker, 2021; Franklin Lindsay, 1993.

[6] Matthew Jones, *Britain, the United States and the Mediterranean War, 1942-44* (Basingstoke: Macmillan in association with St. Antony's College, Oxford, 1996), Jay Jakub, *Spies and Saboteurs: Anglo-American collaboration and rivalry in human intelligence collection and special operations, 1940-45* (London: Macmillan, 1999), Carleton S Coon, *A North Africa Story: The anthropologist as OSS agent, 1941-1943* (Ipswich, Mass.: Gambit, 1980) and Tommaso Piffer, 2015.

[7] Rolf Steininger, *Austria, Germany, and the Cold War: From the Anschluss to the State Treaty, 1938-1955* (New York: Berghahn Books, 2008); Warren Wellde Williams, "British Policy and the Occupation of Austria, 1945-1955" (Swansea University, 2004).

[8] Peter Pirker, *Subversion deutscher Herrschaft*, 2012.

Index

Allina, Heinrich, 77, 80, 99
Anschluss (Annexation of Austria), 8, 42, 46-47, 51-52, 57-58, 63, 66, 68, 94, 102, 121, 137, 153, 165, 178-179, 183, 196, 207, 217
Atkins, Don, 5
Austrian State Treaty, 1, 7, 207
Austro-Hungarian Empire, 47, 54, 55, 82, 102, 145, 170
Badoglio, Marshal Pietro, 120, 154
Barker, Sergeant Charles, 149, 164
Beaumont, Sergeant, 25
Behron, Oskar, 110, 125
Bellasis House, 179
Benton, Kenneth, 60, 73
Blagodatov, General Aleksei, 35
Bloom, Marcus, 174
Boncompagnie, Lieutenant Madeleine, 35, 37
Bonzo, 92, 172, 177, 178, 186, 188
Bottome, Phyllis, 62
Bristol Bombay (aircraft), 17
British Broadcasting Corporation (BBC), 41, 97, 100, 171, 194
Bruckner, *Unteroffizier* Heinrich, 14, 20
Bruckner, Wilhelm, 102, 169, 170, 186
Bruzzoni, Piero, 145
Bryant, 2nd Lieutenant George (Georg Breuer), 194, 195, 200, 201, 202
Buck, Captain Herbert, 13, 14, 15, 16, 17, 18, 19, 23
Buckingham, Captain Harold, 175, 186
Burgess, Guy, 67
Butler, Lieutenant-Colonel Euan, 104, 124
C-47 Dakota aircraft, 70, 142
Castellano, Brigadier-General Giuseppe, 121

Catholic Church, 9, 52, 55, 66, 86, 101-102, 108, 153, 169, 192, 211
Cator, Major Henry, 10-11
Central Intelligence Agency (CIA), 188
Chamberlain, Neville, 45, 56, 65, 109, 134
Churchill, Winston, 3, 7, 14, 17, 49, 63-64, 66, 71, 74-75, 82, 88, 97, 110, 121-123, 136, 142, 197, 206, 210, 220, 253
Clark, Lieutenant-General Mark, 152
Clarke, Lieutenant-Colonel Brien, 83, 211
Clement, George, 174
Cold War, 7, 8, 47, 141, 144, 206-207, 209-210, 212, 217, 218
Countries
Abyssinia (Ethiopia), 11, 46
Albania, 97, 131, 132, 174
Australia, 3, 92, 196, 197
Czechoslovakia, 46, 56, 67, 73, 78, 134-135, 170, 179
Egypt, 12-13, 26, 87, 101, 125, 130-131, 180
Eritrea, 11
France, 3, 9-10, 21, 44, 46, 69, 71, 79-81, 85, 97, 106-107, 115, 142, 147, 152, 168-170, 174, 179, 183-184, 192, 203, 215-217
Germany, 1, 4, 8-9, 23, 29, 38-39, 43-48, 51, 61-63, 65-66, 68-70, 77, 80-87, 91, 97, 103-108, 113-114, 116, 118, 120-123, 125, 130, 135-137, 147, 192, 196-197, 203, 205-207, 209, 217, 219-220
Italy, 6, 23-29, 46, 50, 102, 108, 120-123, 127, 129-133, 136, 138-140, 143-146, 148, 153-

154, 156-158, 160-166, 168-170, 172-173, 175-177, 179-180, 186, 188, 191-193, 197-199, 201-202, 209-210, 215-216, 218
Japan, 197
Poland, 8, 24, 134, 193, 206
Portugal, 78, 89
Slovenia, 66, 81, 102, 120, 131, 134-136, 138-143, 152, 165, 169, 216
Spain, 97, 192, 210
Sweden, 85, 91, 104, 105
Switzerland, 61, 69, 78, 85, 90-91, 101, 104-109, 117, 124, 130, 134, 159, 169-170, 186, 202, 209, 215, 218
Turkey, 85, 104, 109, 110,-112, 115, 118, 125-127, 209, 218
USA, 15, 24, 26, 34, 36, 38, 40, 44, 50, 53, 55, 57, 78, 83, 87-88, 92, 99, 103-104, 108, 111, 115, 121-122, 124, 143, 155, 169, 178, 182, 184, 192, 194, 197-198, 200, 203-204, 206-207, 211, 219
USSR, 33-36, 40, 43, 47, 54, 57, 64, 66-67, 70, 87, 102, 122-123, 126, 134-135, 138, 141, 143, 162, 174, 187, 197, 202-203, 205-210, 215, 219
Yugoslavia, 24, 25, 65-66, 77-78, 97, 120, 131-132, 134, 136, 138, 154, 207, 215
Czernin, Squadron Leader Manfred, 99, 145-146, 220
Dale, 2nd Lieutenant Stephen (Heinz Günther Spanglet), 151-152, 163-164
Dalton, Hugh, 63, 71-72, 156, 158
Dansey, Claude, 59, 73, 84
Danube River, 6, 65
Darton, Major James, 25, 31, 130, 133, 150, 153-156, 159-162, 166, 169, 175, 179, 191, 198, 202
Davies, Brigadier E F 'Trotsky', 174, 186
Dobretsberger, Josef, 110
Dollfuss, Chancellor Engelbert, 48, 55, 57, 102, 108, 115, 153

Drava River (German *Drau*), 140, 163
Duke of Windsor, HRH The, 43-44
Dunera, Hired Military Transport, 196
Eden, Sir Anthony, 44, 46, 49, 98, 122
Egarter, Hans (*Barbarossa*), 171
Essner, *Feldwebel* Walter, 14, 22
Fellers, Colonel Bonner, 15, 22
Feuerlöscher, Herbert, 110, 112-114, 120
Fielding, Major George, 146, 148-150, 223
First Aid Nursing Yeomanry (FANY), 24, 130, 154
Formations, Units, Organisations
(Soviet) Red Army, 30, 33-35, 176, 201, 203, 205-206
148 Squadron, 5, 20, 177
51 Commando, 11-12
8th Army (British), 14, 22-23, 209
A Force, 155, 165, 202, 211
Abwehr, 66, 119, 125, 127
Afrikakorps, 13-17, 23, 29
Austria Office, 77, 86, 93, 131
Austrian Centre, 86, 99, 165
Auxiliary Military Pioneer Corps, 3, 7-8, 10, 23, 38, 92-94, 116, 131, 133, 157, 159, 193-194, 197
British Security Coordination (New York), 92
Deuxième Bureau, 70
Electra House, 64, 67, 71, 75, 100
French Foreign Legion, 9, 12, 14
Gideon Force, 11
Heimwehr, 93
Joint Broadcasting Committee, 67-68, 90, 101
Lex, 69, 105-108, 124-125
Long Range Desert Group, 15, 17
Maryland, 24, 27, 130, 142, 148, 158, 165, 179
Military Intelligence (Research) (MI(R)), 63, 71

No 6 Special Force Staff Section (6 SFSS), 38, 154, 166, 208
O5, 103, 124, 204
Patria, 102, 170
Political Warfare Executive (PWE), 75, 90, 100, 122, 215
Provisional Austrian National Committee (POEN), 124, 204, 211
Servizio Informazioni Militare (SIM), 15
Sicherheitsdienst, 66, 175-176, 201
SOE Austrian Section (X/Aus), 1, 80, 82, 86, 88-90, 92, 94, 98, 109, 133-134, 156, 165, 178, 216, 217
SOE German Section/ Directorate (X), 3, 25, 39, 84-85, 89, 92-93, 96-99, 101, 106, 115, 120, 124-125, 130-134, 143, 161-163, 165-166, 168-169, 180, 187, 191, 210, 216-218
Soviet People's Commissariat for Internal Affairs (NKVD), 35, 40, 126, 130, 141, 162, 203
Special Air Service, 14-16, 23
Special Allied Airborne Reconnaissance Force (SAARF), 35-37
Special Interrogation Group (SIG), 13-18, 21, 23, 29, 32
Special Operations Executive, 1, 3, 4, 6-8, 20, 22-42, 62-65, 71-72, 74, 77-80, 82, 84-91, 93-94, 97, 100-168, 172-187, 193-204, 208-224, 235, 253
SS *(Schutzstaffel)*, 31-34, 37, 47, 52, 79, 91, 138, 149, 151, 163, 172, 180-181, 184, 188, 197, 206
Volkssturm, 30-31, 33
Wehrmacht, 26, 28, 31, 33, 51, 102, 105, 117, 131, 155, 158, 162, 164, 171-172, 175, 178-180, 191-192, 200-201, 203
Formations, Units, Organisations Section D (MI6), 63-72, 82-83, 90, 100, 102,107
Franckenstein, Sir George, 88

Franco, General Francisco, 46, 147
Free French (or Fighting French), 15
Freud, 2nd Lieutenant Anton Walter, 166, 194-196, 198-200, 210-211, 219
Fuchs, 2nd Lieutenant Emil, 99, 126, 172-175, 186-187
Funkspiel (Radio game), 120, 126, 174, 187
Gaiswinkler, 2nd Lieutenant Albrecht, 177-178, 180-182, 185, 187-188, 219
Gedye, G E R (Eric), 52-56, 58-60, 62, 73, 87, 109-120, 125-127, 141, 204, 219, 221, 224
Gerber, *Obergefreiter* (alias of Leo Hillman), 28, 31
Gerold, Karl, 105, 106, 107
Gestapo, 9, 24, 28-32, 35, 37, 39, 41, 53, 59-60, 67, 85, 90, 102, 104, 107, 111, 118-119, 127, 151-152, 173-175, 181, 201, 216-217
Ghent Altarpiece, 183
Goebbels, Joseph, 91
Göring, Hermann, 50
Grafl, 2nd Lieutenant Josef, 177, 180, 187
Grand, Major Laurence, 63-65, 67-69, 72, 82-83, 90, 100, 102, 107
Groehl, Karl, 69-71, 106
Gubbins, Major General Colin, 64, 84, 134
Haas, Roman (Roman Spreitzhofer), 176, 186
Hacker, 2nd Lieutenant Walter (Walter Harris), 41-42, 126, 158, 209, 212
Halifax aircraft, 5, 177, 180
Hanau, Julius (*Caesar*), 65
Hapsburg, Archduke Otto von, 87
Harvey, Captain Betty, 57, 130, 161
Haselden, Lieutenant-Colonel John, 16-18
Hauber, 2nd Lieutenant Richard (Klaus Huetz), 151-152
Hemetsberger, 2nd Lieutenant Josef, 172-173, 175
Herberger, Elsa, 106

Hersberger, Elsa, 105
Hesketh-Prichard, Major Alfgar (Squadron Leader Cahusac), 134-136, 139-142, 144, 152, 162
Hillman, Leo, 7-21, 23, 25-26, 28, 30, 32, 34-39, 92, 156, 159, 175, 219
Hitler, Adolf, 3- 4, 8- 9, 22, 30, 39-40, 44-51, 56, 63, 66-67, 70, 72-73, 80- 81, 87, 91, 102, 120-122, 147, 161, 167, 175, 178-179, 182, 184-185, 188, 196-198, 202-203, 210, 217
Hladnik, 2nd Lieutenant Hans, 157
Hochleitner (*Thunder*), 118-120, 126
Hodgson, Elizabeth ('Betty'), 60, 62, 67-68, 72, 90, 101, 105-108, 130, 154, 161, 169, 175-176, 179, 191
Holdsworth, Commander Gerald, 130
Holland, Major Jo, 63- 64
Hollitscher, Dr Hans, 108
Holmes, Clara ('Midge'), 60-62, 67-70, 72-73, 77, 79, 81, 83, 86-90, 93, 98, 102, 106-107, 109, 112, 121, 124, 131, 153, 156-157, 161, 178, 198, 217, 219, 224
Hopkinson (née Holmes), Prudence, 61-62, 67, 73, 89, 157, 219
Hughes, Sergeant-Major 'Ginger', 134, 136
Innitzer, Archbishop Theodor, 103
Inter-Allied Missions, 201
Jedburgh teams, 203
Jellinek, 'Peter', 108, 125, 221
Jones, Sidney, 174
Jourdain, Lieutenant Augustin, 15-16, 21
Kaiser, 2nd Lieutenant Charles (Carl), 191-194, 202, 210
Kaltenbrunner, Ernst, 181, 188
Keir, Lieutenant Allan, 84, 95-96, 100-101, 125, 131-132, 142
Kelley, 2nd Lieutenant Frank (Franz König), 194-195, 200

Kendrick, Captain Thomas, 59-60, 62, 67, 72-73
Kennedy, Captain Charles (see also Leo Hillman), 4-5, 7-8, 20, 28, 36-38
Kesselring, *Generalfeldmarschall* Albert, 152, 203
King Victor Emmanuel III, 120, 129
Knatchbull-Hagessen, Sir Hughe, 110, 114, 125
Kolmer, Eva, 87
Kreisky, Bruno, 104-105, 124
Langton, Lieutenant Tommy, 18
Layton, Captain Julian, 197
Le Chêne, Pierre, 174
Leckie, Flying Officer Bill, 177
Lee, Major Peter Murray, 100
Lepper, Alice, 111, 126
Leslie, Flight Sergeant Charlie, 75, 177
Lindsay, Franklin, 138
Locations
    Algiers, 24, 130, 158
    Anderson Manor, 198
    Ankara, 110
    Arisaig, 95, 197
    Bad Aussee, 177-178, 180-185, 188, 219
    Bari, 24, 26, 130, 132, 146, 150, 158, 204
    Beaulieu, 106, 124
    Bellasis House, Dorking (STS 2), 179
    Berchtesgaden, 45, 48-49, 168
    Bern, 105-108, 169, 175
    Bolzano, 160-161, 171
    Braunau am Inn, 9
    Brenner Pass, 108, 145, 155, 170, 204
    Brickendonbury Manor, 84
    Brock Hall (STS 1), 95, 197
    Budapest, 205
    Cairo, 11, 14-17, 22-23, 97, 101, 132
    Cambridge, 47, 57, 83, 97, 116, 135, 253
    Carinthia (*Kärnten*), 26, 38-39, 45, 102, 119, 133, 135-137, 142-143, 155, 207
    Cassibile, 120
    Ciapovano, 135-136

Dachau, 36, 151
Derna, 14-15, 132
Dunkirk, 71
El Alamein, 164
Fasano, 25, 27, 41, 158
Forni Avoltri, 148
Geneifa, 11
Gibraltar, 83, 192, 210
Glein, 193, 194
Graz, 155, 159, 162-163, 171-173, 178-179, 192-193
Haifa, 10, 112, 114, 123
Hammamet, 148, 164
Hatherop Castle (STS 45), 157, 166, 198
Hay, NSW, 196
Hotel Metropole, Vienna, 31-32, 42, 59
Innsbruck, 108, 133, 147, 151, 160-161, 170-171, 203-204, 209
Isle of Man, 3, 92, 131, 196
Istanbul, 87, 109-110, 112-120, 127, 158, 204
Judenburg, 173, 194, 199, 201, 203
Karawanken Mountains, 140
Khartoum, 11
Klagenfurt, 37, 38, 140, 207
Knittelfeld, 194
Krems an der Donau, 6, 28, 156, 173
Linz, 36, 37, 38, 51, 183, 203
Lisbon, 70, 75, 107, 120, 121
Llangollen, 78
London, 2, 22, 29, 36, 38, 42, 49, 53-54, 57-59, 64-65, 67-70, 72-73, 77-79, 83, 85-86, 88-89, 93, 98-99, 101, 106-107, 112,-114, 119, 121, 124, 130, 132, 134, 136, 139-140, 145, 153, 155-158, 161, 168, 170, 175, 186, 192, 193, 198, 204, 209, 221, 223
Malta, 14, 16
Manhartsberg, 6, 28
Martuba, 14-16
Massingham, 24, 41, 121, 127, 130, 132, 148, 164
Mauritius, 9, 21, 92
Mauthausen, 38, 42, 173-175, 186-187

Monopoli, 24, 120, 130, 136, 142, 150, 154, 156, 158, 162, 174, 179, 191
Moscow, 1, 120-122, 127-128, 143, 151, 156, 162-163, 175, 205, 217
Murau, 201
New York, 53, 87, 92, 99, 111, 114-115, 128, 165
Normandy, 123, 152, 168, 178, 179
Obdach, 172
Ostmark (Austria after *Anschluss*), 8, 51-52
Palestine, 7, 9-11, 13, 21, 24, 41, 87, 101, 110, 113-114, 125, 130-132
Paris, 62, 69-70, 83, 91, 106, 126, 135, 178, 184, 200
RAF Ringway, 96, 131
Rheinland, 9
Ringwood, Manchester, 198
Rome, 15, 26, 50, 73, 120-121, 145-146, 152-156, 158, 162
Salzburg, 47, 59, 151, 173-175, 209
Salzkammergut, 177
Schiefling, 199
Schloss Thalheim, 201
Sepino, 26
Sicily, 24, 120
Siena, 130, 158, 162, 179, 191
Siwa, 15
St Ermin's Hotel, 64, 134
Stockholm, 104, 124
Stodham Park (STS 3), 197
Styria (*Steiermark*), 112, 119, 126, 135-136, 140, 143, 157, 176, 187, 193
Tobruk, 14-19, 23
Trieste, 135, 212
Tyrol, 47, 93, 101-102, 133, 146-147, 150, 153, 160-161, 164, 170-171, 204, 219
Vienna, 2- 3, 7-9, 20, 27-44, 47-48, 50-51, 53-55, 57, 59, 61-62, 69, 73, 77, 80-82, 85, 87, 94, 103-104, 108-109, 111-112, 116-118, 122, 127, 151, 156, 159, 161, 163-164, 169, 170, 173-174, 176, 178-179,

183, 192-193, 195, 203, 205-207, 209, 219-220, 242
Washington DC, 15, 22, 156, 204
Western Desert, 15, 23
Wolfsberg, 38-39, 194, 202
Zeltweg, 193-195, 199-203, 211
Lzicar, 2nd Lieutenant Karl, 177, 179, 187
MacDonald, 2nd Lieutenant 'Mac', 18
Mallaby, 1st Lieutenant Cecil Richard 'Dick' (*Olaf*), 121, 127
Maquis, 179
Martin-Smith, Captain Patrick, 146-149
Matthey, Squadron Leader Bill, 169-171
Mayr, Hubert (*Georgeau*), 146-147, 150-152, 164-165
McCaffery, John 'Jock', 108
Mehlich, Franz, 117-118
Meinl, Julius, 54, 87, 99
MI5 (Security Service), 62, 70, 74, 87, 94, 117, 192, 239
Mockler-Ferryman, Brigadier Eric, 100
Montgomery, General Bernard, 23
Morton, Desmond, 88, 136, 142
Mur river, 199, 202-203
Mussolini, Benito, 22-24, 45-46, 120
Neumann, Theo, 6, 126, 156, 158, 162, 173, 209
Newman, Isidore, 174
Norman, Gilbert, 174
Novy, Franz, 104
O'Hara, 2nd Lieutenant Michael (Egon Berliner), 159-163, 167, 176
Office of Strategic Services (OSS), 40, 103, 124, 138, 143, 155, 162, 165, 174, 184, 203-205
Operations and Missions
  Agreement, 16, 18, 20
  Anvil (later Dragoon), 142
  Aunsby I and II, 146
  Bakersfield, 146, 148
  Barbarossa, 171, 197
  Bellington, 155
  Bobby, 126, 209
  Brandon, 148, 164

  Clowder, 26, 132-136, 138-145, 153, 163-164, 169, 187-189, 209, 216
  Dilston, 158, 159, 162, 202
  Duncery, 187, 194-195, 200, 202, 210
  Duval, 172-173, 175, 186
  Ebensburg, 177-180, 182, 185, 187-188, 191
  Electra, 7, 20, 30, 39, 42, 64, 67, 71, 75, 100, 175, 191
  Evansville, 159, 162
  Eveleth, 176, 191
  Greenleaves, 131-134, 138, 142
  Greenup, 204
  Hamster, 192, 194, 200, 202, 210
  Historian, 194-195, 200, 202, 210
  Icecream, 161
  Pickaxe, 130, 141
  Pyx, 139, 143
  Rankin, 168
  Seafront, 151
  Seathrift, 146, 152, 163
  Seelöwe (Sealion), 71
  Torch, 24, 147
  Unthinkable, 206
Osoppo partisans, 149, 150
Otten, Karl, 69, 70, 71, 106
Patton, Major General George S, 203
Philby, Kim, 47, 57, 64
Pickering, Major Frank, 140, 141, 143, 144
Pirker, Dr Peter, 20, 41, 66, 88, 99, 100, 119, 127, 143-144, 152, 164, 186, 188, 221, 224
Pollak, Oscar, 86, 98, 104, 117, 156, 165
Prager, 2nd Lieutenant Hans, 172-175
Preiss, Franz, 78-79, 97
Priestley, 2nd Lieutenant [Michael] Peter (Egon Lindenbaum), 151-152, 164
Reitlinger, Friedrich Franz ('Freddy'), 93-96, 101, 123, 131-133, 219
Renner, Karl, 206
Republikanischer Schutzbund, 30

Rhodes, 2nd Lieutenant Eric (Erich Rohde), 194-195, 200
Ritchie, Lieutenant-General Neil, 14
Rommel, *Generalleutnant* Erwin, 13-16, 22, 29
Roosevelt, President Franklin D, 66, 123, 167, 197
Rothschild, Baron Eugene de, 44
Russell, Lieutenant David, 17, 22, 84
Sailer, Karl Hans, 115-116, 204
Sanders, 2nd Lieutenant Eric (lgnaz Schwarz)., 73, 93, 99-100, 138, 141, 157, 158, 162, 166, 202
Sanitzer, Johann, 126, 174-175, 187, 217
Sattler, Matthias, 172
Schaepdryver, André, 174
Schuhbauer, Theodor, 77-79, 89, 94, 97, 112
Schuhbauer, Valerie, 79
Schuschnigg, Chancellor Kurt von, 9, 44, 46, 48-50, 59, 63, 81, 153
Sebba, Dr Gregor, 87, 99
Sehmer, Major John, 174
Selassie, Emperor Haile, 11
Selby, Sir Walford, 44
Senter, Commander John, 80
Seyss-Inquart, Arthur, 50, 57
Sheppard, Bob, 174
Shirer, William, 50, 55, 57
Simpson, Wallis, 44
Sinclair, Admiral Hugh ('C'), 63, 67, 95, 96
Smallwood, Major Bill, 149
Social Democrat Party, 7, 30, 34, 53, 55, 99, 165, 204
Spanish Civil War, 46, 130, 147
Special Intelligence Service (SIS or MI6), 40, 42, 54, 59, 60-68, 70-71, 73-74, 82-84, 90, 102, 107, 113, 116-117, 120, 126, 139, 155, 160-162, 165, 174, 187, 198, 209, 210
SS *Jonathan Holt*, 79
Stalin, Marshal Josef, 66, 122-123, 206-207
Stamper, Evelyn, 60, 62, 67-68, 70, 72-73, 77-78, 81, 83, 86-90, 98, 101-102, 109, 114-117, 121, 131, 153, 156, 161, 178, 216-217
Standhartinger, 2nd Lieutenant Karl, 177-178, 187
Starr, John, 174
Stephenson, William, 92
Stevens, 2nd Lieutenant Harry (Hans Schweiger), 194-195, 200
Stiers, Valère, 174
Stirling, Captain David, 14, 16, 23
Stonehouse, Brian, 174
Stout, Lieutenant George (ALIU), 184
Sweet-Escott, Lt Col Bickham, 241
Taggart, 2nd Lieutenant William (Wolfgang Treichl), 151-152
Tambornino, Karl, 30
Taurus Express, 113
Terwind, Beatrice, 174
The Third Man (film), 205
Thornley, Major Ronald, 83-88, 91, 99-101, 106, 113-117, 120-121, 130, 132-134, 141-142, 156-157, 160, 162
Threlfall, Major Henry, 104, 124
Tiefenbrunner, Private 'Tiffen', 13
Tito (General Josip Broz), 25-26, 66, 134-135, 140, 142, 145, 154, 207, 209, 212, 215
Trautmannsdorff, Count Norbert von, 155
Truman, President Harry, 206
Trumpe, 117-118, 120
Vichy French regime, 79, 192
Villiers, Lieutenant-Colonel Charles, 38, 136-140, 142, 198, 208
Waldenegg, Egon Baron von Berger, 153
Waldenegg, Heinrich Berger, 154
Wanborough Manor (STS 5), 179
Warndorfer, August, 174
Warner, 2nd Lieutenant Fred ((Manfred Werner), 12, 21, 25-26, 159, 194, 195, 202
Weinzinger, Erich, 110, 125
Widmayer, Heinrich, 119

Wilkinson, Lieutenant Colonel Peter, 123, 132, 134-137, 142-143, 163, 198, 207, 209, 220

Williams (Wunder), 2nd Lieutenant Harry, 192-194, 210, 220

Wingate, Colonel Orde, 11

Wirlandner, Stefan, 115-120, 158, 166, 202, 209, 212

Wise, Captain Ernest (Ernst Weiss) and Mrs Enid, 153-154

Zeff, Edward 'Teddy', 174

ABOUT THE AUTHOR

Dr Peter Dixon is a researcher, author and lecturer. He served over 30 years as a Royal Air Force pilot and spent the next decade leading the charity Concordis International in its conflict resolution work in Sudan and other divided societies. He completed his doctoral research at the University of Cambridge in 2015, studying outside intervention in civil wars, and now teaches International Relations at the same university. His writing has included *Amazon Task Force*, the story of a medical expedition in the Peruvian Amazon, *Peacemakers: A Christian view of war and peace* and, on SOE, *Guardians of Churchill's Secret Army: Men of the Intelligence Corps in the Special Operations Executive* and *Setting the Med Ablaze: Churchill's Secret North African Base*.

Bibliography

Aga Rossi, Elena. *L'Inganno Reciproco: l'armistizio tra l'Italia e gli Angloamericani del Settembre 1943 (Mutual Deception: the armistice between Italy and the anglo-americans of September 1943)*. Rome: Ministero per i Beni Culturali e Ambientali.

Aldrich, Richard. "Unquiet death: The post-war survival of the Special Operations Executive (1945-51)." In *Contemporary British History 1931-61: Politics and the limits of policy*, edited by Tony Gorst, Lewis Johnman and Scott Lucas. London: Institute of Contemporary British History, 1991.

ALIU. *Art Looting Investigation Unit Final Report*. Washington DC: Office of the Assistant Secretary of War, 1 May.

Andrew, Christopher. *Secret Service: the making of the British intelligence community*. London: Heinemann, 1985.

_____. *The Defence of the Realm: the authorized history of MI5*. London: Allen Lane, 2009.

Anglim, Simon. "MI(R), G(R) and British Covert Operations, 1939–42." *Intelligence and National Security* 20, no. 4 (2005): 631-653.

Ashdown, Paddy. *Nein!: standing up to Hitler 1935-1944*. London: William Collins, 2018.

Atkin, Malcolm. *Fighting Nazi Occupation: British resistance 1939-1945*, 2015.

_____. *Section D for Destruction: forerunner of SOE*. Barnsley, South Yorkshire: Pen & Sword Military, 2017.

Bailey, Roderick. *Target Italy: the secret war against Mussolini, 1940-1943*, 2014.

Barbina, Enrico, and Jurij Cozianin. "Autunno 1944, Danbury sul Monte Pala." *La Panarie* 2018.

Barker, Ernest. *Behind Enemy Lines with the SOE*: Frontline Books, 2021.

Barker, Thomas M. *Social Revolutionaries and Secret Agents: the Carinthian Slovene partisans and Britain's Special Operations Executive*. New York: Columbia University Press, 1990.

_____. "The Ljubljana Gap Strategy: Alternative to Anvil/Dragoon or Fantasy?" *The Journal of Military History* 56, no. 1 (1992): 57.

Barneschi, Gianluca. *An Englishman Abroad: SOE agent Dick Mallaby's Italian missions, 1943-45*. Oxford: Osprey Publishing, 2019.

Baxa, Paul. "Capturing the Fascist Moment: Hitler's Visit to Italy in 1938 and the Radicalization of Fascist Italy." *Journal of Contemporary History* 42, no. 2 (2016): 227-242.

Beevor, Antony. *The Second World War*. London: Weidenfeld & Nicolson, 2012.
Benton, Kenneth. "The ISOS Years: Madrid 1941-3." *Journal of Contemporary History* 30, no. 3 (1995): 359-410.
Bernhardt, Daniel, Sarah Braun, Victoria Koller, and Denise Ribul. "Albrecht Gaiswinkler - Held oder Hochstapler." Austria, 2009.
Biber, Dušan, *Allied Missions in the Slovenian Littoral 1943-1945*, at IWM Personal Papers 12751 Peter Allix Wilkinson.
Bierman, Colin, and Colin Smith. *Alamein: war without hate*. London: Viking, 2002.
Bottome, Phyllis. *The Goal*. London: Faber & Faber, 1962.
Bradsher, Gregory, "The Monuments Men in August 1945: The Belgian Treasures", National Archives and https://text-message.blogs.archives.gov/2015/10/15/monuments-men-august-1945/ (accessed 12 September 2022).
Brown, Anthony Cave. *Bodyguard of Lies*. New York: Quill/William Morrow, 1991.
Cadbury, Deborah. *Princes at War: the British Royal Family's private battle in the Second World War*. London: Bloomsbury, 2015.
Calvocoressi, Peter. *World Politics, 1945-2000*. 8th ed. Harlow: Longman, 2001.
Coon, Carleton S. *A North Africa Story: The anthropologist as OSS agent, 1941-1943*. Ipswich, Mass.: Gambit, 1980.
Courtney, G B. *SBS in World War Two: the story of the original Special Boat Section of the Army Commandos*. London: Hale, 1983.
Cowles, Virginia. *The Phantom Major: the story of David Stirling and the SAS Regiment*. London: Grafton, 1988, 1958.
Cunningham, Cyril. *Beaulieu: the finishing school for secret agents 1941-1945*. London: Leo Cooper, 1998.
Darton, James, interviewed by Professor David Dilks, IWM Private Papers 14089 Maj James Garwood Darton, 23rd January 2002.
de Jaeger, Charles. *The Linz File: Hitler's plunder of Europe's art*. Exeter: Webb & Bower, 1981.
Derry, Sam. *The Rome Escape Line: the story of the British organization in Rome for assistingescaped prisoners-of-war, 1943-44*. London: Harrap, 1960.
Dilks, David. *The Diaries of Sir Alexander Cadogan, OM, 1938-1945*. London: Cassell, 1971.
Dixon, Peter. *Guardians of Churchill's Secret Army: men of the Intelligence Corps in the Special Operations Executive*. London: Cloudshill Press, 2018.
_____. *Setting the Med Ablaze: Churchill's Secret North African Base*. London: Cloudshill Press, 2020.
Evans, Richard. *The Third Reich in Power*. London: Penguin, 2012.
Foot, M R D. *SOE in France: an account of the work of the British Special Operations Executive in France 1940-1944*: [S.l.] : HMSO, 1966 (1976), 2006.
_____. *SOE: an outline history of the Special Operations Executive 1940-1946*. London: The Bodley Head, 2014.
_____. *Resistance: European resistance to the Nazis, 1940-1945*. London: Biteback Publishing, 2016.

Foot, M. R. D., and J. M. Langley. *MI9: escape and evasion 1939-1945*. London: Biteback, 2011.
Franks, Norman L R. *Double Mission: RAF fighter ace and SOE agent, Manfred Czernin DSO MC DFC*. London: Kimber, 1976.
Fry, Helen. *Freuds' War*. Stroud: History Press, 2009.
_____. *MI9: A history of the secret service for escape and evasion in World War Two*. New Haven: Yale University Press, 2020.
_____. *Spymaster: the man who saved MI6*. New Haven: Yale University Press, 2021.
Gaddis, John Lewis. *The Cold War: a new history*. New York: Penguin Press, 2005.
Gaiswinkler, Albrecht. *Sprung in die Freiheit*. Salzburg, 1947.
Garnett, David. *The Secret History of PWE: the Political Warfare Executive, 1939-1945*. London: St Ermin's Press, 2002.
Gedye, G E R. *A wayfarer in Austria*. London: Methuen, 1928.
_____. "Austria's Dark Outlook." *The Fortnightly* (1934).
_____. *Fallen Bastions: the Central European tragedy*. London: Gollancz, 1939.
Gildea, Robert. *Fighters in the Shadows: a new history of the French Resistance*. Main ed., 2015.
Goldenberg, Anna, and Alta L Price. *I belong to Vienna: A Jewish family's story of exile and return*. New York: New Vessel Press, 2020.
Hainzl, Wolfgang. *Die Luftstreitkräfte Österreichs 1955 bis heute*. 3rd ed. Gnas, Austria: Weishaupt Verlag, 2000.
Harclerode, Peter, and Brendan Pittaway. *The Lost Masters: the looting of Europe's treasurehouses*. London: Gollancz, 1999.
Hastings, Max. *The Secret War: Spies, codes and guerrillas, 1939-1945*. EPub edition. ed., 2015.
Howarth, Patrick. *Undercover: the men and women of the Special Operations Executive*. London: Routledge and Kegan Paul, 1980.
Jakub, Jay. *Spies and Saboteurs: Anglo-American collaboration and rivalry in human intelligence collection and special operations, 1940-45*. London: Macmillan, 1999.
Janeschitz, Hans. *Felieferhof: ein Bericht über die amtlichen Untersuchungen der Massenmorde in der Schießstätte Felieferhof*. Graz, 1946.
Jefferson, David. *Tobruk: a raid too far*. London: Robert Hale, 2013.
Jeffery, Keith. *MI6: the history of the Secret Intelligence Service, 1909-1949*. London: Bloomsbury, 2010.
Jenner, C. J. "Turning the Hinge of Fate: Good Source and the UK-U.S. Intelligence Alliance, 1940–1942*." *Diplomatic History* 32, no. 2 (2009): 165-205.
Jones, Matthew. *Britain, the United States and the Mediterranean War, 1942-44*. Basingstoke: Macmillan in association with St. Antony's College, Oxford, 1996.
Keelan, Brendan, *Eric Redmond and the Secret History of the SS Jonathan Holt*, unpublished article.
Keyserlingk, Robert H. *Austria in World War II: an Anglo-American dilemma*. Kingston: McGill-Queen's University Press, 1988.
_____. "Die Moskauer Deklaration: Die Alliierten, Österreich und der Zweite Weltkrieg." In *Österreich im 20. Jahrhundert*, edited by Rolf Steininger and Michael Gehler 2. Vienna: Böhlau Verlag, 1997.

Knight, Robert. "British Policy towards Occupied Austria 1945-1950." London School of Economics, 1986.
———. "The Waldheim context: Austria and Nazism." *Times Literary Supplement*, no. 4357 (1986).
———. "Ethnicity and Identity in the Cold War: The Carinthian Border Dispute, 1945-1949." *The International History Review* 22, no. 2 (2000): 274-303.
———. "Life after SOE: Peter Wilkinson's journey from the Clowder Mission to Waldheim." *Journal for Intelligence, Propaganda and Security Studies* 2009, no. 1 (2009): 71-82.
Knightley, Phillip. *Philby: the life and views of the KGB masterspy*. London: Deutsch, 1988.
Kocjancic, K, "Klagenfurt Trial (Sept.-Nov. 1947)", Axis History Forum, https://forum.axishistory.com/viewtopic.php?t=120852 (accessed 27 June 2021 2021).
Lamb, Richard. *The Ghosts of Peace, 1935-1945*. Salisbury, Wiltshire: M Russell, 1987.
Landsborough, Gordon. *Tobruk Commando: the raid to destroy Rommel's base*. London: Greenhill, 1989, 1956.
Leighton-Langer, Peter. *X steht für unbekannt: Deutsche und Österreicher in den britischen Streitkräften im Zweiten Weltkrieg*. Berlin: Berlin Verlag, 1999.
Lewis, Damien. *SAS Ghost Patrol: the ultra-secret unit that posed as Nazi Stormtroopers*. London: Quercus, 2017.
Lindsay, Franklin. *Beacons in the Night: with the OSS and Tito's partisans in wartime Yugoslavia*. Stanford, CA: Stanford University Press, 1993.
Linortner, Johann. *Die Kunstgüter im Altausseer Salzberg 1943-1945*. Bad Aussee: Salinen, 1998.
MacDonald, Charles B. *The Last Offensive*. Vol. CMH Pub 7–9 United States Army in World War II: The European theater of operations. Washington, DC: US Army Center for Military History, 1973.
Macintyre, Ben. *A Spy among Friends: Kim Philby and the great betrayal*. London: Bloomsbury, 2014.
———. *SAS Rogue Heroes: the authorized wartime history*. London: Viking, 2016.
Mackenzie, W J M. *The Secret History of SOE: the Special Operations Executive, 1940-1945*. London: St Ermin's, 2000.
Macmillan, Harold. *The Blast of War, 1939-1945*. London: MacMillan, 1967.
Maimann, Helene. *Politik im Wartesaal: österreichische Exilpolitik in Grossbrittanien 1938-1945*. Vienna: Hermann Boehlhaus Nachfolger, 1975.
Marks, Leo. *Between Silk and Cyanide: A codemaker's story 1941-1945*. Stroud: History Press, 2008.
Martin Smith, Patrick, and Peter Pirker. *Widerstand vom Himmel: Österreicheinsätze des britischen Geheimdienstes SOE 1944*. Wien: Czernin, 2004.
Mauch, Christof. *The Shadow War against Hitler: the covert operations of America's wartime secret intelligence service*. New York: Columbia University Press, 2003.
Mayerhofer, Rainer. "Rettl, Lisa / Pirker, Peter: Ich war mit Freuden dabei." *Wiener Zeitung*, 3 December 2010 2010.

McCarten, Anthony. *Darkest Hour: how Churchill brought us back from the brink.* London: Viking, 2017.
Meixner, Wolfgang. "Engineer Friedrich Reitlinger (1877-1938). Industrialist and economic functionary in the Tyrol between "Heimwehr" and National Socialism." *Zeitgeschichte* 29, no. 4 (2002): 191-201.
Molden, Fritz. *Fires in the Night: the sacrifices and significance of the Austrian Resistance, 1938-1945.* Translated by Harry Zohn. Boulder: Westview Press, 1989.
Mommsen, Hans. *Germans against Hitler: the Stauffenberg plot and resistance under the Third Reich.* Translated by Angus McGeoch. London: I B Tauris, 2009.
Nelles, Dieter. *Widerstand und internationale Solidarität: die Internationale Transportarbeiter-Föderation (ITF) im Widerstand gegen den Nationalsozialismus* Veröffentlichungen des Instituts für Soziale Bewegungen Schriftenreihe A, Darstellungen. Essen: Klartext, 2001.
Neugebauer, Wolfgang. "Zur Struktur, Tätigkeit und Effizienz des NS-Terrorsystems in Österreich." In *Krieg im Äther: Widerstand und Spionage im Zweiten Weltkrieg,* edited by Hans Schafranek and Johannes Tuchel. Vienna: Picus Verlag, 2004.
_____. *The Austrian Resistance 1938-1945.* Translated by John Nicholson and Eric Canepa. Vienna: Edition Steinbauer, 2014.
O'Connor, Bernard. *Operation Ebensburg: SOE's Austrian 'Bonzos' and the rescue of looted European art,* 2018.
O'Sullivan, Donal. *Dealing with the Devil: Anglo-Soviet intelligence cooperation during the Second World War.* New York: Peter Lang, 2010.
Ogden, Alan, and Martin Fielding, *The Clowder Mission in and around Forni Avoltri, June - November 1944,* unpublished paper.
Pauley, Bruce F. "From Splinter Party to Mass Movement: The Austrian Nazi Breakthrough." *German Studies* 2, no. 1 (1973): 7-29.
Pelinka, Anton, and Rolf Steininger. *Österreich und die Sieger.* Wien: W. Braumuer, 1986.
Philby, Kim. *My Silent War.* London: Grafton, 1968.
Piffer, Tommaso. "Office of Strategic Services versus Special Operations Executive: Competition for the Italian Resistance, 1943–1945." *Journal of Cold War Studies* 17, no. 4 (2015): 41-58.
Pirker, Peter. "'Tomorrow John Kitterer will play': the SOE Operation Duval and the Mauthausen Survivors Josef Hemetsberger and Hans Prager." In *Who resisted? Biographies of Resistance Fighters from entire Europe in the Mauthausen Concentration Camp and Lectures from the International Conference 2008,* edited by Andreas Baumgartner, Isabella Girstmaier and Verena Kaselitz, 515–531. Vienna: Edition Mauthausen, 2008.
_____. *Gegen das "Dritte Reich": Sabotage und transnationaler Widerstand in Österreich und Slowenien 1938-1940.* Klagenfurt: Kitab, 2010.
_____. "Partisanen und Agenten: Geschichtsmythen um die SOE-Mission Clowder." *Zeitgeschichte* 38, no. 1 (2011): 21-55.
_____. *Subversion deutscher Herrschaft: der britische Kriegsgeheindienst SOE und Österreich* Zeitgeschichte im Kontext. Goettingen: Vienna University Press, 2012.
_____. "Transnational Resistance in the Alps-Adriatic Area in 1939/40: On Subversive Border Crossers, Historical Interpretations and

National Politics of the Past." *Acta Histriae* 20, no. 4 (2012): 765-788.

———. ""... a credit to the British army and to his own country, which is Austria": Dokumente zu Leo Hillmans Kampf gegen den Nationalsozialismus." *Täter: Österreichische Akteure im Nationalsozialismus* (2014). www.doew.at.

———. "Die Remigration sozialistischer Exilanten nach Österreich: Exilpolitik – Netzwerke – Nachkriegsintegration." In *Vision and Reality: Central Europe after Hitler*, edited by Richard Dove and Ian Wallace, 119-156. New York: Brill, 2014.

———. "British Subversive Politics towards Austria and Partisan Resistance in the Austrian-Slovene Borderland, 1938–45." *Journal of Contemporary History* 52, no. 2 (2017): 319-351.

———. *Codename Brooklyn: ju¨dische Agenten im Feindesland, die Operation Greenup 1945*. 2. Auflage. ed. Innsbruck: Tyrolia Verlag, 2019.

Pirker, Peter, and Ivo Jevnikar. "So geheim wie möglich." *Die Presse*, 14 April 2018 2018.

Pitt, Barrie. *Special Boat Squadron: the story of the SBS in the Mediterranean*. London: Corgi, 1985, 1983.

Porch, Douglas. *The French Foreign Legion: a complete history of the legendary fighting force*. London: Macmillan, 1991.

Prenninger, Alexander, Regina Fritz, Gerhard Botz, Melanie Dejnega, and Verlag Böhlau. *Deportiert nach Mauthausen* Europa in Mauthausen / Band 2. Wien Köln Weimar: Böhlau Verlag, 2021.

Pridham, Geoffrey. *Hitler's Rise to Power: the Nazi movement in Bavaria, 1923-1933*. St Albans: Hart-Davis MacGibbon, 1973.

Rathkolb, Oliver. *Fiktion "Opfer" Österreich und die langen Schatten des Nationalsozialismus und der Dollfuss-Diktatur*. Innsbruck: StudienVerlag, 2017.

Rauchensteiner, Manfried. "Österreich nach 1945: der Weg zum Staatsvertrag." In *Österreich und die Sieger*, edited by Anton Pelinka and Rolf Steininger. Wien: W. Braumuer, 1986.

Reitlinger, Friedrich. "Als Tiroler in der britischen Armee." In *Österreich und die Sieger*, edited by Anton Pelinka and Rolf Steininger, 53-66. Vienna: Wilhelm Braumueller, 1986.

Rettl, Lisa, and Peter Pirker. *"Ich war mit Freuden dabei!": der KZ-Arzt Sigbert Ramsauer: eine o¨sterreichische Geschichte*. Wien: Milena, 2010.

Richards, Brooks. *Secret Flotillas Vol 2: clandestine sea operations in the Mediterranean, North Africa and the Adriatic*. 2nd ed. London: Whitehall History Publishing in association with Frank Cass, 2004.

Sadler, John. *Operation Agreement: Jewish commandos and the raid on Tobruk*. Oxford: Osprey Publishing, 2016.

Sanders, Eric. *Emigration ins Leben: Wien-London und nicht mehr retour*. Vienna: Czernin, 2008.

Schafranek, Hans. "Unternehmen 'Nordpol': das 'Englandspiel' der deutschen militärischen Abwehr in den Jahren 1942-1944." In *Krieg im Äther: Widerstand und Spionage im Zweiten Weltkrieg*, edited by Hans Schafranek and Johannes Tuchel. Vienna: Picus Verlag, 2004.

Schmidl, Erwin A. *Der "Anschluss" Österreichs: der deutsche Einmarsch im März 1938*. Bonn: Bernard & Graefe, 1994.

Seaman, Mark. *Special Operations Executive: a new instrument of war.* London: Routledge, 2006.
Selby, Sir Walford. *Diplomatic Twilight, 1930-1940.* London: John Murray, 1953.
Seydi, Süleyman. "The Activities of Special Operations Executive in Turkey." *Middle Eastern Studies* 40, no. 4 (2004): 153-170.
Shirer, William L. *Berlin Diary: the journal of a foreign correspondent, 1934-1941.* New York: A A Knopf, 1941.
Shirer, William L. *The Rise and Fall of the Third Reich: a history of Nazi Germany.* New York,: Simon and Schuster, 1960.
Simms, Brendan, and Charlie Laderman. *Hitler's American Gamble: Pearl Harbor and the German march to global war.* London: Penguin Books, 2021.
Smith, Peter C. *Massacre at Tobruk: the story of Operation Agreement.* London: Kimber, 1987.
Stafford, David. *Britain and European Resistance, 1940-1945: a survey of the Special Operations Executive, with documents.* Toronto: University of Toronto Press, 1980.
_____. *Endgame 1945: victory, retribution, liberation.* London: Little, Brown, 2007.
_____. *Mission Accomplished: SOE and Italy 1943-1945.* London: Bodley Head, 2011.
Stargardt, Nicholas. *The German War: a nation under arms, 1939-45.* London: The Bodley Head, 2015.
Steinacher, Gerald. "'Der Einzige Österreicher in der Schweiz, der den Nazis Effektiv Widerstand Leistete': Wilhelm Bruckner und der österreichische Wehrverband Patria 1943-1946." In *Jahrbuch 2001-2*, edited by Christine Schindler, 147-183. Vienna: Dokumentationsarchiv des österreichischen Widerstandes, 2001.
Steininger, Rolf. *Austria, Germany, and the Cold War: From the Anschluss to the State Treaty, 1938-1955.* New York: Berghahn Books, 2008.
Stephenson, William S. *British Security Coordination: the secret history of British intelligence in the Americas, 1940-1945* Secret history of British intelligence in the Americas, 1940-1945. New York: Fromm International, 1999.
Sweet-Escott, Bickham. *Baker Street Irregular.* London,: Methuen, 1965.
Tennant, Sir Peter. *Touchlines of War:* Hull University Press, 1992.
Thomas, Gordon. *The Pope's Jews: the Vatican's secret plan to save Jews from the Nazis.* First Edition. ed. New York: Thomas Dunne Books, 2012.
Ullrich, Volker. *Hitler: Volume II, Downfall 1939-45.* London: The Bodley Head, 2020.
Van der Bijl, Nicholas. *Sharing the Secret: the history of the Intelligence Corps 1940-2010*: Pen & Sword Military, 2013.
Warner, Fred, *Don't You Know There's a War On?*, unpublished.
Weinzierl, Erika. "Vor- und frühgeschichte der Zweiten Republik." In *Österreich und die Sieger*, edited by Anton Pelinka and Rolf Steininger. Wien: W. Braumuer, 1986.
West, Nigel. *MI6: British Secret Intelligence Service Operations 1909-1945.* London: Weidenfeld & Nicolson, 1983.
Wilkinson, Peter. *Foreign Fields: the story of an SOE operative.* London: I B Tauris, 1997.

Wilkinson, Peter, and Joan Bright Astley. *Gubbins and SOE*. Barnsley: Pen & Sword Military, 2010, 1993.
Williams, Warren Wellde. "British Policy and the Occupation of Austria, 1945-1955." Swansea University, 2004.
Wylie, Neville. "SOE and the Neutrals." In *Special Operations Executive: a new instrument of war*, edited by Mark Seaman, 157-178. London: Routledge, 2006.
Wynter, Brigadier H W. *Special forces in the Desert War, 1940-1943*. Richmond: Public Record Office, 2001.
Ziegler, Philip. *King Edward VIII: the official biography*. London: Collins, 1990.
Zwergbaum, Aharon, David Saks, and Zvi Loker. "Mauritius." In *Encyclopaedia Judaica*, edited by Michael Berenbaum and Fred Skolnik 13, 690-691. Detroit, MI: Macmillan Reference USA, 2007.